FAMILIES OF EDEN

FAMILIES OF EDEN

Communes and the New Anarchism

Judson Jerome

A CONTINUUM BOOK
The Seabury Press · New York

The Seabury Press
815 Second Avenue
New York, N.Y. 10017

Copyright © 1974 by The Twentieth Century Fund
Designed by Paula Wiener
Printed in the United States of America

Library of Congress Cataloging in Publication Data

Jerome, Judson.
    Families of Eden.

    (A Continuum book)
    1. Collective settlements—United States. I. Title.
HX654.J46   335'.9'73   73-17877
ISBN 0-8164-9198-4

DEDICATED TO:

Jessie, John and Sarah, Susan and Ralph, and Livvy,
  who helped us start in communal life,
to Marty, who bears with all the changes,
to our children—Polly, Topher, Jenny, Beth and Michelle,
  and their friends, who teach us why it should work,
to Wilma, Ralph, Bo, Jethro, Rufus, Baby and the Senators,
  who greeted us here,
to Joseph and Jacky, Mary, Isham, Sophie, Pete, Ira, Ned,
  Greg, Eric, Bill, Nona and Chinaberry, Steve, Claudia, Andi,
  Bob, Kathy, Diane, and Reggie, who left their imprint on
  Downhill Farm, though they moved on,
to Herb, Robb, Til, Maple, and Lisa,
  who lived the book and helped write it,
to Joel, Ann, Rhonda, and Freddie, who have come since,
to dozens of visitors such as Michael, Bob, John, Steve
  and Judy, Anella, Paul, Jil, and Mildred,
  who shared their knowledge of communal life with us,
to Charles and Pat, Lucy, Craig, Dick, Larry, Hugh, Frank,
  and David—staff members and those who sent in reports,
to Chuck, who may have lost his job over this,
to Arthur, Brian and Ellen, John, Robert, Rosabeth, Ken,
  Stew, and two Davids, who read early versions
  and made suggestions on the manuscript,
to other scholars of communes—including some of those above,
  and Jay and Heather, Bennett, Richard, Keith, Ron,
  and two Johns—whose work has helped extend and
  confirm our own,
and to hundreds of fellow communards whose membership
  we joined with this project, especially Peter Rabbit and
  Nancy at Libre, Molly at Hillhouse, the folks at
  Grimmet's Chance and Frog Run and Total Loss Farm and
  Wooden Shoe and Heathcote and Magic Mountain and
  Dragon's Eye and Goodheart and Nethers and
  Iris Mountain and Twin Oaks. I love you all.

And my thanks to the Twentieth Century Fund for the grant
  that made the study possible.

Contents

Foreword

I have never in my writing tried to draw a clear line between what I regard as the illusion of "objective truth" and my own needs and concerns. My last book began:

As an educator, a poet, husband, lover, father, citizen, as a man in mid-life no less desperate than blacks and youth and women for self-realization, I find myself lying on the glare-bright table of the seventies like a fish whose gills are pumping insubstantial air. I write about colleges because I have been observing them most closely, but the issues of this book could as easily be seen in politics or churches, theater, law, the family, industry or commerce, drugs or drink, styles or amusements, the class struggle or the mass media. A culture is dying. A culture is gasping to be born. These themes permeate this book, which only incidentally uses higher education as its evidence of a larger transformation in which we are all participating.*

In this book, often explicitly, I continue the autobiography which, in a sense, all my books have been. As all of us must, I am searching for meaning, fulfillment, salvation,

* *Culture Out of Anarchy: The Reconstruction of American Higher Learning*, Herder and Herder, 1971, p. vii.

for the best use of life, not only for myself but for those I love.

When we moved to the commune where we now live, Downhill Farm, my wife and I had a sense that it was just in time, that we were getting ourselves and our children out just ahead of a tidal wave of infection. Three of our children had escaped ahead of us. Our eighteen-year-old daughter had dropped out of high school as soon as she was sixteen, the first day she legally could do so, and left home (with our blessing and encouragement) for an independent life. For awhile she was a member of the Bear Tribe, a communal group learning the ways of the American Indians—how to live off the land compatibly with nature. Our twelve-year-old daughter had preceded us to the commune by a couple of months, and in that short time had begun to flower as a self-reliant, joyful, maturing woman, cured, as it were, overnight, of the sick preoccupations and insecurities of adolescence in suburbia. Our eight-year-old daughter, who is aphasic, had been living for nearly two years in Camphill Village, a communal school for brain-damaged and retarded children. But our sixteen-year-old daughter was mechanically and indifferently serving time in an elegant, progressive public high school, gradually being drawn into the competitions, vanities, and tensions of vacuous social life dominated by the record player, the telephone, drugs, and sexual jealousy and possessiveness (with relatively little sexual joy). And our five-year-old son, in kindergarten, was changing before our eyes as he adopted the values his friends adopted from their parents and older siblings: secretiveness, competitiveness, shrillness of desire, silliness, his curiosity growing duller by the day. He was becoming money-conscious; and his friends stole from their mothers' purses. He was picking up neighborhood attitudes of giggling shame about sex. His head was feverish with "I want" and "Mine!" and trips to stores were becoming ordeals of saying no to his nascent, raw, and mindless consumerism. Television and the *Sears Catalog* were his *Playboy* magazines of possessive fantasy. We lived in the gleaming new planned city of Columbia, Maryland, which advertises itself as "The Next America," and our children were not safe on the streets because of the mounting racial tension, drug problems, gangs, and interpersonal violence. My wife's life had become one of housekeeping and childcare and perpetual shopping. The more successful I became in my profession, the less meaning it had for me and the more it separated me from family and friends. I had contracted the endemic disease of American males—the association of personal worth with annual income—and though it was well over twenty thousand a year, it was never enough, not because of rising prices or exorbitant standard of living, but because it was a surrogate for love, and especially for self-esteem, and made hungry where most it satisfied. The very activities which meant progress in my life progressively cut me off from the satisfactions I most yearned for. I decided to retire.

I am deliberately emphasizing the personal, what might be judged the selfish, elements in my motivation. One does what he has to do, and I could do no other than what I have done. I have reams of rhetoric to supply on demand about the value of the social experiment in which I am now engaged—which, incidentally, is much more demanding of energy and heartache and painful self-examination and punishing change than any way of life I have been engaged in in the past. It is not *mere* rhetoric, but earnest belief, that if our own commune can demonstrate some viable alternative to the prevailing system, that if it can be first a haven and then a generative source of energy and action for a number of people who are as fed up with or defeated by the other options in our society as I am, my efforts here will be of greater significance for the world at large than they would be if I had continued functioning as an increasingly jaded professor of literature in an elite private college. But the rhetoric, even when genuine, invites argumentation and suggests threat. Many of my friends and former colleagues, not to mention those I encounter when I go to lecture or participate in conferences or otherwise deal with in the noncommunal world, react with hostility, as though there were some implication that my choices should be their choices. I don't know what other people should do—either to save themselves or to save the world. All I can do is explain as honestly as possible why what I have done seemed necessary to me.

Aside from the gratifications of daily life (e.g., this morning, before I got to my typewriter, I invented an alternative to a turnbuckle to stabilize the new screen door—built from scratch—in the communal kitchen), I occasionally get reaffirming signals from other sources that there is more sanity than madness in having picked this curious route. The sixteen-year-old daughter I mentioned had been hitchhiking across country and on the West Coast with a twenty-year-old man of Guatemalan family whom she loved. In one letter she said:

I know that a lot of things have happened to change my life. Mainly Downhill Farm. Because if it didn't come, things would have changed in a much different way. I'm thankful for the things happening the way they have.

Only she and we knew the terror behind the words: "things would have changed in a much different way." But no more needed be said between daughter and parents: a life had been salvaged from the debris of a dying culture. And we never had to say that to her. She knew.

My son—who is no genius, just an alive young mind—is learning plumbing, electricity, auto mechanics, the joys of sharing. He strikes off into the woods alone to find blackberries because he knows the people here love them.

He knows the weeds in the garden—by name—better than any adult on the place. He hasn't said "I want" for any commercial product in a year. We will enter a court fight, if necessary, to save him from school. For the first time in more than a quarter century of marriage my wife and I are engaged together in labor and love of other people, a life in which work and play and education and spiritual growth are inseparable. This book is a diary to which all around me contributed.

FAMILIES OF EDEN

1

What is a Commune?

America has always been a land of communal experiments. The first European settlers often formed communal groups —and, before them, Indian tribes lived communally: the pueblos are the most ancient American communes still functioning. This book concerns the resurgence of interest in communalism after 1965, when Haight-Ashbury and other hip urban communities disintegrated into scenes of drugs and crime, and thousands began looking for relatively isolated and secure enclaves where the new culture could develop. There has been a similar movement in Canada and western Europe—and the phenomenon is related to that of the kibbutzim in Israel, communes in Japan, and, more recently, in Africa (again, a return to the communalism of tribal society), and even to the huge communes of China. But the focus here is specifically upon the United States.

The new communes received much attention in the media in their early days, but, interestingly, public attention waned precisely when the movement began to get serious and to grow, becoming more practical and positive in its efforts to create viable alternatives to the prevailing system, especially after 1968. In that year a shattering series of disillusionments—including the assassinations of Martin Luther King and Robert Kennedy, the invasion of Czechoslovakia, the emphasis on black separatism, the Democratic Convention in Chicago—drove many dissidents in our society to abandon militant and overtly political tactics and to turn to building a system within the system. In a few brief years have emerged recognizable patterns and viable structures of a new culture—in some ways a mirror image of present society, in some ways a refurbishment of strong elements of the American heritage. Communal structures (both in living and working arrangements) are a definitive characteristic of that new culture.

In contrast to communal societies of other eras and places, contemporary communes in the United States are typically domestic units (i.e., homes, as opposed to communal villages, towns, or mini-societies), averaging less than a dozen adults plus attendant children. Other communes have tended to be first of all conscious social experiments, with explicit beliefs, rules, patterns of governance, and customs —visible as an exoskeleton. The structures of the new communes are more like skeletons under the skin, which can be intuited and hypothesized, but remain implicit—to the extent that the communards themselves are often unaware of them. Few of the new communards would call themselves anarchists, but that is the most accurate term for their most characteristic philosophical and political disposition. Like flora and fauna, they live by natural, organic laws, unstated. The new anarchism depends upon a revolution in consciousness which will restore humankind to its Edenic harmony with the universe.

After magazines, newspapers, and television lost interest in communes, academic researchers and journalists writing books began sending out questionnaires and commune-hopping, tripping continually over one another's traces. Lucy Horton, one of the staff members for this study (who was simultaneously gathering recipes for her *Country*

Commune Cooking, Coward, McCann & Geoghegan), describes arriving at one in California. The house was deserted. She wandered until she found the sweat hut (bent saplings covered with rugs, burlap, and mud). Sure enough, steam was seeping out of the entrance flap, so she peeled off her clothes and popped in, finding the hut full of naked people. "Are you from the commune?" one asked. None of them were; they were all visitors. We fantasized that they might have answered in chorus: "We're all sociologists." Some communes have one day a week when they are open for visitors, and the members are quite likely to disappear on those days, so that the visitors may look over the architecture and interview one another.

Because of their small size, intimacy, and need for privacy, communes are much like family homes, and one may easily imagine how families would react to a continual stream of crashers and investigators knocking at their doors. I had not visited more than a couple of dozen communes (mostly in rural New England) before I realized that this mode of investigation is, in every sense, a bad trip. Some dozen other staff members made field visits and several kept long journals of visits from commune to commune around the country. All of us developed a great distaste for such visiting and abandoned the method, though not before we had a substantial amount of material. A number of us lived together at our own commune, Downhill Farm, in the Allegheny Mountains of Pennsylvania, and began experiencing the flood of visitors ourselves—and, ironically, found ourselves turning investigators away.

If visiting is unsatisfactory, so are other standard means of social inquiry. One man, collecting data for a dissertation, was shown a stack of questionnaires gathering dust in the corner of a communal living room—received through the mail from hundreds like himself. One of our staff members, also working on a dissertation, threw his questionnaires to the winds after visiting some twenty communes in New Mexico, Colorado, and on the West Coast. As happens to many academics who undergo this exposure, he also threw his doctoral plans to the winds.

One advantage of this wholesale invasion of communes by writers and scholars has been the appearance of a number of books which may make further commune-hopping less essential for others. I believe our own study is unique, however, in that it combines impressions and observations from a wide range of reporters, almost all of them communards themselves. Moreover, there is an autobiographical dimension in this book which, I believe, makes it somewhat different from other studies. Though by now the story of middle-aged professionals leaving the system with their families to commit themselves to the building of the new culture is a common one on the American scene, it has not yet been told in print—certainly not in the context of a comprehensive survey of the movement and a topical discussion of contemporary communal living.

Rather than reporting on individual communes (our data cover far too many to permit that, and our respect for the privacy of specific communes prohibits it), we organized our information in terms of economics, communications, political structures, interpersonal and sexual relations, education, religion, and changing consciousness, attempting to generalize on bewilderingly disparate phenomena. We used the books and articles resulting from other studies, but the bulk of our secondary material consists of items in the underground press, correspondence, and publications of the communes themselves—material unfortunately unavailable to the general reader. And our primary material—on which most of this book is based—consists of experiences, memories, reports on individual communes, and substantial journals of travelers. Five of us have lived together at Downhill Farm for over two years, and this immediate involvement in communal living has taught us more than any other source about what it means —and how misleading generalizations may be.

There is no satisfactory way to define a commune. Early in our study we said we would consider one to be a group of more than two adults and attendant children living together whose relationship was not limited to economic and legal ties. That, however, included everything from some families to Scout camps to the astronauts traveling to the moon. We found that some who considered themselves communes did not live together (though they had done so for a period), and many groups that do live together do not regard themselves as communes. By eliminating those communes formed before 1965 we substantially disregarded the "intentional communities" (as they were often called) such as Tanguy Homesteads—many of which were started, often by Quakers, in the thirties and forties, and especially in a wave of idealism in the aftermath of World War II. We similarly disregarded for the most part traditional religious groups such as the Bruderhof, Hutterites, and Sons of Levi (not to mention monasteries and convents), and perhaps the best-known commune in the United States, Koinonia, founded in 1942. Our concern was with what we called the *new culture*—though that term, too, eludes precise definition.

Though it may be somewhat tedious, I will review in the next few pages some of the considerations required by a comprehensive survey. A taxonomy of the new communes must make a basic distinction between urban and rural. There are relatively few suburban communes, and those which exist are primarily residences of people working in cities, so share characteristics of urban ones. There are few communes in small towns, though some (e.g., Georgeville Trading Post, in Minnesota, which simply took over an abandoned town) *are* towns, and some rural communes (e.g., Pandanaram in Indiana, Steve Gaskin's Farm in Tennessee) are large enough to qualify as villages, though they are not so incorporated.

Across the axis of urban and rural we may draw another, distinguishing communes in terms of purpose. Some are organized for purposes external to themselves and others are primarily oriented internally. In the first case a cause, or belief, or task, or professional or artistic interest brings people together, and they may decide that by living together they can achieve their purposes better. A craft commune is a good example: leatherworkers, potters, jewelers, and weavers may decide that by forming a community they will be able to create an agreeable atmosphere, share resources, work cooperatively on marketing, and benefit by mutual stimulation. That is quite different from a situation in which people decide that they want to live together, and as it turns out, many become involved in crafts. In urban situations many people are simply looking for a place to live, and for some of them to join an existing commune or to form a new commune is one possible solution for their problem. In rural settings it is often the place which attracts members—the woods and fields and farming life. Many join communes on the basis of friendship. That friends may decide to engage in some industry together, or articulate common beliefs, may be incidental to their primary interest in one another's company. The commune for them is primarily a home, not a structure.*

---

* The term *collective* is sometimes used to refer to people organized around a task, profession, or political objective. They may or may not live together. For example, there are dozens of law communes, in most major cities, where all staff members, including lawyers, secretaries, researchers, participate equally in decision making, share income equally, and spend much of their energy in movement cases, often without fees. But living together is not essential to their purposes. Other collectives, such as the radical political group who lived together in Washington, D.C., for several years and published *Quicksilver Times*, are communes as well, regarding the intimate interaction of daily life as an advantage in achieving their external purposes.

But the grid must be multidimensional—a ball grid, or sphere—with axes radiating in many directions. Communes have been distinguished as pluralist and monist, depending upon whether they tolerate a wide spectrum of purposes or are oriented politically, religiously, or follow the dictates of a charismatic leader. Somewhat different is the distinction between noncreedal and creedal, the latter being those in which members are expected to subscribe to a specific set of beliefs.

All these distinctions are useful—and necessary. For example, Twin Oaks, in Virginia, is based on B. F. Skinner's *Walden II.* Thus it is externally oriented: people came together to create a model which they hoped would be followed by others (and, indeed, has been, resulting in the formation of a number of other "Walden II" communities). At the same time it is very importantly a home, engaged in a number of economic enterprises such as manufacturing hammocks and printing for self-support. Though it eschews group political and religious commitment, it cannot be classed as creedal. It is monistic in its commitment to behaviorism, which provides a unifying *raison d'être.* But its very commitment to scientific experimentation insures an openmindedness about belief. (Though it was characterized by rather dogmatic antireligious views in its early days, it has become more tolerant as it matures.)

The Canyon Collective (California) lives together in order to do the work of Vocations for Social Change and publish *Workforce.* The Ant Farm (Texas) is organized to take on projects in art, architecture, and design. Heathcote (Maryland) is sponsored by the School of Living, publishes a newspaper, *The Green Revolution,* holds workshops on various aspects of communal living and homesteading, and welcomes visitors on a regular basis, introducing them to communal life. All are externally oriented, and because of their common commitment to a particular kind of social action, the Canyon Collective might be classed as monistic, but none are creedal, and Heathcote is exceptionally pluralistic. Such communes as these may be quite fluid in structure and may encompass a broad range of purposes and contain (at least for periods) individuals who do not particularly identify with their external purposes, though the commune as a whole regards living together as a means toward some defined aims.

An internally oriented, pluralistic, noncreedal commune is likely to regard communal living as an end in itself. Its purpose is to facilitate the multiple purposes of its members, and its vector of growth and change is a composite made up of these. The distinctions are by no means hard and fast. Some groups begin as pluralistic and noncreedal, but a monistic purpose or creed evolves (e.g., quite a few communes in one valley in Oregon began without any religious basis, but converted to Christianity in 1971–72). I believe the more common drift is in the opposite direction, as was the case of two communes which intended to run Liberation News Service from a rural base, but soon gave it up and continued as rural, pluralistic, internally oriented communes.

The Lama Foundation (New Mexico) is both creedal and monistic. Its permanent members share a belief in the teachings of its charismatic leader. At the same time this group performs a number of more ecumenical educational functions, from publication and workshops to summer-long work-study programs, making a spectrum of religious practices and teachings available to the public. The Family of Mystic Arts (Oregon) is creedal (primitive Christianity), but more pluralistic, as tolerance of diversity is embodied in its creed. Living together is much more an end in itself for this group, and though they have many visitors, this is almost an inadvertent function (resulting from publicity in the media in its early days), and so the group would probably best be classified as internally oriented.

Still another axis distinguishes the public and private communes. All those I have mentioned by name have in some sense gone public. They are listed in directories, reported in publications, and, like businesses and institutions, include dealing with outsiders as part of their explicit function (with the exception of Family of Mystic Arts). By far the largest number of communes are unlisted and prefer to remain that way. Like private families, they primarily exist to serve the needs of their own members; their dealings with the public are practical and secondary considerations. They are, of course, well known in their local areas, particularly to other communes and freaks—a name members of the new culture gladly call themselves—and may participate in information and communication networks regionally and nationally. Some (e.g., Panther cribs, Weatherman collectives) are deliberately secret to those outside their organizations. But most private communes simply avoid publicity and make no arrangements for structured contacts with outsiders. A communal scholar once said to a university audience, "If you've heard about a commune, it isn't typical."

One communard noted, "There are basically two kinds of communes—rich and poor." Some, indeed, are quite middle-class and even prosperous, including an old-age home in Florida taken over and communalized by the residents. Most live below the poverty level, relying to some degree on various forms of welfare, though some members may come from wealthy backgrounds. Another axis distinguishes open and closed. Some, like Morningstar (New Mexico), Wheeler's Ranch (California), and People's Park (Vermont), are deliberately open, on principle accepting any who go there to visit or live. One such, in Virginia, which I cannot name because it is private and its policy is to avoid all publicity, is nonetheless open land for any who choose to come—and is well known within the movement. Some communes are in fact, if not by intention, crash-pads, with a continual flow of visitors and changing residents. Most, like families, are not particularly interested in growth or accommodating visitors, and so are relatively closed (though rarely absolutely so).

Other useful axes distinguish organic and nonorganic (regarding diet and consumption patterns, and food-raising methods on rural communes), vegetarian and omnivorous (though the latter usually have a contingent of vegetarian members), those with and without cottage industries or businesses, those who rent and those who own their house or land, those with total and those with partial pooling of expenses and income, those which have and have not formed legal entities such as corporations or trusts, unisexual groups and those containing both sexes, those monogamous on principle and those which are not (though the latter may be fairly monogamous in practice), peer groups and those with wider age range, those with and without children. "Academic" is a recognizable and large category—i.e., those made up predominantly of students and teachers (or other educational staff) as opposed to those with a minority of such members. Areas around colleges are usually thick with academic communes, many of which exist only for the school year.

One might include a simple distinction between small and large, with the breaking point at about twenty. But there are important qualitative differences all along the scale, more critical in the small numbers. That is, the difference between a group of three and one of four is more substantial than the difference between one of four and one of five, and so on. The anthropologist John B. Calhoun has demonstrated experimentally that there is an optimal size for social units of many mammals, including human beings—about a dozen adults and attendant young. "It is in the context of social networks made up of clusters of about this size that human beings achieve their fullest degree of health and creativity." * Our research indicates large numbers of communes with six to eight members, and those of about a dozen are fairly common. Relatively few seem to stay in the middle ranges—between about fifteen and fifty. If they are larger than twenty, they are likely to grow into the hundreds (almost always under charismatic leadership). An exception is Twin Oaks, which limited its size on its first site to fifty members and began spawning new communities with mixtures of old members and new applicants—and which scrupulously avoids charismatic leadership.

A combination of these characteristics provides a fairly informative profile permitting some standardization and comparison. Our guess as to the statistically typical commune today is one which is urban, internally oriented, pluralistic, noncreedal, private, poor, closed, organic, omnivorous, unincorporated, without industry or business, in a rented house, with partial economic sharing, both sexes, nonmonogamous, nonacademic, composed of six to eight peers with one or two children under six. How many such communes are there? They are not, of course, officially identifiable—e.g., by the Census Bureau. Many rent or buy property in violation of local zoning regulations, and so are reluctant to acknowledge that they are communes. Many, in fact, do not call themselves communes, though they share all the above characteristics. Most are highly resistant to questionnaires or formal studies (and the several attempts at quantitative studies done by these methods are misleading because the respondents are a self-selected group, atypical by definition). Nor is there any assurance that they will participate in organizations of communes, subscribe to newsletters, or allow themselves to be listed even by sympathetic parties.

---

* Don Benson, "Optimal Size," *The Modern Utopian*, vol. 4, nos. 3 and 4, p. 31.

Efforts to extrapolate statistics from the scattered evidence we have may be as dry and vain an exercise as developing a taxonomy, but before encountering more concrete descriptive material, I think it is valuable for a reader to have an overview of the dimensions of the phenomenon insofar as we can determine them from our data. For example, we have some suggestive figures from several cities. New Communities Project in Boston had (as of fall 1972) "about 200 communes" on its mailing list for the Greater Boston area. This did not include groups that were exclusively student co-ops existing for the duration of the school year. A staff member reported, "I would guess that figure represents a fairly accurate estimate of the number of communes in Boston," but I doubt that he is right. More likely, for every one on their list there are several more who do not know of New Community Projects, or choose not to be identified by that organization. *Kaliflower*, a very exclusive newsletter, hand-delivered to verified communes in the San Francisco area (and to a few in Berkeley), circulated to over 350 groups. That same year a newspaper estimated the number of communes in Berkeley at 200. Neither of these included the southern Bay area. In New York City in 1971, according to the *New Yorker*, there were at least 1,000. In considering all such estimates I think it is realistic to project an iceberg of unknown groups beneath the tip of the known, at a ratio of at least four or five to one. Moreover, any estimate should allow for a growth rate, though this, too, is difficult to determine. Most observers agree that the number of urban communes is growing, probably at least doubling annually, even allowing for a substantial rate of dissolution.

In addition to Boston, the San Francisco Bay area, and New York City, there are similar concentrations of communes in Chicago, Philadelphia, Washington, and Baltimore, with lesser, but still large, numbers in Los Angeles, Seattle, Portland (Oregon), Minneapolis, Milwaukee, Detroit, and Pittsburgh. Many other cities, such as Atlanta, Fort Worth, Dallas, San Diego, Saint Louis, Albuquerque, Buffalo, Cleveland, Cincinnati, and Miami, also have numerous communes. All cities with universities have them in large numbers, which makes for disproportionate numbers in such smaller cities as Ann Arbor, Boulder, Ithaca, Bellingham, Lawrence, and Eugene. There are over 2,500 campuses in the country, and though, of course, many of these are small, isolated schools, outside the new-culture mainstream, an estimate of an average of ten per campus seems reasonable, even excluding the temporary housing arrangements which do not outlast an academic year. Many of these would not be classed as academic, as defined here, since university neighborhoods attract large numbers of people with no direct association with the institution, who may be inclined toward communal living. That implies 25,000 communes—many of which, of course, overlap with estimates for the thirty-odd cities mentioned.

Given all these factors, it seems conservative to say that urban communes, more or less fitting the profile given above (with allowance for large numbers of them being academic), number in the tens of thousands, and that even with a low average size of six to eight members, the people living in them number in the hundreds of thousands, certainly more than a quarter million. These do not include the creedal and monistic communes and commune-complexes (e.g., New Life, in Philadelphia, a Quaker-oriented social action organization of about a dozen communal houses; the Fort Hill Community—headed by Mel Lyman —in Boston, with several hundred members; Reba Place, in Evanston, a Christian social action group with a couple of hundred members), which tend to be much larger in size. For example, about 1,400 Jehovah's Witnesses live in the communal Bethel complex in Brooklyn, and, of course, thousands in cities live in convents, monasteries, and other sectarian communal arrangements. All in all, I would estimate that over half a million people in our cities are currently living communally, with the number rapidly increasing.

Though urban and academic communes are by far the most numerous variety and may be highly significant in predicting future patterns of urban life, they are less significant than rural communes for the purposes of this study. In the first place, urban communes tend to be variations on the rooming houses or shared apartments that have always been part of urban and academic life.* In these settings, communalism is largely a convenience. Many members are heavily involved in social action, community service, studies, or religious practices, which makes sharing quarters a desirable means of keeping down costs and maintaining communication. Many urban people shift from commune to commune, year after year, as interests, jobs, or needs change. One's important membership, in that context, is in a wider community of similarly committed people rather than in a specific, familial group.

While rural communes are less transitory and might seem easier to identify (i.e., to distinguish from closely related living arrangements), they are no easier to count. The figure "over 2,000" was picked up from a *New York Times* story** and spread broadly by writers about com-

---

* In the late forties and early fifties my wife and I—like many of our peers in graduate school—almost always lived in shared apartments, usually with communal meals, often with communal budgets, and even with experiments in group marriage, though the word *commune* was never used, and we did not think of such arrangements as a way of life except as a means to an end—getting through school economically, so we could launch professional lives and private families. A young woman from a group in Washington, D.C., told me that she and half a dozen other people were sharing an apartment in 1969 when she saw a story in a newspaper about communes. She went home with the news: "Guess what we are! We're a commune!" And she had to explain the term.

** Bill Kovach, "Communes Spread as the Young Reject Old Values," *New York Times*, Dec. 17, 1970. Kovach actually said, "Nearly 2,000

munes, such as Robert Houriet, Richard Fairfield, and Benjamin Zablocki. We believe that figure does not even indicate the order of magnitude of numbers of rural communes today. Staff members for this study, and a number of other travelers visiting communes whom we have interviewed, have been in most parts of the country and have discovered no area without its complement of rural communes, i.e., at least one within a hundred square miles of wherever one happens to inquire. If there are, indeed, at least one per hundred square miles, that implies some 30,000 in the United States (excluding most of Alaska), a figure that does not seem unlikely if the barren and low density areas are averaged with those of high commune concentration, such as California, Oregon, New Mexico, Colorado, and New England.

Almost none of these would be revealed by any survey less intense than personal visitation, as most are private, nameless, uncommunicative. When we moved to Downhill Farm, in an unfrequented area of the Alleghenies where freaks are especially rare, we knew of one other commune within a forty-five-minute drive. It had started about a year before and immediately began publishing a newsletter and making its name known. We discovered another already in existence, closer to us, unnamed and unpublicized

---

communes in 34 states have been turned up by a *New York Times* inquiry seeking to determine how many permanent communal living arrangements of significant size could be found in the country, why they existed and who lived in them. The number is believed to be conservative because it no doubt missed some smaller communes and does not include hundreds of small, urban cooperatives and collectives. . . . No accurate count exists, largely because official agencies —except the police, who watch urban collectives and communes for narcotics—generally ignore the development. In addition, most are quiet and sometimes secretive, and thus go unnoticed by neighbors." The methodology of the inquiry was not reported, nor was there any definition of "commune," "permanent," or "significant size," and it should be remembered that most communes have started since 1968 and the annual increase in numbers is large.

(consisting of six adults and three children living together on a common budget). Within another year four more had started in the same radius, making a total of six, of which only our own and the one with the newsletter would be likely to be known by anyone, except personal friends, outside the immediate area. A member of Heathcote—on the Pennsylvania border above Baltimore—said, "There are at least seven rural groups within a twelve-mile radius, but Heathcote is the only one I ever saw on a list." David Riesman, who has a farm near Brattleboro, Vermont, reports that "now there are far more communes than farmers in the area," of which only a handful would be likely to be picked up by any survey. As one moves into the Midwest, with its expanses of flat land farmed largely by agribusiness, communes are, of course, less frequent—yet they exist, as they do throughout the culturally inhospitable South.

Shaky as the original figure is, as well as the permutations I will base upon it, we might guess that if the *Times* found 2,000 communes in 1970, there are at least 5,000 in 1973 in roughly the same category of prominence. If our local situation and that of Heathcote are in any way typical, the ratio of public to private communes is between one to three and one to six—let us say one to four as a conservative estimate. That would imply that for 5,000 identifiable communes there must be some 25,000 as a total, a figure not far out-of-line with the 30,000 estimated on the basis of geographical distribution. The average number of members is somewhat larger in rural than in urban communes—more like ten to a dozen. Thus, some 250,000 to 300,000 people must currently be living in rural communes. Combine that with the estimate for urban communes, and the total is over three-quarters of a million, or over. 3 percent of the population, or more than three persons in each thousand. The proportion of Israel's population living in kibbutzim is ten times as large (3–4 percent), but there is no such growth rate there, and no indication that contemporary kibbutzim are part of a movement toward massive cultural change, as seems to be the case in the United States.

While our own files on about 1,000 communes are obviously quite incomplete, their distribution is suggestive. By far the largest number (135) are in California. The next largest (80) is New York, of which nearly half (35) are in Greater New York City. Illinois, Massachusetts, Oregon, Pennsylvania, and Vermont are represented by some 25–40 each, and the remaining states by smaller numbers, with none listed in Idaho, Nebraska, Nevada, South Carolina, and Wyoming. To a large extent, of course, these files indicate where the staff has traveled. There are no doubt communes in Idaho, but we were unable to go there to find them. As in other phenomena of growth, the more communes there are in an area, the more likely is their number to increase and the more likely are some to be publicly known and listed—to a point. The number of communes in the Taos area has probably actually decreased since the bad summer of 1969, when local tensions resulted in violence and a strong reaction among communards themselves against more coming into the area. Similarly, there is a strong antifreak bias among communards in the Brattleboro area: it is possible for a population to increase to the point that it unbalances the ecology, and the survival intuition is to limit further growth.

Since our focus here is on communal living as an end in itself, the more isolated and stable rural communes provide our most valuable evidence. These are found in the hundreds in any part of the country where marginal farms are being sold. The person-power of a commune makes it possible to rejuvenate old farms which could not be operated effectively by blood families, especially where the land is too rough or broken up to be of interest to agribusiness. Though, as the discussion of taxonomy above indicates, communes are bewilderingly diverse, we also found an astonishing consistency. Those which are bizarre tend to be the few that are publicly known. It is the numberless and anonymous communes which never appear on any list and are never noticed by the media—which even tend to escape the visitors on their circuits—that define a type.

We found ourselves joking about "the Great Commune in the Sky," meaning not an ideal, but a model our study led us to base our generalizations upon. We tested this model against our own experience and that of a number of other travelers (each of some half-dozen, for instance, who had visited at least thirty communes; one who had visited at least two hundred over a three-year period, several of them being places he stayed for long visits). We interviewed ourselves and these other travelers with a standard format of questions, then tested our description by reading it back to them and asking for comments, reservations, and exceptions. We can be surprisingly specific about what we regard as a typical rural group. This is not a statistically accurate description, nor might any single group have all these characteristics, but it is an attempt to give the flavor, style, and outline of the sort of communal farm you might find if you went to the local organic food store, record or book store, free clinic, or other hip hangout, asked for directions to a rural commune, and went out to visit.

There are from a half-dozen to twenty adult members (average age in the late twenties, with few over fifty), a few children (usually five or under), living on a run-down, marginal farm of some thirty to a hundred acres. The degree of commitment of the adults varies from mere visiting, trying, exploring, through a kind of provisional membership status, to a core group of four or five who have some confidence that they will remain together for the forseeable future, and who bear the major responsibility for the commune. Usually one or several of the core group are buying the farm, and there are probably mortgage payments of something like a hundred dollars a month. They may not even have a name and are probably unincorporated, but think vaguely that they should be; they are not yet motivated strongly enough to undertake the legal expense and bother. (Besides, the ambiguity of status and commitment makes it difficult to identify a specific group which might incorporate. When you ask how many live there, the answer is invariably, "About twelve," or some other number: from day to day one is not quite sure who's there, who's in, who's out.)

Maybe half are vegetarians, and the garden is organic. There is little homogeneity of political or religious belief, though many tend to be disenchanted with political action, and most are tolerant of a wide range of religious concerns of other members—from astrology to devotion to Jesus. At any given time most are living monogamously. One or more couples in the group may be married, but most are not. Several have been divorced. Some few have jobs that take them off the farm. There are probably at least incipient efforts to set up a cottage industry, produce crafts, run a garage, or engage in some other nonfarming business for cash. Several, or even most, get food stamps, and eligible mothers among them are receiving Aid to Dependent Children. Some may receive Unemployment Assistance. A few have college degrees (perhaps even advanced degrees), and one or two have abandoned promising professional careers. Others did not complete high school. Most are white, from solid middle-class backgrounds, though increasingly there are young communards of blue-collar or rural background; occasionally there are blacks, chicanos, or American Indians in the membership. Usually such farms have little or nothing in cash crops: they hope to raise a large proportion of their food for subsistence and to pick up needed cash from odd jobs (often day labor on other farms), gifts, or welfare.

In many there are something like encounter meetings to work out group problems, and group decisions are made by consensus, though there is little emphasis upon governing structure. There may be some kind of rotating schedule for chores (in which all participate: there is little distinction of sex roles, and people consciously try to pick up skills they do not have), and there may be amorphous areas of individual responsibility (based on knowledge and interest); but for the most part people participate in the work of the commune without assigned tasks or expectations, as they feel like it. There is a fairly strong work-orientation in most, especially in the Southwest and the East. One works about as hard around the place as he would on a paid job —and weekends are no exception. Expenses are generally shared (e.g., for food, vehicles, mortgage and utilities, construction and garden and animals). Sometimes income is pooled; more commonly, however, a dual system is maintained in which individuals have their own savings and income aside from what they put into the group budget, and they buy certain things (e.g., cigarettes, liquor, dope, gifts, gas for personal trips, clothes) out of their "own" money. Similarly, ownership of things is vaguely dual. Some let their cars be used fairly freely by the group and some maintain various degrees of private control. Clothes are washed together (often at a laundromat), but sorted according to owners. Such things as records and phonographs may be used by the group, but everyone knows to whom they belong. Responsibility for taking care of the children may be shared, at least in theory, but the major burden is likely to remain with the mother or father.

Bathrooms are shared freely, for all functions, for as many as can fit, at all times, without embarrassment. Individuals or couples tend to have private rooms, but there is a good deal of traffic through them, and no one minds sharing a room with others, even strangers (and rarely are there sexual implications in such sharing). There are usually no rules against alcohol or dope, and most members occasionally use both, but for the most part they can't afford and don't keep either around. (A case of beer disappears in an evening with so many helping themselves, so one does not often buy beer.) A few may engage in yoga or meditation. There are lots of books around, but at least when the weather is good there is little reading. Subscriptions to newspapers or magazines are rare and are likely to be either to underground publications or to local, country papers that carry more news of auctions than of the international or national scene. Some communes have television or radios, but they are seldom used. Often there is no telephone. Contact with the outside world is primarily maintained through visitors—of which there are a great many, most often friends of members. Activities such as music (playing dulcimers, recorders, banjos, and guitars, singing), cards, chess, or nude massage are common in the evening. The kitchen is the social center; most conversation takes place in the course of snacking, or with coffee or tea, and is more likely to be about getting the hay in or the yogurt made than politics or poetry or personal problems. Nudity is common and casual, as are physical demonstrations of affection—regardless of sex, age, or couple-relationship. Bickering is usually over chores—e.g., cleaning up after snacks. Pets are another source of interpersonal tension (a number of seasoned communes have absolute rules against them), and cars are another sensitive issue (the approach to most country communes is cluttered with disabled or abandoned vehicles). Most people at least dabble at crafts such as embroidery, weaving, leatherwork, woodwork, and many are creative bakers and cooks. Meals are a central ceremonial and aesthetic activity. There is a disposition toward coziness and quiet; many find irritating loud music on the record player, boisterous humor or play, outbursts of anger, and rackety machines. Sometimes the daily bustle is overwhelming, and the commune's reaction is often toward a phase of seclusion and quiet.

When the term *commune* is used in this book without

other qualification, it may be assumed to refer to that Great Commune in the Sky just described, though the picture is like a line drawing of a grasshopper in a biology text, which depicts no actual insect that ever whirred across a summer field. As the next chapter will indicate, the picture is bound to be misleading, though the bits and pieces of observation of communes speckling all sectors of that taxonomic ball grid lead one to imagine a prototype in Plato's realm of the ideal. If one were to travel the American frontier in the early nineteenth century he might have found just such diversity in the stockades and outposts hewn from the wilderness, and from those clues might have deduced—both as accurately and inaccurately—the characteristics of the civilization to follow.

2

Cabbages and Kings

As one begins to experience communes, the homogeneity suggested by the generalizations in the last chapter is impossible to imagine. To illustrate, I will include here some adapted excerpts from a journal of my early travels. Before starting research for this book I had incidentally visited and stayed in a few academic and urban communes, but had made little conscious effort to understand the nature of the phenomenon. In July of 1971 Marty (my wife) and I, with various of our five children, set out in a camper to visit some of the places we had heard about in New England— some listed in commune directories, some we had learned of privately. Beth, then fifteen, accompanied us on some visits. Jenny, our aphasic daughter, then seven (whose rather random behavior made long or intense visitation difficult), and Topher, then four, were with us most of the time. I include here one commune in Colorado I visited alone. As throughout the book, the names of communes are generally fictional—except when they themselves want or do not mind publicity.

CATHOLIC WORKER FARM.* The ninety-acre farm at
Tivoli, New York, is one of several country hospitality
houses established in conjunction with urban hospitality
houses by the Catholic Worker Movement, which was
started by Dorothy Day in 1933. It is located in an old
estate, which must have been elegant in its day, on the
banks of the Hudson. Eleanor Roosevelt spent her summers
there as a child. Now there is a large stone gate house, a
thirty-odd room manor, a women's dormitory attached to
the kitchen, a small, beautiful chapel, and several other out-
buildings. Part of the program of the CWF (in addition
to publishing the newspaper, *The Catholic Worker*, and
serving the poor) was to create decentralized farm communes which could take over functions of the state. The
older members now—in reaction to the current movement
—deny that the place is a commune. "We're a hospitality
house," Stan Vishnewski (who has been in the Movement
since the beginning) said gruffly.

Their function is to take in indigent travelers and dere-
licts, many of them sent from a related hospitality house
in the Bowery. But currently they are visited by many
younger freaks, and there are definite generation-gap problems. Of the transients there, many are senile or sick, alcoholics or addicts; others are young people who, especially
in the summer, sleep in bedrolls on the grounds. I once
visited a County Farm in Ohio, where the indigent were
taken in and, to the extent they were able, put to work.
The Catholic Worker Farm is much like that—with an
overlay of a hippie crash-pad, and an almost invisible but
important substratum of political and religious idealism.

We first encountered John, a young long-hair who had
just spent several weeks at the Brotherhood of the Spirit

* For a good general account, including recorded conversations with
members, see Richard Fairfield, *Communes: USA; a Personal Tour*,
Penguin, 1972, pp. 334–44.

(which we were later to visit), and he had the spaced-out, joyous, evangelistic manner of most Brotherhood members. "Something big is about to happen here," he told us intently. "I feel it, like at the Brotherhood, a gathering of energy." Our principal guide was Will, a gray, burr-headed, athletic man, former folk singer and Broadway actor, who has lived at CWF for several years with his wife and two children (both of whom he delivered on the farm). He immediately insisted we come into lunch, which the others inside were just finishing.

The main room of the manor is a kind of lobby, shabbily furnished, with a dusty library well-stocked with radical and Catholic publications. A couple of ancient ladies sat entranced on couches. The dining room has about a dozen bare board tables, each for about eight people. A group was sitting around Dorothy Day talking business. Two or three people pitched in to get lunch for our family—rice casserole, salad, green beans from the garden, milk, and tea. Will sat with us while we ate, earnestly, simply describing his mystical relationship with God (unlike any version of Catholicism I have ever encountered). Beth and I cleared the table and washed dishes, put food away in the institutional kitchen. The able-bodied, mature men were all out in the fields—except for Will—so those around were the very old and the hippies. Will took us to three beehives he tended and proudly explained what he was learning from them (chiefly patience).

One solemn man in his thirties, Walter, taught philosophy part-time at a nearby college, had lived at CWF with his wife for several years and they recently had a baby. He was about to leave CWF with some others to start a hospitality house in Toronto—because he was sick of "hippie bullshit" from such as John. Stanley Vishnewski, a writer, had just had a piece accepted by *The New York Times* on commune-hopping—and he, also, was scornful of young drifters. "It's a sickness they have," he said, "like alcoholism or drug addiction. It takes them a couple of years to get over it—if they ever do." On the other hand service was the spirit of the original intent, and he recognized that that sickness, like any other, needed to be served. What brought you into this in the first place? I asked Stanley. "The Catholic religion," he said—and gave no further explanation. "This place is too luxurious for our purpose," he said, as it attracted too many of the "wrong" type of visitors. But on principle, none are turned away.

Permanent residents have various assigned jobs. The place is run without pretense of democracy by Dorothy Day and the older staff. The newspaper is edited there, and most support comes from it (circulation about thirty-five thousand) and donations. Some two hundred dollars a week go for groceries for a summer population of about sixty, down to thirty or forty in the winter.

An example of the sort of case CWF was intended to serve was that of a mother and little girl, either abandoned by the father or, as the mother put it, waiting until he found a job. John and his generation were more inclined to see community as an end in itself—and were waiting for the new age to dawn. I heard one of what were apparently typical squabbles—an oldster bawling out a young girl for playing her flute in the empty dining room. She was very hurt and confused. Far from the vibes John felt, I thought both energy and morale were low. Things weren't getting done. After our short visit a friend of mine stayed there a couple of nights with her two children, and she confirmed this impression. She spent delightful hours in the evening on the river bank with the hippies, listening to guitars and singing, but generally she found a dissolute, depressed atmosphere, great tension, slovenliness, and a contingent of young people with energy and creativity who could not relate well to the idealism, discipline, and moral seriousness of the Catholic core group.

CAMPHILL VILLAGE. In Chapter III there is a brief description of Beaver Run, one of the Camphill villages that specializes in the care of retarded and brain-damaged children—where our daughter Jenny lives most of the year. At Copake, New York, is an older village, for adults, begun in 1955. If the Catholic Worker Farm has only an inadvertent and somewhat uncomfortable relation to the new culture, the Camphill villages have almost none at all. Freaks show up at them from time to time, having found an address in some directory of communes. They are treated hospitably, but soon leave. "They say we are too good for them," a staff member at Beaver Run commented wryly. Indeed, the abstemious and disciplined life of these communities would be attractive only to people thoroughly dedicated not only to service but to the educational and religious ideals of Rudolf Steiner. There is a severity of purpose and commitment in the staff which is likely to make an outsider feel inadequate and somewhat uncouth, in spite of the staff's warmth and friendliness.

To travel to Copake on the same day one leaves CWF is something of a jolt and an irony. CWF grew out of an explicitly anarchist social design. But if one wants a vision of how an anarchist society made up of decentralized, relatively self-sufficient communities might work, he might visit one of two communes, based on almost antithetical philosophic principles: Twin Oaks and Camphill. In their very different ways both have achieved a high degree of efficiency and internal order, of happiness and self-fulfillment for their members, and of compatible and effective relationships with the outside world. (A third example might be the villages of the Bruderhof, which I omit because I have not visited.)

Camphill seems on the one hand like a village of the old Europe of our imaginations, on the other like a glimpse of a future in which human potential is more fully realized than it generally is today. It is located on some five hundred rolling green acres (another seven hundred nearby are being acquired) in central New York. Staff families live with six to eight retarded adults in cottages (which look somewhat like suburban ranch-style houses, except they are larger and have an architectural distinction peculiar to Camphill) scattered over the grounds. Lanes wind among the houses, shops, and other buildings, recreational areas, and surrounding fields. There is a bakery which provides bread not only for the village but in large part for the nearby town of Copake, a shop where toys are manufactured, and another for copper enameling, productive gardens, livestock. Each villager has a job, as it is important to the Camphill philosophy that each person be a productive contributor to the community. Physically the village is a model of beauty, order, and economical plenitude (though they are by no means wealthy, deriving most of their support from their industries and an extremely modest "tuition" from the families of the retarded or various state programs). To see the villagers strolling in the evening, or playing soccer on the green fields, or herding cows in for milking, or earnestly, happily working in the shops, is to sense what power resides in even the severely handicapped in the liberating atmosphere of mutual acceptance and loving support.

We parked our camper near one of the cottages where lived a young couple (in their thirties), their three-year-old curly-headed son, and eight retarded adults—two men and six women. The yard was neatly fenced and dappled with well-kept flower gardens. We had dinner—fruit salad, rolls, bread and cheese, fruit punch—on a long table in the yard. Each person had a role in preparing the meal, setting the table, or cleaning up—most roles performed with agonizing difficulties, easily absorbed in the prevailing patience. Except for the large number of rooms, the house was like that of a conventional middle-class family, with the usual kitchen appliances, furnishings, and decorations, all immaculately maintained.

We talked with the couple, Karl and Ellen, respectively Swiss and Scottish (nationalities which are characteristic of the Camphill staff) about how they met and became committed to the movement in Europe. I asked whether they thought of their lives as involving sacrifice and service. Karl laughed. "No—except self-service. It satisfies us, or we wouldn't do it." After dinner he took us on a walk around the village. We are always impressed by the way our Jenny responds to and is responded to by other retarded people: there is an intuitive mutual recognition, a kind of eye-talk across the chasm. Since Jenny was accustomed to the Camphill style of life, she seemed quite at home, as though she recognized that she might someday live at this village herself. The central building of the village is the Hall, used for religious services, meetings, and other community functions. I mentioned a distinctive style of architecture—and it is most magnificently embodied in the Hall. There is only one right angle in the building—from which all other measurements had to be taken. The windows, for instance, are all irregular quadrangles or other rectilinear shapes. Karl, a wood craftsman (as well as gardener), responded with pride to my admiration of the intricate banister, smoothly finished and joined from dozens of irreguar shapes. He explained that when getting the job done is less important than the doing, time is unimportant, and incongruity can be absorbed.

BROTHERHOOD OF THE SPIRIT.* (Name now changed to Metelica Aquarian Concept, Inc.) In 1968 Michael Mete-

---

* For a good general description and report of a long stay, see Robert Houriet, *Getting Back Together*, Coward, McCann & Geoghegan, 1971, pp. 346–61.

lica, a high school dropout and former Hell's Angel, removed himself to a tree house near Leyden, Massachusetts,
and gradually gathered around him the nucleus of what
was to become the Brotherhood. The group settled at various places before buying an old inn and restaurant between
Warwick and Northfield, Massachusetts, which is now
their chief encampment (though as they have grown they
have opened settlements in a number of other places around
the country). Near the inn they erected a gigantic rustic
dormitory (mainly with lumber from old barns), which is
pictured on the album cover of their rock group's first issue
from Metromedia, *Spirit in Flesh*. (The group's name has
been changed to "Metelica!") In the photograph some two
hundred wild, energetic, joyous young people are crowded
in the windows and doors around the porch of that dormitory, with blond, grinning, mesomorphic Michael in the
foreground. That depicts exactly what one encounters on
a visit. The place swarms with life and joy—mostly young
people who seem in many cases to have been strung out on
drugs and have desperately seized this form of salvation.

When I wrote asking if I might visit, I was immediately
answered:

Dear Jud,
  Glad to receive your letter. You will find the Brotherhood
of the Spirit different from any place you will visit. We have
achieved the togetherness, the peace of mind others search for.
And we are now beginning our greater purpose to be a living
example of this brotherhood to humanity. . . .
  The best preparation for coming here would be to get our
album and absorb it. It's on Metromedia Records. At this time
we are taking overnite visitors for one night. Come any time
you want. You could probably stay longer if you want to.
However, we currently are sleeping from 11 A.M. to 5 P.M. &
12 AM..–4 A.M. . . .
  We would prefer you to be most intrusive, the more you
plunge into things the more you will see. What we have must

be experienced, it just can't be studied or learned. And we're glad to share with anyone that is interested. . . .

Spirit in Flesh will help you to better understand your own life and what you want. (After all, that's what you're really interested in.) Feel free to write any time you want.

Michael, then age twenty, is lead singer of the rock group and a reincarnation of Saint Peter and Robert E. Lee. It was his whim which introduced the unusual sleeping schedule, which, again at his whim, was changed to a more normal one the night we visited. There are five rules at the Brotherhood: no smoking, no drinking, no dope, no promiscuity, and all property belongs to Michael. The rule against promiscuity means, a member explained, that people should not have intercourse unless they feel "infinite love" toward one another. Since prospective members, or PMs, sleep in large open rooms in the dormitory, it would be difficult to engage in sexual activity without detection, and several who have spent time in the Brotherhood report that there is, indeed, much less intercourse there than among people of the same ages outside. The property rule was explained as intended to relieve members of the taint of materialistic possession. Michael has the spiritual strength, and it is his karma, to bear it.

An anecdote pertaining to this rule was told me later on this journey at a commune I will call Maple Mountain. One of the early locations of the Brotherhood was Maple Mountain, owned by a folk singer I will call Sally, a beautiful woman in her mid-thirties who was then a PM of the Brotherhood. There were then about sixteen members. Michael wanted Sally to turn over the deed for the four-hundred-acre farm to him, but she was not ready to do so. According to Sally, Michael began claiming that she had said things she hadn't said and calling upon one or more of the seven elders (in seniority, not age) of the Brotherhood as witnesses in his behalf. Sally then went to the medium,

Elwood Babbitt, a local farmer in his fifties who is Michael's own spiritual adviser, for guidance. Babbitt consulted *his* spiritual adviser, a seventeenth century English physicist, who said that in his last incarnation Michael had been a leader of many troops, and still had to work off much bad karma because of that. Babbitt told Sally that she was probably right in her perception that Michael was manipulating her. He advised Sally to ask Michael to leave. "I can't do that," she said (she is an extremely sweet, nonaggressive person), but Babbitt told her she could if she had to. Finally she did, and the Brotherhood left. Sally told of another woman who was asked to turn over her house to Michael. The day after she did so, she was asked to move out. She moved, and remained a member.

Though the members are predominantly in their late teens or early twenties, there is a higher proportion than in most communes of people from various races and social classes and of various ages. They describe themselves as, and appear to be, continually stoned—on life, love, the spirit. They are as evangelical as Jesus Freaks; from the moment we arrived they were persuading us to join. Characteristically, they stood close to us as they talked and stared us down with soulful eyes. Absence of sexual threat seems to make the women astonishingly open and intimate; I found myself (and this is unlike me!) embarrassed to have young girls lean against me, hold my hands, and gaze rapturously in my eyes on first meeting.

But the rap is tedious. One must get rid of negativity. One must believe that the renewal of the world was beginning right there outside Warwick, Massachusetts. One must be honest, love everyone, feel joy, and work to attain higher consciousness. Our guide for most of our visit, Ted, was a Yale graduate, a highly sophisticated, intellectual young man, who uncritically accepted Michael's authority and the strange amalgam of the world's religions, of spiritualism and reincarnation, derived from séances of

Elwood Babbitt (many of which, taped and transcribed, were available for members to study), and from pronouncements of Michael.

Along with a number of other overnight visitors, we camped in the parking lot. Several expensive cars were there, of parents of members; those we talked with were grateful that their children had found the Brotherhood—probably because it saved them from drugs. The members seemed deliriously happy, bounding down the path, playing games, hugging one another, singing, spontaneously throwing themselves into work projects. We lined up cafeteria-style for the evening meal, eating in the packed dining room of the old inn, on whose vaulted ceilings were transcribed in beautiful, gilded Gothic lettering, statements from Babbitt's transcripts about the Seven Universal Laws: Order, Balance, Harmony, Growth, God-Perception, Spiritual Love, and Compassion. The statements were dignified, eloquent, and coherent.

That night, while we were standing around the campfire near our car, a number gathered to continue evangelizing. A young East Indian from Trinidad carried on endlessly and unintelligibly about the Bible. A wasted, illiterate woman in her late thirties, with her little girl, looked haunted in the firelight. Her artist husband had abandoned her. The Brotherhood had been her salvation. One of the long-standing members, Klondike, a tall, quiet man, softly urged us to stay, to join. They all spoke with the same orthodox intensity. No one acknowledged any problems. All were studiously vague about such things as finances, duties, the hierarchy, how things get done. Material things just take care of themselves, or Michael takes care of them. They claimed to operate completely without structure or governing procedures—by intuition, spontaneity, and loving cooperation.

Michael himself, to whom we talked the following morning, dressed colorfully—in contrast to a general drabness of other members—with leather wrist and headbands, a bright vest, an ornate belt. He had been jogging—and coughed a great deal while he talked. He lives away from the group, drives a sporty car. A number of young girls stood around looking at him adoringly, wanting to accompany him wherever he went, hear his every word. Four blacks were in the conversation; they had come back with the Brotherhood from New York City, after a recent publicity trip: two hundred freaks running through the streets papering the city with posters showing a gigantic head of Michael, advertising the album. Michael was persuading the blacks to join. One of the girls said good naturedly but seriously that she might like to come back, but she had to get down to the city to get shot up with a little scag one more time before she joined.

Michael struck me as quite an ordinary young man— unpretentious, good-humored, modest. He told me that most people lose their native spirit when they grow past childhood, but for some reason he didn't. About fourth grade he recognized that he was different. He was unhappy, alienated for awhile, and after his stint with the Angels he lived as a hermit in his tree house. Now his parents, who visit often and help out the Brotherhood, are very happy about it and him, and he feels close to them again. It was all for a purpose. There is no such thing as circumstance. He assured us that we had come there for a purpose, though we could not yet determine what it was. It was important that we be witnesses to the beginning of the new age. I asked how members are taken in. Prospective members live for two or three months in the dormitory, and ask for membership when they think they are ready. Michael makes the final decision—which is almost invariably positive. "But I can tell when a person is dishonest," he said, looking at me with unsettling eyes. It is said that he can read auras. I wondered how mine read.

AN URBAN GROUP. Their house, in Newtonville, a suburb of Boston, has no communal name. Like thousands of other urban communes, they have come together tentatively, as near strangers, sharing living space and expenses, working toward a stronger sense of group consciousness, which in one way or another all desire. Our friends the Coxbergs are impatient with the process, though they recognize that in less than six months the house could hardly have come together any more than it has. Some members, including the Coxbergs, see their urban situation as temporary—a means of getting money and friends together for a move to the country. Others, for various reasons, plan to remain in the city, and for them the commune is not so much an end in itself as an agreeable and stimulating living arrangement which takes its place in importance alongside professional work, political work, and other urban-oriented activities. There are various ways of describing the tensions among the eight people sharing the house, but this rural-urban polarity in orientation is certainly one factor. It has less to do with country as opposed to city than to community as opposed to convenience. A move to the country would require a degree of commitment to one another and to communalism which the urban-oriented people neither have nor aspire to.

Had we not been told about such tensions, we would not have known they existed in our visit of a few days. The atmosphere was much like that of a busy rooming house, with people coming and going, mostly absent during the day, the evening meal being the major communal focus. There was no schedule for shopping, cooking, or cleaning. Each adult member put ten dollars a week into a grocery budget (and shared monthly rent and utilities, with individual responsibility for long-distance calls), and money was taken from an envelope in the cupboard by anyone who felt the need to buy food (and such household items as soap, toothpaste, toiletries, paper goods, cleaning materials). At about five someone would begin poking around the kitchen to see what was available and start motions toward dinner. Others would drift in, and before the meal was served, nearly everyone was present and helping out. We held hands in silence around the table before eating, then sang the familiar Shaker song as a group:

> 'Tis a gift to be simple,
> 'Tis a gift to be free,
> 'Tis a gift to come down
> Where you want to be,
> And when you have come down
> In your place just right,
> It will be in the Garden
> Of Love and Delight.

I told them another verse, as I remember it:

> I will vow to be simple,
> I will vow to be free,
> I will bow and be humble,
> Just like the willow tree,
> I will wear this as a token,
> I will bear the easy yoke.
> I will bow and be broken,
> Yea, fall down upon the rock.

But they didn't like that one and decided not to incorporate it in their ceremony.

Four were employed at regular jobs outside the house, all at more-or-less professional levels (the most highly paid being a computer salesman). One, a psychologist, saw patients mostly at home in his study, but met some groups outside. One was a full-time graduate student. One mother with a young baby was home most of the time. Another mother, a divorcee with two little girls, four and nine, received Aid to Dependent Children—the only one receiving any kind of welfare. She was very busy taking classes and participating in various encounter-type training groups, so the children were often left in charge of others in the house.

One evening there was a gathering in the house of people from a number of other communes, from New Communities Projects, and from the New Towns Project of the Cambridge Institute, for discussion and socializing. The New Towns Project's goal is to build a communal town of large scale (at various times the aim has been for as high as ten thousand residents, as low as one thousand). New Communities Projects was in the process of getting out a People's Yellow Pages (such as have appeared in some thirty cities around the country), listing services and businesses particularly attuned to the new culture, including lists of communes and "want ads" for communes seeking members or individuals seeking communes. The flavor of the discussion was primarily political and organizational, with some concern for interpersonal problems and group process—very different from the tone of discussion in rural communes or in the religious communes we had been visiting.

BEAVER ROAD FARM, in Vermont, as I will call it, has suffered from overexposure to publicity and visitors, so I will disguise it as much as possible here. In its fifth year when we visited, it is one of the more stable communes, and one of those most successfully functioning as farms (for subsistence, not market). Several of its original members had been political activists who became discouraged by the increasing militancy of the left. Several have advanced degrees in esoteric majors such as Oriental history. A British woman member described it as "very literary," and, indeed, among its dozen members there is a surprisingly large and gifted component of poets and writers of fiction and nonfiction, though very little about the run-down farmhouse, antique farming methods, and earthy daily life suggests that it is an intellectual's haven.

Two of its members were professors when we visited and so were at the farm principally on weekends and during the summers, though their salaries were the mainstays of financial support. Since then, income from publishing has become more than sufficient for their needs. They pay two hundred dollars per month on a mortgage for over a hundred acres—their chief cash outlay, as they eat little meat, have their own eggs, milk, and vegetables, make their own cheese, bread, and wine.

Shortly after our arrival we spun out on a wild truck ride to load bales of hay from the field to store in the barn before an oncoming storm: a neighbor had given them the bales in exchange for labor in haying, which both men and women contributed. We camped at some distance from the house (since they have no children, our two little ones were an unaccustomed aggravation) and saw them mostly during the day, when we helped in the remarkably lush garden, drove people on errands, swam in a nearby pond.

There is an almost mythic, tragic air about the place because of the number of poignant events in their shared past (including close relations with several neighboring communes) and the fantasies of high-strung, imaginative members. The living room contains a stage for performance and a loft that looks like a theatrical set. Around the property and buildings are signs and mementos with evocative histories. On a pasture hill visible from the house fluttered an abandoned maypole from their May Day festival (a gathering of the tribe), standing askance, its faded streamers fluttering, like a prop from a Bergman film. Here, more than at any other commune I have seen, the deeper cultural dimensions of the new age are apparent, encompassing a vision of evil as well as good, of ancient roots as well as future promise and a sometimes almost unbearably intense and vivid present.

At the end of the day they gather in the kitchen, stoking up the wood stove by kerosene light, preparing vegetables. A brown mood seemed to prevail, a sense of stories lurking in the shadows beyond the yellow light. (They have electricity, but rarely use it.) "We are just a bunch of people who went to college together and who wanted to live together in the country," one man said, though several present members were not of that original group. "One thing we do," a woman said, "is eat well." As a joint was passed a man commented sadly that they were down to seeds and stems, but the philosophy of acceptance extended to more than marijuana. "We've never had a meeting about finances," a woman said. "Things come to us." In fact, another member commented, they hardly ever had anything one might call a meeting at all. "I don't know how we have escaped the personal tension that has destroyed other communes," a woman said. Certainly not by resort to what one of the men called "encounter bullshit." One man said there was a good deal more tension, especially sexual, than was apparent. His personal grievance was that one of the women, with whom he had been mated for several years, now wouldn't even speak to him. "It would be nice to get a hello in the morning," he said, and he blamed women's liberation for turning things sour. But the sourness may have been mostly in his head, for to our superficial observation there was more stability and family feeling than in most communes. We were sorry to leave after several days, but recognized that visitors like ourselves were one of their main problems. ("We have turned a man away who arrived with a knapsack on foot through deep snow," one man said.) It was a house of rose one must not go too near.

Maple Mountain Center, as I called it earlier, was the one commune we encountered on this journey which we considered joining—and in fact we did some investigation of real estate in the area in case we decided to settle nearby.

It is a good lesson regarding these brief impressions of communes that we were thoroughly mistaken. What seemed to us a remarkably solid, together group of people in July had experienced an almost complete change in membership by September. In October we visited again, and again were very optimistic about the group's possibilities. Again we were wrong. The commune folded within a year, with some bitterness.

Probably both its strength and weakness was its owner, the woman I called Sally, one of the most magnetic personalities I have ever encountered. She seems to be soft, warm, endlessly giving, almost helpless in her lack of authority—though surely there are more difficult aspects of her personality which may emerge as acquaintance deepens. The danger of charisma is that it may wear thin, or eventually be resented by the very people who are drawn to it. Or it may prevent the growth of complementary strength in others. Maple Mountain was Sally. For personal reasons she left the property in charge of the others (mostly much younger), and the commune fell apart. She returned to unpaid bills, which were justified by a departing man on the grounds that "no one has the right to own so much property."

The huge old house is decorated by an exotic mural on one exterior wall, painted by the Brotherhood when they lived there. The commune rang with music. Guitars and dulcimers were hanging in the living room, and several members (as well as Sally) would pick one up from time to time and break into spontaneous song. Sweetness, joy, and shy kindliness characterized each human contact—all strangely sexless. Sally wanted Maple Farm to be a kind of ashram, and there was theoretically a strict discipline, with hours posted for meditation, chores, meals, relaxation, and bedtime; but this was only loosely followed, and several did not participate in the group meditation. Daily life was much as it is on any farm commune.

I helped the two young men bring in hay, an awkward process pulling with a tractor a rake that was supposed to be horse-drawn. No one knew much about farming, vehicles, house maintenance, cooking, or the country, though all were earnestly learning, and they were getting a lot of help from friendly neighbors. In addition to Sally and her two young children, and the two men, there were four young women. We rototilled and weeded squash plants nude, used the tractor to haul teepee poles out of the woods, gathered beans, helped tend the prize goats. Mealtime was preceded by a long period of holding hands in silence, then singing, as one person after another started a song, then reading of short paragraphs Sally or others had found during the day—thoughts. (There was a lot of reading in Sally's well-stocked library.) A business meeting was held one afternoon, punctuated by a lot of singing, drifting good humor, languor, though there was a steady, subtle pressure from Sally to get responsibilities assigned, the work done. They took turns in the mornings, for instance, getting the children up, fed, and dressed and the older one off to the free school this commune ran nearby. Each member was supposed to contribute $100 per month toward expenses, but almost none did, and I gather Sally bore most of the cost. They bought almost nothing, but seemed comfortable in their hardship.

In my inexperience the ingredients here seemed excellent for a successful commune, and I don't know now what I might have observed that would have tipped me off that it would not succeed—except for the domination, however benign, of Sally herself. What I fear for the movement, from this experience, is that communal living may be better equipped to accommodate weakness than it is to accommodate strength. In order to function without adverse effect on the group's own life, a woman with the many talents and superior qualities of Sally might have to be surrounded with others with equally strong characteristics.

Sweet as they were, the young people with her were relatively ineffectual and submissive, neither equipped to sustain themselves on their own nor to incorporate an individual with sufficient personal power to sustain them.

SECRET RIVER. In a wilderness area of southern New Hampshire is a tract of some four hundred acres with seven houses on it, a community I will call Secret River. As we entered we first encountered a white frame, rather small, and ordinary house by a pond. There was a garage open, and a long-haired VW mechanic was working under a car. About five young people with a couple of kids lived in the white house. It was jokingly called the white commune (in contrast to the yellow commune up on the hill), though the people who lived there did not regard themselves as a commune. The young man had been a teacher until recently in New York, hated it, was busted on a drug possession charge, and for that and various reasons had split to New Hampshire. He was hoping to make a go of the newly opened garage, drawing trade from the surrounding area and charging much less than other garages.

The yellow commune, which we next visited, was the most thoroughly communal commune I have ever seen, with complete, obligatory sharing of property, sex, child care, space, and expenses. (A woman friend who later spent some time there said they tried to make up for everything with sex: no smoking, no drinking, no dope, not even any coffee or tea, but it was required that each woman sleep with each man.) It was a run-down, large house, teeming with flies, dirty babies underfoot, and the vibes abominable. Another visitor, a woman in her twenties, was there—had been for four days—with her husband. He was certain he wanted to join, but she was in doubt. When we arrived she was talking with a woman member in the kitchen, who was tending babies and cooking. Everyone else was out stripping an old barn for lumber, for the commune building which was under construction: it would, when completed, have three open rooms on three levels—one for cooking and eating, one for socializing, one for sleeping. The present yellow house would be for overflow and visitors.

Because from what we had heard about the place we thought Secret River might actually be a place we would like to join, we asked many questions—about how work was distributed, where money came from, how children were cared for, how decisions made. I was astonished to find that the visiting woman, who was trying to make up her mind whether or not to join, learned the answers to these questions for the first time from this conversation. Either she had been too shy to ask—or, more probably, the communication was so difficult that it was impossible to find out in ordinary interaction. A teen-age boy was around the kitchen during much of our conversation. He lived mainly with his mother, in a house down the road (still part of Secret River, which is composed of several private homes and these two communes). His father was one of the founding members of the yellow commune, and the boy spent a good deal of time there. Later we talked to his father, a chemistry professor at a nearby college (hour's drive away). He was a very reserved man in his mid-forties, trying to be friendly, but not quite knowing how. Certainly no one made any effort to entice us to stay, even overnight, and, after a few hours, we left in haste with relief.

SPICELAND. Four young people live in a little log cabin (a converted barn) in eastern New Hampshire. They had hardly moved into the place when they got a letter from me asking if my family might visit their commune. This blew their minds. They didn't even know they were a commune, much less how a stranger might have found out about them. The name I am calling Spiceland was on the mailbox when they moved in, and they liked it and kept it, not knowing that, apparently, a commune had been there earlier and was listed in *The Modern Utopian*.

They were extremely hospitable, truly remarkable and lovable people—three men and a woman in their mid-twenties. They had grown up in that area, known each other in college, and decided to try to live on the land together—hardly aware of the fact that there were such things as communes. In just a few months they had completely rebuilt the barn into a clean, cozy, very attractive home. The outside is all log slabs. Inside, the interior walls are similarly rustic, but very well finished. One of them, a cabinet-maker, had built fancy kitchen fittings. They carry water to the house from a nearby spring. They had cleared a road through heavy thicket and cleared and planted a garden (apparently the land had not been used for years). The three men worked at full-time jobs in town (e.g., one was a laborer for a landscape architect), while Milly, the wife of one of them, stayed home.

The couple relationship between Milly and her husband was steadfastly monogamous, and tension over this had caused one man of the original five to leave. They entertained us—dinner, pot, beer—as they might in suburbia, then came down to our camper to talk long into the night by the fire. Mostly they were interviewing me, like earnest students, about social change, education, communes. They were strongly idealistic, revolutionary in intent (about building a better world), and felt guilty about dropping out of the political struggle to find happiness in building their house and getting closer to the earth and one another.

TAIL OF THE TIGER. That is the actual name of an ashram near Barnet, Vermont, which welcomes visitors. In fact it is run like a kind of inn, with rates (seven dollars per day, and visitors are expected to work). Rinpoche, their guru, is a Tibetan Buddhist. He started a couple of ashrams in

Scotland, had an automobile accident that seems to have altered his character somewhat, married a very worldly English girl considerably younger than he is; he smokes cigars, drinks brandy, apparently is a very earthy guy. He lives at still another of his ashrams in Colorado but spends long periods at Tail of the Tiger, offering seminars and workshops for substantial fees.

There is a large farmhouse and a large barn. The third floor of the house is the meditation room, elaborately decorated with mats and an altar. We were a large group visiting (my brother, his wife, and his three children had joined our family), so we were given a kind of tour. In the meditation room our guide, a thin woman in her thirties who had been in the Peace Corps for several years, sat us down for a discussion of the unique mode of meditation taught by Rinpoche (you let your mind wander, you meditate in action, doing whatever you would otherwise do; nonetheless, your mind finally comes round to the white space that is the goal of meditation). Much of the barn has been adapted into various studios for crafts (e.g., jewelry-making, weaving). Then we had lunch in the communal dining room.

I was impressed by the sincerity and openness of those we met—a very well educated, articulate, experienced group, mostly in their twenties and thirties. About twenty (including four or five very young children) live there regularly. A young woman, a model, married to an artist, told us how they happened through for a weekend, looking for a place to crash, met Rinpoche, and their lives were utterly changed. (She goes into the city for modeling jobs occasionally to pick up cash; her husband stays in the community, working and painting. She pointed to an ornate, carved and painted doorway he had done, under Rinpoche's detailed instruction.) Several members had just returned from a crafts fair at Putney, Vermont, where they had picked up a little money. Members are expected to contribute something like seventy dollars per month each for subsistence. Most of what they earn above that goes to Rinpoche. What does he do with it? I asked. "He has lots of expenses, doing his work around the world," I was told. He flies around and gives lectures—from which he doubtless also gains income. I find myself suspicious of such arrangements; but there was no question about the dedication of the members, who lived on a detailed schedule Rinpoche established for them.

NATURE FARM was a school in organic gardening near Putney, Vermont (since closed). Some fifteen young apprentices of both sexes lived communally in a work camp, and put in long, hard hours, beginning at 4:30 A.M. Apparently they paid no tuition or living expenses, but the farm made a profit from their labor. We visited very briefly, mostly talking to the young, wealthy man who put up the money for this operation, and a visiting consultant on bioenergetic composting (methods derived from the teaching of Rudolph Steiner). Nature Farm was connected to the New England People's Cooperative and the National Organic Farmers Association, both of which have a number of communes on their membership lists.

WOOLMAN HILL is another communal school, near Deerfield, Massachusetts. It is a Quaker conference center that was taken over in 1970–71 by a group of graduate students in education to be run as a community high school. Some fifteen to twenty students and about that many staff live in the several houses and out-buildings. There is a large organic garden. They have a number of animals, several craft studios. The students' tuition is scaled according to ability to pay. Each is expected to work a certain number of hours per week on chores and in the garden. All students and staff participate equally in governance, including the setting of tuition. All recognize that community itself is the basic educational experience, rather than formal instruction.

Though our visit was very short, I was quite positively impressed by a successful blend of school and commune. We worked that evening in the lush garden, putting up strings for bean runners. The spirits of students and staff seemed high, and it was clear that their interaction was mutually educative. I felt sorry for one little girl, under six, who played with my son while we were there but seemed quite isolated among so many older people.

POTTER'S FANCY, as I will call it, is a curious mixture of phenomena near Franklin, New Hampshire. The land (some forty acres) is owned by a Quaker-oriented, highly individualistic craftsman in his late thirties—Joe. Though Joe has no interest himself in communalism, he doesn't mind other people using the land so long as they don't interfere in his life. He is a little scornful and distrustful of lazy hippie types, but is tolerant, and helps them learn gardening and crafts if they are so inclined. In 1970 the Study-Travel Community School was started by two young men, who set up their base at Potter's Fancy. Their idea was that the high-school-age students would travel around the world together and camp at Joe's between trips. A couple of the staff and several students got very much involved in yurt building and became experts. (A yurt is an inexpensive Mongolian building, round, with fluted sides like a muffin paper.) On the sandy land, among scrub pines, they built ten scattered yurts, each out of sight of the others, plus a double-sized yurt as a common room, with two smaller yurts (kitchen and entrance way) attached.

During the year, students and staff alike decided that they were more interested in becoming a commune than in traveling and schooling. But when that decision was made, everyone split, except two of the senior students (who also happened to be expert yurt builders). A couple of brothers of one of these moved in, then a couple of women, then another man who happened by. Thus, at the time of our visit, there were five men and two women, all in their late teens through early twenties, living in the dozen yurts—and having a ball.

Two of the men were rock guitarists and loved to sing— so, as at Maple Mountain, the place rang with continual song. They worked in the garden, loafed, swam, worked at various crafts, and had a good life together, with no plans or intentions, not even of becoming more of a commune. We hated to leave after a few days.

THE ROCK PEOPLE, as I will call them, were having a party, showing a double feature (*How to Marry a Million-aire* and *Red Planet Mars*). Only 1 percent of the people on earth live above nine thousand feet, the approximate altitude of several communes in southeastern Colorado. They have almost no water supply, a nine-month winter, at best a rugged life. All the communes and many other residents of the immediate area had been invited. As we wound up several miles of rocky, rutted road there was a chain of headlights ahead of and behind us, and the parking lot was full. Perhaps a hundred people gathered in a geodesic dome—the largest ever built by nonprofessionals, sixty feet in diameter, thirty feet high, with four-by-four beams as structural members and white styrofoam triangles between them. The whole building seemed to float, as though it were made of match-sticks and tissue paper, because of its size and delicate, aerial design. Inside was a single, enormous room, divided by a curved loft across one end, ringed by a solid banister, and reached by an elegant timber stairway. The dozen adult members sleep up there, and their children sleep below. Art works, musical instruments, electronic equipment, and a large open cooking area were dispersed around the lower level. The whole building was heated by two small wood-burning stoves whose flues extended in graceful suspension all the way up to and out of the external skin.

Before the film we chatted, smoked (tobacco and marijuana), passed wine around in gallon jugs, while children scurried around happily joining in. Many of the guests were dressed in Basic Communard—jeans or bib overalls, long dresses and shawls. Others wore whimsical costumes; one man was dressed as an Arab. Others wore such spiffy clothes as sleek dresses or sports jackets. There were several gray-headed people among the group of predominantly young adults. "There are so many new people in the valley I feel I don't know anyone," a woman complained, but it seemed to me that everyone knew everyone else. The dome warmly overflowed with embraces and kisses, eager gossip in knots of conversation, and the drifting aroma of pot.

Eventually we settled down on blankets, benches, in one another's arms, for four hours of incredibly trite film which seemed nonetheless to be appreciated (except that the second feature, a religious, anticommunist tract in the guise of science fiction, was too much of a bummer to be funny). At midnight there was more embracing and chattering, hushed now, and weary, and the cars filed down the difficult mountain road.

A stockade on the frontier? The new society gathered there was not shockingly different from the old, but one in which the tone was nonetheless distinct and significant. The ingenious and highly crafted architecture, the fine equipment, the electricity (thanks to a generator), represented an intelligent absorption of technology. Here was no hippie slovenliness, but a scrupulous concern with function and order. (One woman said they "were getting their shit together on the material plane.") There was no pretense of independence from the economy of the larger society; they could not have scrabbled their subsistence without working (e.g., at jobs in the nearest town). But the degree of self-sufficiency under conditions of real poverty and hardship was impressive, as was the creativity of the life style.

I was particularly struck by the easy integration of children (most of them under six) into the adult community without the behavior problems—the fussing and restlessness and attention-getting pranks—one might expect at, say, a church picnic or a neighborhood movie. Compared to middle-class social events in the outer society, there was relative ease and affection at this gathering, freedom from posturing and arguing, from put-downs and gamesmanship and neurotic sarcasm, flirtation and phony modesty, drunken or drugged excess, or prudishness. Here was pleasure in the context of civility and moderation: a middle-class ideal the middle class is seldom able to approximate. One felt welcome, safe, loved, and such good vibes are more sustaining than any luxury on the market.

SABOT is a commune of a dozen adults and two children on a farm of less than forty acres outside a small town in New Hampshire. That name means "wooden shoe" and is the root of *sabotage*, a reference to the wooden shoes French workers are said to have used to clog the machinery of employers, and the commune originally had a militant political intent. However, they have decided that they can achieve more through cooperation with their neighbors, and today the people of the town are as proud of their local commune as of any local feature. Sabot advertises for odd jobs in the local paper, and meets requests with teams of men and women sent without regard to conventional sex roles. There was some local resistance at first to women digging ditches, men cleaning houses and tending children, but this passed when it became apparent that the communards worked hard and well, that they would go out of their way to help, that their concern for cash was minimal (though they needed some to survive). Their farm has no electricity, no running water, no source of heat except wood stoves—and that's the way they like it. They use rags (washed each time) instead of paper in their open-air outhouse, for ecological reasons.

My wife and children and I went there with some other communards for a house-raising, which turned out to be a regional festival. Dozens of communes in the area had been invited as well as neighboring farmers and townspeople—and over a hundred people of all ages showed up that winey October weekend to help and watch. We lifted the sides into place for a twenty-foot cubicle addition to the existing old farmhouse, hauling the huge pieces up into place with ropes and pikes. Eight-inch-square oak beams had been cut with hand tools for mortise and tenon joints, to be held together with oak pegs (not a nail was used in the entire superstructure). All these pieces had been measured, cut, and laid out, but not assembled. As each was laboriously hauled into place there arose a cheer, because everything fit—neatly, exactly, a miraculous degree of precision work considering the tools and conditions. It *had* to fit—or there would have been serious delays (wasting the assemblage of labor) or accidents.

Home brew and cider went round the gathered crowd in jugs as each new joist or section was locked into place. Imagine a wiry little man, one of the town's selectmen, in his sixties, walking a beam twenty feet in the air, then, with incredible balance, swinging a huge mallet, with an iron-banded wooden head six inches in diameter, to drive pegs into the joint under his feet. Imagine a strapping beauty of a woman with long swinging blonde braids and a headband that made her look like an Amazon princess setting her baby aside to swing a sledge hammer, pounding in a stubborn peg with a cheer from the crowd at each blow. All around the house preparations were going on for the potluck festive dinner in the autumn fields. My son and I tossed apples into the maw of a cider press while a young man turned the crank, sending juicy pulp flying in the faces of the crowd gathered there waiting turns.

"How did you learn to build a house this way?" I asked one of the women members. Not even the selectman on the high beam had ever used this method, though he had attended a similar house-raising when he was a child. "From books," she said. She went on to tell me that they had gone down to Providence to a naval museum to read early nineteenth century publications of the British navy on sail making, to learn how to stitch tipis securely. Whether it is to make soap or slaughter hogs or build compost, the communards are recycling skills that have nearly disappeared from our heritage—just as they are recycling horse-drawn farm equipment, grain mills, and lumber mills.

And people. Though several of the adults (ranging in age from sixteen to late twenties) are from affluent backgrounds, with degrees from Dartmouth and Bryn Mawr, others had redeemed lives from the squalor and crime of ghetto streets. Their life is an unending seminar in the meaning of love. They know that in the new world such things as rules and regulations and contracts and agreements and boundaries must fall away, to be replaced by bonds of affection and trust and mutual respect. But how to do it? They have as much difficulty with problems of jealousy, possessiveness, fear of risk, defensiveness, abrogation of power, and use of others as objects, as do people in the old culture, but at least these communards are working at such problems, which are upfront and on the agenda. They know that unless they overcome the artificial scarcity of love, their whole venture is a waste. The seclusion of their farm, the isolation from other people and stimuli, the pressures of working together as a family under conditions of hardship, these factors enhance a vital, difficult, advanced course in human relations, as necessary to survival as bread and shelter. By deliberately choosing to live without some options—such as electricity—they open up a whole new range of options for themselves, knowing more about the quality of light at dawn and evening, the depth of darkness, the precious gray of winter and abundant gold of summer, than do those of us who cancel nature without a thought by flipping a switch.

Such festivals as the house-raising provide a context which resembles in many ways the gathering of energy and dedication of spirit in the churches and the marches of the civil rights movement. I have seen it at an urban warehouse commune, when a huge boiler was lifted five stories (to supply a heating system) to the cheers of strangers on the street, laborers and communards on the derrick, hanging out of windows, leaning over a roof ledge—along which walked a freaky violinist playing songs from *Fiddler on the Roof*. I have seen it in a Vermont commune where we went to help with sugaring, as did friends from neighboring communes, friends from other distant places, and local French farmers and other neighbors. In knee-deep mud and snow we built corduroy roads for the heavy sled drawn by a team of two workhorses, up the rocky mountain to the sugar bush. We strung pipe from the gathering tank to the sugarhouse, raised the giant smokestack, and fired the arch beneath the bubbling pans. At night we gathered around the circular table in the crowded kitchen, stepping over one another to serve ourselves from the wood range, carrying water in from the spring, chatting, laughing, and passing a joint by kerosene lamps, early to bed to rise at dawn.

These are the work/play/demonstration festivals now welling up volcanically around the country to complete the agenda of the unfulfilled American dream. One should not be confused by the apparent yearning backwards in many rural communes. It is true that the house-raising in New Hampshire recreates a piece of an older America, and that much of its charm is that of nostalgia; but the deeper point about the revival of archaic processes is not that they are old-fashioned, but that they are gratifying in themselves. As my wife and I carved pegs with drawknives we were not wishing we had a lathe, or a cache of manufactured substitutes. Efficiency in the sense of finishing quickly or saving effort was not a relevant consideration at that point —which is not to say that these are never important considerations. In choosing how to do a task, or how to live, many kinds of efficiency must be weighed against one another. What brings people together in constructive, joyful ways? Where is the common ground which unites young and old, rich and poor, educated and uneducated? What is *fun* to do? What challenges and extends oneself? What best conserves the resources of the earth and its ecological balance? When I show visitors the twenty-by-forty log cabin we built here on the farm from our own timber, I always hear myself saying, "And it cost less than seven hundred dollars." It did—that cash going for such things as a very modern metal heatolator for the fireplace, bricks, mortar, shingles, flooring, gable boards, and glass. But the value of the cabin is that building it is a reward in itself. It is a home hewn from the woods, each log and line of chinking bearing memories and experiences, a home one puts self into, grows with, becomes part of, symbolizing a life in which work and leisure, self and environment, joy and pain, are melded. If you enjoy sailing, you have no envy of the motorboat roaring past, for the point is in the doing— not in quick arrival (where? to do what?). As we waded and shouted on the horses up the rutted trails of the sugaring road in Vermont, no one wished for a snowmobile, or for a vacuum system that would pump the sap directly from the trees to the tanks.

The house-raising does not symbolize a romanticized past, but a realistic future. That is not to say that we will become a nation of people hewing beams with hand tools, but that we will insist upon finding ways of working joyfully together, of doing tasks rewarding in themselves. At a time of unprecedented disenchantment with work extending from the assembly lines to the highest levels of management, the rediscovery of meaning and fulfillment in daily life may well become a priority as compelling as the civil rights which were demanded in recent decades.

Human dignity itself is at stake, as it was in the desegregation of schools and public facilities, in the fight for open housing and voter registration. People gather in resistance to a narrowly functional definition of self and soul. Beyond equality and material welfare there are yet further horizons on which human integrity and spirit must be affirmed, which no legislative sop nor technological advance can satisfy.

As we sat at our campfire at Sabot the night after the festival one of the young men from the commune came by, late, to visit. Everyone else at the house was asleep, finally, including the baby he had been tending. It was not his child, but he had taken a major responsibility for it—and was exasperated. "That fucking kid!" he said. "He has everything. He had been cuddled and played with, fed and burped, changed, rocked, nestled in a dry clean bed, but he just wouldn't quit. Just one more rush. Give him everything that reason demands, and he wants just one more rush before he surrenders!" There was a kind of admiration in the man's voice, a recognition of a fellow spirit, already, at a few weeks of age, indomitable, yowling across a generation gap.

What do people want? Something beyond sustenance and reason, even beyond affection, beyond justice. Just one more rush. Insatiably. Their signals flicker their unity across the night. Already they are bathing the horizon in transforming fire.

3

From Utopia to Eden

The term *utopian* is often used to describe the resurgence of interest in communalism, and it has, indeed, utopian elements. But I believe the major thrust is in the opposite direction—away from the planned society and toward what is imagined to be a blessed state of nature, an effort to regain Eden. The extremes in either direction are absurd—and can be illustrated from contemporary communes. Benjamin Zablocki, one of the best analysts of communes, once said that if you can imagine a way to live, someone somewhere is out there trying it in a commune. I will give examples here of communes which touch upon the absurd in these opposite directions, then trace the impulse in my own life to flee Utopia in search of some kind of natural redemption.

First I would like to comment on the connotations of the two terms. Utopia is popularly a positive concept, its negative implications limited to those of impracticality and escapism. But one of the major scholars of utopianism, Lewis Mumford, sees it as an aspect of *The Pentagon of Power:*

Strangely, though the word Freedom is sometimes included in the descriptions of utopia . . . the pervasive character of all utopias is their totalitarian absolutism, the reduction of variety and choice, and the effort to escape from such natural conditions or historical traditions as would support variety and make choice possible. These uniformities and compulsions constitute utopia's inner tie to the megamachine.

The problem of oppressive utopianism is made critical in contemporary Western civilization by the potentialities of automation, system design, surveillance, mind alteration, and computer technology, as discussed by Robert Boguslaw in *The New Utopians:*

These new utopias resemble classical utopias in their approaches to system design; in their assumptions about system states, system environments, operating units, and operating principles; in the quest of their designers for operating modes free from human imperfections; in their foibles and in their strengths. They differ from the classical variety primarily in the scope of their operations. . . . They involve plans for orbiting the earth as well as the neighboring planets. They receive their impetus from the newly discovered capabilities of computational equipment rather than from the fundamental moral, intellectual, or even physical requirements of mankind. These are the utopias that are well along on the drawing boards of system designers throughout the contemporary world. They are the systems that are being planned and constructed in the utopian renaissance.

A utopia created without reference to man's "moral, intellectual, or even physical requirements" is a paradox indeed —as though the good life were too good for man or even for life itself, and the Perfect State, in its majestic stability, suffered no intrusion from organic processes.

Just such an ideal society seems to be planned by a modern commune, which publicizes itself this way in the underground press:

We are a community of intellectual artists and musicians with a lifelong commitment to utopian ideals and building community. We see our planet at a crossroads. The choice, as we see it, is to either utopianize now or face extinction within the next 300 years. We are looking for intellectual individuals or groups of individuals with the maturity to state a lifelong intention of involvement and join with us in the building of the first utopian community in the history of mankind. If you are interested in becoming part of P.A.S.S. Free U please call or write first and we will give you more of the details.

They mean every word of it. A telephone number and address in San Francisco are given. An inquirer will be invited promptly to be considered for membership. In 1971 this group, which I will call the Orange Helicopter Exercise, consisted of eight members living in two large houses. Tomorrow the World.

What is the structure which the world must accept within 300 years—or be destroyed? These eight people are the nucleus of the first house, which will consist of twenty-four people evenly divided between the sexes. Four houses (ninety-six people) constitute a unit at the second level, and ninety-six groups of four houses form the third level, or neighborhood. The fourth level consists of ninety-six third-level groups in close proximity, or a utopian city of 884,736 people. (We did not hear any discussion of children in this plan.)

There is a strict rotation of sleeping partners in each house, each woman sleeping with a different man each night (an arrangement which must be complex for the nucleus group, which consists of five men and three women). When a visitor enters the comfortably furnished living room, the whole group assembles to interview him. (They do not interact with persons outside their group except to interview prospective members.) A man in his fifties, whom I must admit is named Jud, has been working out this utopian design over the past fifteen years. Jud does most of the talking, but all members say "We think . . ." because individual deviation is unheard of.

One of us who has lived for several years in communes

visited the group. At that time there were thirty-one explicit standards used to judge prospective members. Before he realized he was being considered for membership he was being grilled. His journal says:

It was bothering me that everyone was looking at me in shifty judgmental eyes—no smiles—and holy shit! now they've all got their thumbs down at me! I focking failed. Jud said, "Our evaluation of you is that you're hung up in old ways, and that you'll never live in a community. We haven't met anyone yet from Los Angeles that isn't freaked out. Thank heavens our standards have protected us from you."

In explaining why this visitor had failed, Jud said, "We're miles different from you. We think vegetarianism sucks. Bisexuality sucks. Rural decentralism sucks." If one failed on any of the criteria he was automatically out, and there was not even an educational program to help people overcome monogamy or bisexuality, vegetarianism, or wishy-washiness such as thinking that cities might contain more or less than 884,736 people in 300 years and the planet might still survive.

But Eden also is no dappled landscape bountiful with fruit and rosy-skinned athletes. I think of a commune in Vermont which I will call The Lunatics. As one approaches a rural commune he is almost bound to see first a lot filled with "junkers," abandoned car bodies. The Lunatics' junkers are at the bottom of the hill, however, and the last steep quarter-mile of wooded road must be walked. The next evidence one is likely to see of the presence of a commune is half-finished, experimental architecture—particularly the skeletons of geodesic domes. The Lunatics have one covered with chicken wire, a space-age pen of squawking fowl. Over the hillside are sheds and piles of junk surrounding a rustic, square, two-story house walled with rough planks. Out front in the yard is a wood-burning range, its stovepipe jutting comically into the air. Eight young men and women are standing around in bare feet and bib overalls, poking the fire and stirring huge pots on the stove. They are rendering fat from a hog which a neighbor helped them slaughter. (They are planning to slaughter another tomorrow on their own.)

This commune had recently undergone mitosis over some disagreement, another eight or so going off to live together elsewhere (including the young man to whose father the land belonged where the remaining Lunatics were squatting). Those that remained were in their early twenties, all Jewish, all friends from high-school days. Like characters from that cartoon strip about cavemen, *Alley Oop*, they were studiously unkempt. One of the men wore random, knotted pigtails sticking up with twigs or bones in them. Slovenliness had been developed into a conscious style.

They immediately shared a joint they were passing with my wife and me and a woman friend as we came up to the stove. Did we know how to render lard? The stench of scorching rind was suffocating in the autumn air, and one of the women jabbed at it ineffectually with a wooden ladle. We pooled our ignorance, and eventually the scorching gave way to the spattering of melting fat. Up at the house a crew was wrapping the pork in paper to store it in a commercial freezer about ten miles down the road. Afterward we sat awhile by a potbellied stove in the house chatting and smoking. Upstairs (or up-ladder) and the first floor were each a large, open room. They all slept together in the loft; the first floor was kitchen and social space. One wall was lined with the largest hubbard squashes I have ever seen—the size of beach balls. There were photographs tacked up of one of the women giving birth, including one with the baby's head emerging, the mother grinning, propped up on her elbows to watch. That was the last photo in the series, we were told, because at that point the photographer fainted. The baby, born there in that room, looked a little scrawny. His mother's milk was insufficient, and they were reluctant to switch to bottle-feeding. While we talked, another woman pacified the restless child by letting him nurse her dry breast.

The commune had cleared the land and built the house from scratch, starting in the fall a couple of years before our visit. The local farmers called them lunatics for undertaking such an impossible task, but they finished the house, got in wood for the winter, and survived—and happily kept the lunatic label (as Shakers and Quakers and freaks before them had accepted opprobrious labels with pride). But the neighbors had not been hostile: rather, affectionately disbelieving, as they watched green ignorance hew survival from the intractable forest.

They were an endearing group. One young man seemed silent and sullen during most of our visit—and we discovered before we left that he was moping because he was afraid that he had insulted one of us with an unnoticed, chance remark. That quality of hypersensitive love and fear of hurting permeated their lives. They were city kids who learned everything they knew about rural life from hard knocks, eager experimentation, advice from helpful neighbors, and study of a few old books around the house (one I saw on gardening was published in the 1890s). Of course, they had no heat but wood, no light but candles and a kerosene lantern, no water except what they carried from the spring, no income except food stamps, gifts, and Aid to Dependent Children for the one baby. (Bennett Berger, a sociologist studying communes, calls such economics W & W—windfall and welfare.) The father in this case was one of the men who lived there, but some women in communes deliberately avoid knowing which man is the father of their children.

The Orange Helicopter Exercise demands a "lifelong intention of involvement," but the Lunatics thought little beyond tomorrow. Yet in a very real and total sense, their lives were already on the line. Had Hobbes visited he could not describe that life as "solitary," but he might have judged it "poor, nasty, brutish, and short." I wonder whether he would have caught the good vibes, the affection, humor, pluck, and indomitable optimism of the group.

It is confusing to some who hear of such communes that the communards have no theory. Their primitivism is not a head trip. They are not, like Helen and Scott Nearing (authors of *Living the Good Life*), trying to prove something by living independently. When critics point out that they are using the commercial freezer, the manufacturers of buckets and kerosene lamps and iron stoves, the welfare system of the outer society, they would probably respond with a shrug. So? They never pretended otherwise. They use what is available. They do not imagine a future 300 years from now in which the world is populated by bands of Lunatics, rendering fat on antique stoves.

If one complains, as their elders often have, that it is irresponsible for them to live as they do without a plan for how the rest of the world should live, the same charge can be made against most of the people in the world who muddle through without theory—most damagingly against the more fortunate residents of Utopia USA, which circa 1974 projects an ideal of each nuclear family having a private home, probably on about a quarter-acre lot, with air-conditioning, central heating, a complex set of appliances, a couple of automobiles, telephones, television, prepared, prepackaged meals, free schooling through at least the bachelor's degree for each person, high-quality medical, police, and fire-protection services, and so on. Social groups within the country are ranked as "disadvantaged" until they have achieved that level of consumption, and other nations are merely "developing" until they have attained it. If we try to imagine the populations of Asia, Africa, South America, and Europe living on the earth at comparable cost, we can see graphically the meaning of irresponsibility. A child born in the United States will consume twenty times more and contribute fifty times more pollution to his environment than will a child born in India.

Edenism (a friend asks if that is cockney for "hedonism") differs from utopianism specifically in lacking a plan. Some feel hostile toward the way of life of the Lunatics because they feel challenged—as though the Lunatics were saying, "If all you people lived as inoffensively on the earth and with one another as we do, we could somehow figure out the minor technological and economic problems that need to be solved so that we could all survive." The challenge is threatening because it contains much self-evident validity, and few of us are willing to live as the Lunatics live. But it is important to remember that the Lunatics, unlike the Orange Helicopter Exercise, lay no trip. They never issued such a challenge. They only wanted to know how to render fat into useful lard—another question the world might well ponder.

Our Christmas Carol might tell of Tiny Tim inundated with goodies on Christmas morning. Scrooge and his parents have provided him with everything television taught him to ask for, at fantastic cost in world resources and human energy. By that evening all the toys are broken, the candies nibbled and discarded, and the child has made himself a wagon by tying a string to a cardboard box, happy with the only satisfaction his spirit recognizes—personal creativity, self-determination, primitive delight.

That describes the Great Refusal of American youth in the 1960s. While the poor were subverting their utopian housing projects, the prosperous young were making a shambles of suburbia. As Kenneth Kenniston and others have documented, the revolution began in privileged communities such as Scarsdale. Their bodies surfeited, many young people began to recognize the suffocation of their spirits. A temper tantrum erupts by the Christmas tree. Parents wring hands and gnash teeth. Drugs. Protests. Hitchhiking back and forth across the continent. Communes. Jesus Freaks. Imagine: after everything we gave him for Christmas, what did he want—but Jesus! Many have experienced glut without satiation. The business of the new culture now is to discover and make functional some way of achieving satiation without glut.

It is five-thirty in the morning. I am sitting naked at my typewriter. Our five ganders (we call them the Senators, as they waddle around the farm, caucusing) let out another of their coordinated, apparently unmotivated cries. Gray light is pouring over the eastern mountain. My last paragraphs sound like railing to me, like rhetoric having wandered too far from experience, calling out to find itself and getting back only echoes.

My friends tell me from time to time that I exaggerate, and I wonder whether I have worked myself up into melodrama. What am I really talking about? I turn to a book on communes, which directs my thoughts back to my own life:

The only modern equivalent of Robert Owen, the British industrialist who funded and founded New Harmony, seems to be James Rouse, developer of the New Town of Columbia, Maryland, a community with a projected population of over one hundred thousand, but far from communal.*

I remember my last conversation with Jim Rouse, a man of whom I am very fond and for whom I have great respect. We were on a jet from Boston to Baltimore. He was explaining to me why he hoped to have a gigantic Disneyland-type amusement park on the periphery of

* Rosabeth Moss Kanter, *Commitment and Community: Communes and Utopias in Sociological Perspective*, Harvard University Press, 1972, p. 166.

Columbia. It would be wholesome. There were to be no alcoholic beverages. It would provide exciting employment opportunities for our young people. Like Owen indeed, Jim is a man of social vision and profound conviction. Unlike Owen, he is also a deeply committed Christian, one of the leading members of a sect whose founder sees Columbia as potentially the New Jerusalem. With a midway.

He is also a very practical capitalist, believing that a good plan rides on its own grease. Convinced that planned development is better than unplanned urban sprawl, he sought the help of the best available experts in designing a city to be "completed" over a ten-year period. In order to borrow the money to buy the land and to bring the plan into reality, he had to convince large investors (Connecticut General, Chase Manhattan, Teacher's Investment Annuity Association) that the economic plan was sound, that the real estate would accrue in value at a predicted rate *because* of the excellence and attractiveness of the city design. For example, though some thought it wise to exclude private automobiles from residential sections, this provision was realistically excluded from the design on the grounds that it might lack popular appeal, so the real estate might not be sold rapidly enough to make the remainder of the plan—with its many excellent features—work.

Eventually real live people such as our own family began to move onto the bulldozed soil of the nascent utopia ("The Next America," it is described in its advertising). They were attracted by the design, right on schedule. Immediately they, the new citizens, wanted to participate in the designing process. Sorry. Few variations were possible, because of the developer's responsibility to his investors. To alter the economic plan during the first ten years might be to endanger the whole enterprise. In the first couple of years there was widespread discontent as citizens protested the policies of the developer—whom they projected as Big Daddy. But discontent was a relatively healthy response. More disturbing was the paralysis, indifference, sense of impotence, which developed as more and more people—especially teenagers—perceived little opportunity to exercise control over their lives. Ironically, one of the objectives of the plan was to achieve a heightened sense of community. From the way the village centers and walkways to the residential cul-de-sacs were laid out to the progressive plan for gradual citizen control (over the ten-year period), community involvement, informal relationship, and democratic feeling were laid in like the wiring and sewage.

But the plan itself became the dictator. The developer could quite honestly shrug and point to the graphs he was not authorized to change. It was not that there was something "wrong" with the plan. It was, of course, in many ways imperfect, but that is not the central point. However well conceived, its predictability—even its planned variety—became oppressive. As one drives out of the city, the unplanned, surrounding houses, with their television aerials and clothes-lines and fences (prohibited by the plan) suddenly strike one as vital in all their ugliness. As one enters, it is as into a vast Howard Johnson's, complete with subtle variations in harmonious tones, even with tastefully selected art works, waterways, and patches of woodland. It is like the villages alongside model railways, populated by occasional iconographic figurines.

Most houses in Columbia had little gas lights burning in front of them twenty-four hours a day (at a cost of two dollars per month to the householder). When I moved in, that light stood on my lawn as a vestal symbol of the planner's forethought for my happiness. Never mind the heedless pollution of the atmosphere and waste of natural resources entailed by an architect's whimsy. What mattered to me was that the designer was squatting on my lawn day and night. After some weeks of intimidation, and careful reading of the various codes I had committed myself to in buying the house, I went outside one midnight and turned off the bleeding light—then whooped around the neighborhood in liberated joy. I had recaptured some of nature's darkness. I had regained some infinitesimal modicum of control over my life. I had thumbed my nose at the Grand Design.

Commenting on this anecdote, David Riesman writes me:

Regarding Columbia as such an enormous improvement over the urban sprawl of the rest of America, . . . I am less sympathetic than you to the anarchic, bitchy and semi-destructive impulse that leads to . . . messing up Columbia by anarchists who rip it off because it is otherwise agreeable to live there and because they can feel so heroic. I am not talking about captive teenagers but about noncaptive Judson Jeromes.

This noncaptive left, and took his teenagers with him, without bitterness. I agree that Columbia is an "enormous improvement," and yet feel that tragically Jim Rouse and his good intentions have become entrammeled in his plan. The record is not much different from that of other planned cities, such as England's Stevanage:

Such planned communities have been marked by the utopian expectations of their sponsors. Human happiness was to be achieved, in the planners' view, by certain physical arrangements. They were fired by the conviction that universally valid architectural and sociological principles could be developed "for engineering the happiness and success of a neighbourhood or community." *

The stubborn impulses of human beings racketing around the plastic cage produce neglect, vandalism, torpor. The rapid physical deterioration of our own Versailles-like

* Page Smith, *As a City Upon a Hill: The Town in American History,* Knopf, 1966, p. 290, drawing upon Harold Orlans, *Stevanage,* Routledge and Paul, 1952.

blocks of public housing projects reflects the same principle. People will take possession of their lives, even if by pissing in their own hallways or dumping garbage in the courtyards. Every carved school desk in the nation bears witness to the principle.

It may be that our "anarchic, bitchy, and semi-destructive impulse" may be our salvation. The best thing I can say about Columbia is that the amusement park plan was finally rejected because of its unpopularity with the citizens—who had every material reason to benefit.

Designs for new automobiles at, say, General Motors, have to be made some three to five years ahead of the marketing date to enable the production departments to retool. Thus it becomes subtly determined that five years from now a given number of buyers, say nine million, will *have* to want cars of a given design. An advertising (or educational) trajectory has to be planned to intersect the production trajectory: the marketers have to deliver the buyers just as surely as the factory has to deliver the cars. If there is an error, the industry itself may collapse— and with it the economy, not only of our nation but of those nations dependent upon us. In a frightening way it is perfectly true that what is good for General Motors is good for the country—and the world. Our security and comfort, if not our survival, are as dependent upon the consumption of automobiles as a heroin addict is dependent on heroin. Grant one or two first premises, and a maze springs up from which there is no escape.

Except escape. It is not simply a matter of choosing a place to live. The life-style of Columbia is supported by high salaries. To live close enough to the city to work there means to support the local real estate values—e.g., a minimum of two thousand dollars per acre for unimproved farmland in a twenty-mile radius of Columbia. A hundred miles away we found a hundred-acre farm with a house and a number of good buildings for less than the value of our Columbia box. But no salary. I retired, taking a 90 percent cut in steady income. There is some symbolic significance in my sitting here naked at the typewriter. One has less ability to buy, as he has less need of, clothes.

As for Eden, I have formulated my own conception in a poem inspired by the experience of taking Jenny to Beaver Run, one of the Camphill villages I have mentioned. In the fall of 1970 I was experiencing professional demoralization, feeling the hopelessness of reform of institutions to meet adequately the manifest human needs of our society. At that point in our family's life we discovered a village, Beaver Run, shimmering across the gulf as a dream. Jenny had found her place. Would we find ours?

Before repeating that poem here I would like to amplify a couple of things I learned from Jenny. For one thing, because she has few words, she has little concept of the past (what there is must be nonsequential) and almost none of the future. She lives in the Eternal Present—like God. Another way of putting it would be to say she has never left Eden; she does not wander, as most of us do, forever aching for some vague paradise lost, yearning for some vague paradise to be regained. She has a very different sense of reality. It is not that she is always blissful—far from it. But her unhappiness does not stem from our peculiar vexations based upon expectations and disappointments and deferred rewards. Also because she has very little language, she tends not to be judgmental. She is amoral. That is not to say that she is valueless: she has vigorous preferences, clear satisfactions and dissatisfactions. But she is almost entirely free of the sense of oughtness, of propriety. And the love she gives—like the love she demands—is unconditional. She is not about to live up to the standards of others, nor to impose standards upon them as a condition of acceptance. Like nature, she makes do with what is. If you accept Jenny, it cannot be on the condition that she be other than what she is. Finally, and

consequently, she forces one to a reconsideration of the
question of spirit or soul. While Beaver Run is, indeed, a
school, and hopes to change and educate its children, it is
pervaded by a fundamental awareness that the "real" person, the "inner" person, is, as the poem says, "beyond all
damage . . . free of the yoke of time." It is a school in
which it is impossible to fail. The behavior of the outer person may change and improve, may be socialized. But the
inner person simply is. And that is enough. One passes.
More than any other single event, taking Jenny to Beaver
Run and writing this poem were the experiences which
prompted this book. I am reminded of those glimpses of
plenitude which led to these concerns, the glimpses of what
we might find fulfilled in our lives—unless, as the poem
itself implies, our mind-set, like the gates of Paradise, leaves
us irrevocably excluded.

THE VILLAGE

i. *Saturday*

tomorrow we take her to the village
                                        a sturdy seven
Jenny is oval of face her small eyes darting mischief
she looks sideways teasing giggling
                                        her few words
arduous grunts and squeals she runs tottery trounces
her little brother
                        the moment swells a translucent balloon
before her eyes the past *gone gone* the future like
Good Humor meltingly offered just beyond grasp
                                                about
tomorrow she knows her clothes toys books are packed in boxes
I stand at my study door
                                outside she swings on a rope
from the oak happiest by herself
                                        the neighbor children
cannot understand her they are brain damaged
we who lean on tomorrow do not understand

ii. *Sunday*

all of us edgy to leave

                Jenny goes out to wait
in the car flies back flatfooted running ponytail swinging
to fetch her yellow lunchbox one doesn't go to school
without a peanut butter sandwich

                       we laugh and load
for the family trip through rolling Pennsylvania
three hours of autumn Jenny hooting gladly pointing
at passing trucks ponds cows

               she pulls her mother's chin
around to be sure she is getting through

                    and when we find
the gravel road to the village

          the cottage assigned

                  she knows
wing wing! she shouts and scrambles out to try

               the swing
by the door

        adults fumble through introductions while
she darts into bedrooms bathroom locates piano and toys
riding her moment like a surfer carrying her
essential world in her head

             it is distressingly
simple we invent anxieties about
her toilet sleep food language

              it seems as thought there ought
to be more papers to shuffle even death requires
more preparation

        we leave

          the car vacant and still

iii. *The Village*

    "Stupid means nothing in nature. You are what you are."
                —JACQUES COUSTEAU
driving away my mind plays tricks

             suppose there were
a village just for people who lived in care

         of one

another where
           differences were expected
                                judge
not
      with what one has make do
                         I see a village
spreading its cottages and economical gardens
on the verdant hills
                   people sharing whatever
                                    coming
together to work play learn worship in joy
                              no last
names
      ages all relative
                   the sexes mingling
                               the point
of life being
           nurture fulfillment happiness
I try to imagine yearning for nothing having enough
food warmth company
                   reading no ads
                              imagine making
our own music bread and love
                         have we brains enough among us?
imagine congruence of need and delight
                              imagine
sinking into the downy bed of the earth's abundance
letting now be adequate
                   there is nothing but now
I dream a village
           rooted and spreading
                         ready
for seasons
      riding the earth round steadily into
the dawn

                    *   *   *

        we are excluded
                   on the freeway speeding

cursed with the knowledge of our own mortality
striving against that limit
                              believing a living is
something to be earned
                              memory clogged with guilt
future a terror
                    present a point of balance we
have lost

                    *   *   *

              there they believe inside each one is one
dwelling in splendor
                         beyond all damage
                                        beyond all
distinctions   -
                 free of the yoke of time
                                   a self a presence
(I speak with eyes to her in there: hello Jenny)
there they believe the body with its senses
                                        mind
with sense
              are tricks of light on the face of the troubled pool
I try
         to imagine believing
                            flesh is not me
                                        I am not
a sum of deeds
                    these very thoughts are a mere flux
of current
              I cannot think my way to the still depths

                    *   *   *

we are excluded
                 we are normal
                              we would be bored
in that village
              we would organize it for profit

iv. *Monday*

we rearrange the house it is strangely quiet
                                        without
her random energy careening through the day
the night is undisturbed
                            we are guiltily relieved
of soiled pants clutter spills howls fights blaring TV
things put away stay put away
                                    Jenny is guiltless
rolling her day before her like a ball
                                        we call
to find she loved the school slept well
                                            they are overwhelmed
by her relentless curiosity
                            I smile
knowing they will be won
                            wryly knowing
                                            the bother
exasperation weariness the worry
                                    (when sick
she lies so wordless in her body
                                    rapidly breathing)
knowing the lesson she teaches in unconditional love
at home we look at one another newly
                                        there is
much we have neglected between us much we have
poured in a bottomless receptacle much
to be built
                in us are planted
                                    Jenny's slanted humor
trust and desperate vitality
                            we search
out innocent ground
                        the place the friends the strength
                                                        to farm

4

Economics of the Flow

One starts with money. Those who are curious about communes almost invariably ask first about how they support themselves; and though they may not ask, they wonder about sex. Any parent who has tried to explain the latter subject to children can recognize my embarrassment about the former. The mechanical details are neither difficult to understand nor shameful; but they are, in a sense, beside the point. The parent's urge is to lecture on the meaning of love and life. Once *why* is understood, it is easy enough to work out how.

Similarly, economics is ultimately a question of values —for which money is only symbolic, and in communal life of secondary importance. A long-experienced communard said:

We came together for economic reasons—to save money, to escape the rat race. But now the point is being together. We almost never talk about the economic stuff anymore.

Being. Together. How difficult it is to be. How much more difficult to be together. And how it matters. If we understood these things we could easily work out how to pay the bills. If we understood those things about sex, the physiological research of Masters and Johnson would be less necessary to intimate relationships.

The problem is only confused by the fact that, indeed, many communes are productive economic units, in which a group is supported by cash income from group activities. A number of communes grew up around rock groups; The Grateful Dead supported a commune of two hundred people near Mendocino. A number are supported by editing and publishing magazines, newspapers, or books: the Canyon Collective produces and is sustained by *Workforce*; *Quicksilver Times* was an underground paper and commune in Washington, D.C.; The Portola Institute published *Whole Earth Catalog*; the Lama Foundation publishes influential religious books by Baba Ram Dass (Richard Alpert) and other writers as well as running a spiritual school for tuition. There are law communes, medical communes, architectural communes, design communes, engineering communes, video communes. Many communes are schools or therapy centers. Communes run restaurants, garages, bakeries, clothing stores, head shops, bookstores, record shops. One makes tipis. One manufactures hammocks. Many sell craft products. One operates a large orchard, and many sell organically grown vegetables. Some specialize in group relations workshops and encounter group leadership or are growth centers in the human potential movement.

But communes which have a viable economic base are an insignificant fraction of the tens of thousands of communes in the United States today. And though many who do not have such a base yearn to have one, I would be hesitant to predict that the direction of development will be toward economic self-sufficiency. I believe that the norm now is, and will probably continue to be, that the commune is primarily a home, a domestic rather than an economic unit—or, in economic terms, primarily a unit of consumption, like a private family. Some members may work, some may receive welfare or live on savings or gifts. There is a prevailing expectation (realistic, I believe) that some form of guaranteed income is essential in a society where population growth and technology are eliminating jobs faster than economic development can create them. Three separable but interrelated questions are involved: how communes are related to the economic system of the larger society; how an alternative economic system is emerging in the new culture; and how domestic and consumption patterns are changing as a result of an increasing tendency toward living in expanded or intentional family arrangements.

One might contrast the present situation with the utopian communities of the nineteenth century, which were themselves mini-societies, efforts to create models for a society to be. Typically, they raised a large proportion of their food, made their own clothing and furniture, built their housing, and produced goods (not often services) for sale (not often barter) "outside." There were some unsuccessful efforts to link communities economically, but it is surprising, on reflection, that the several hundred communal groups in the United States were so little aware of one another. Jefferson and others had conceived of a decentralized society, but the communitarians were not generally working on any such theory. No one was attempting to restructure the American economy by creating a network of isolated, semiautonomous communities. Like the Bruderhof today, many regarded their villages as examples, dreaming that if only their model were imitated in the larger society, the world would be saved. But if they thought of such questions at all, their hope was that everyone would live in Fourierist phalanxes, or as Shakers or Perfectionists or socialists.

There was little evangelism: the communities did not try to convert others to their own beliefs and forms (exceptions being such public speeches as Robert Owen made, or the newspapers published by Oneida and some other communities). There was also little ecumenism. So far as I have been able to discover, these communities did not see that they had a common cause with other communities of diverse faiths. A pluralism of utopias is a contradiction in terms, for the Way is either wrong or right. Nineteenth century communards did not view themselves, as their modern counterparts are likely to do, as part of a pluralistic new culture. Each community (or group of communities in the case of the Shakers or Fourierists) was primarily a belief system. Secondarily, and perforce, it was an economic system. They were communal within—and clearly recognized and adapted to the fact that they had to be capitalist without, units in a capitalist system.

And they prospered. Ironically, considering the reputation of contemporary communes, one could make the case from historical example that communalism is good business. Rosabeth Moss Kanter summarizes some astonishing records in her study, *Commitment and Community: Communes and Utopias in Sociological Perspective*, such as that of Bethel, which increased its assets a hundred times over in its thirty-six years of existence.

For nineteenth century communities at least, financial prosperity may be associated with the decline of community—partly because it indicated the growth of efficient Gesellschaft organization and partly because of the social consequences of prosperity, such as emphasis on individual consumption. Prosperity may lead to bureaucracy and privatism. Richard Ely wrote in 1885 that whereas poverty can knit members into a compact whole, "prosperity can be fatal."

By the end of the century most such communities had disappeared. Often they broke up because of inability to handle internal dissension, but:

Few colonies, if any, failed because they could not make their living. . . . They failed to like communal housekeeping. They failed to hold their young people. They failed to compete with growing industry and commerce in a new, unexploited country. But they did not fail to make an independent subsistence living—and pay off a lot of debts and help a lot of stranded people.*

Just as industrialization and urbanization made the small, independent farm obsolete, so these were the major forces that wiped out the small, independent villages. The typical size of these communities approached a hundred adults, so there was some hope that they could encompass within themselves enough skills and resources to function with relative autonomy—at least until mass production, improved transportation, and other technological developments made it impossible for them to compete or even to coexist with the increasingly centralized larger economy.

We often forget the cost of progress in its elimination of human skills. As Lewis Mumford says in *The Pentagon of Power:*

While the population of complex and technically superior machines has enormously increased during the last century, the technological pool has actually been lowered as one handicraft after another has disappeared.

Mumford compares the technological skills of a community to a gene pool in their ability to reproduce the artifacts of life. A natural disaster might wipe out almost the entirety of a nineteenth century village, and the skills necessary to support that way of life could be found in the survivors sufficient to recreate the destroyed structure. By

* Ralph Albertson, "A Survey of Mutualistic Communities in America," *The Iowa Journal of History and Politics*, vol. 34 (October 1936), p. 440. Cited by Kanter.

contrast, a modern town can be immobilized by the absence of a few key technicians, or even by power failures in distant cities. Autonomous subsistence requires, of course, certain manufactured items (e.g., washboards, horse-drawn agricultural equipment, hand gristmills) from the larger society. A village might have its own blacksmith, but is unlikely to smelt its metals or do its own mining. But as the life-style changes, the very products which make even relative autonomy possible are likely to go off the market. New-culture publications such as *The Whole Earth Catalog* and *Mother Earth News* are in large part devoted to restoring a disappearing technological pool. Today the Hutterites persist through farming; the Bruderhof and Koinonia persist through manufacture and national marketing of specialties. Amana and Oneida have converted themselves to industries for the most part indistinguishable from other corporations in the system. By this century the isolated mini-society type of commune had almost ceased to exist.

In contrast to the nineteenth century communities, modern communes are consciously involved in setting up an alternative economic system. For example, there is a great deal of overlap between the movement to rural communes and the older homesteading movement (among those, for instance, influenced by the writing of the economic decentralist Ralph Borsodi). Self-sufficiency is an end in itself for many, with aesthetic and moral value. A kind of neo-Puritanism finds satisfaction in liberation from telephones, radio and television, from electric power, plumbing, sewage systems, even from most machinery. Barter is preferred to cash exchanges. Self-employment in crafts and cottage industries is preferred to jobs with large corporations or organizations. The methods of agribusiness are rejected in favor of organic farming and intensive labor.

Homesteading and decentralist impulses combine easily with political motivation in many cases—antipathy to "the system," predictions of ecological disaster and armed warfare as twin threats which make imminent the need for survival skills. Such communards relate with surprising amiability to neighboring farmers who retain the frontier skills of their grandparents like fading daguerreotypes in the family trunk. I remember two middle-aged Ph.D.s on a commune skimming the swill from a septic tank with buckets, delighting in their discovery of how things work and their capacity to cope. It was a political act—a demonstration of the possibility of some degree of personal and communal liberation from the grip of the system's specialists.

Also in contrast to the nineteenth century communities, there are many efforts to combine and connect and relate the scattered communes of the new culture. Modern communes are vastly more diverse and numerous than their predecessors, but they are also more united. The scientific-minded behaviorists of a *Walden II* type of commune may be amused by or disdainful of a mystical, Christian group living gratefully on The Flow, but they nevertheless feel a kinship and recognize a common cause.

When one joined a nineteenth century community the commitment was, at least in theory, for life—for oneself and progeny. But among modern communes such permanence is not even a value. Communards are as mobile as their junior executive counterparts in the straight world. Such impermanence and turnover have many detrimental effects on communes, but among their advantages is providing an information web. The sheer movement of communards from place to place, staying overnight, or a week or a couple of years, as the vibes dictate, keeps information and valuable personal contact flowing—a topic I will return to in the next chapter. Nonetheless, in spite of their cultural cohesiveness and deliberate efforts to create an alternative economy, individual communes are rarely effective economic units.

A visitor to a number of communes in rural Oregon reports:

Economically, to traditionalist eyes, these communes were on-going disasters, yet they were obviously surviving. How? In part, I think, because of the universality of a Thoreauvian economic consciousness—an awareness that wanting less obviates needing more—together with all of the effects induced by affluence rejection, ecological concern and the moral righteousness inherent in the fast-expanding vegetarian/yoga trips. The thrusts of all of these forces, bombarding everyone with their similar ethics from a profusion of quarters, tend to reinforce each other, both rationally and emotionally, and, channeled through peer group conformance, become a new tradition, an acceptable authority, to which the individual can comfortably surrender his prior consumptive habits. Paralleling and further supporting this phenomenon, as the outgrowth of protestant ethic rejection, is a work attitude which is at once a form of physical apathy and an insistence that existence is better lived in than sweated through. Add to this base mix the benevolent superstructure of a benign climate, supportive relatives, tax returns (for recent dropouts), unemployment, welfare, an occasional outside job and gifts (altogether termed "our float" by one of these groups), and angels, stir well and set it out to bake (organically) in the Oregon sun. It rises!*

A commune I will call Enchanted Woods provides a case study in the economics this visitor describes.**

* Bill of Neverland, "Commune Tripping in Oregon," *Black Bart Brigade*, no. 1 (November 1971), pp. 31-32.
** This commune has been described at length in two books about communes; a long transcript of a talk by and interview with one of its members appeared in a newspaper; one of the members has written a book about her experiences; and a staff member of this study had a long visit and reported it in her journal. But in gathering material for this book, we promised communards that we would not identify specific communes. It may seem over-scrupulous not to refer even to published sources; but such references would lead to identification of the communes and therefore associate them with information given

In the winter and spring of 1968, in a West Coast city, a group of strangers in their mid-twenties gathered in a seminar to discuss alternative life-styles. They moved on from reading and comparing such books as Robert Heinlein's *Stranger in a Strange Land*, B. F. Skinner's *Walden II*, Robert Rimmer's *The Harrad Experiment* and *Proposition 31*, and Aldous Huxley's *Island*, to pooling clothing and other belongings and taking camping trips together. Some were more impelled than others to move from talk to action, and began looking for land. After several false starts, on an impulse, a group set out, located land; six people made the downpayment and moved there:

It didn't happen in a logical way. There never was a moment when a group of people sat down together and decided to buy this piece of land. You can't point to any one moment and say, "That's when this family started to exist." Each person made his own decisions, played his own hunches. Somehow, it came together.

Among the motivations operating was a desire for economic simplification, a recognition that "stuff was only stuff."

All the weighty paraphernalia of my old life, that I had possessed, but somehow never enjoyed. There was a piece of

---

in confidence. I do not mean to imply that the publicity given this commune is unfavorable. Quite the contrary. But even favorable publicity plagues a commune with visitors and inquiries disruptive to its existence as a private family. This commune has suffered from exposure that it neither sought nor approved of. I believe communities should be able to control and determine information that identifies them in print. Individuals in the group, even when they know the commune intimately over long periods—as is the case with our sources for this commune—can speak and interpret only for themselves. Moreover, communes change rapidly—and any journalistic account can provide only a snapshot in time. Since my concern is with general accuracy about the movement and not facts about specific groups, I believe that readers have no need of more exact identification than I provide here.

yellow cloth and some carefully chosen embroidery thread.
. . . I had never felt peaceful enough to just sit and embroider.
There were books I had bought to drown out a subway ride.
It was like a meal where there's so much food, and you sud-
denly realize that you haven't really chewed and tasted and
enjoyed a single bite.

Most such stuff was left behind on the faith that when
things are needed, they will appear.

The farm—called Enchanted Woods—is about seventeen
acres, with a stream running through it. Mortgage payments are $100 per month (one month they couldn't make
this, but the landlord accepted five cords of cut oak in
exchange). For most of their four years they have man-
aged on a total budget of about $250 to $400 per month to
support an average of twelve to fifteen. (There are often
about twenty in the summer, dwindling to eight or ten in
the winter.) In an interview, a member said:

Most of us are dropouts from middle-class jobs. We would
rather have physical labor jobs. It feels more honest to me.
We're in a lumber area and we can get jobs planting pine trees
in areas that are being reforested. People will very often go
down to the city and they will work for a month or two or
three. One of us was a gardener and he can still come back
and get gardening jobs.

My father has been sending me money and I figure that it's
OK to take it. We would like to earn our own money, but
we haven't found a way to do it that feels good. . . . I feel
that most of the jobs I worked at were nonsense. I got paid
for doing something that was harmful and I'm not willing to
do that anymore. . . .

*How do you figure that it's all right to take money from your
father when there is a certain kind of work you're not willing
to do?*

I took money from my father to go to college. Why is it all
right for kids to take from their parents for something we all

know is sometimes a shuck . . . ? There's lots of work that I'm not willing to do because it's not really work. My first job after I got out of college was as a social worker in a welfare department. I took the job because I wanted to help people and I found out that I was hurting them. . . . I didn't ask my father for this money. He knows how we're living. He knows that his money is well spent, and I presume he would rather give it to us than do any of the other things that he might do with it. And it's OK with me to take it. We have sometimes had money coming to us from people who didn't really like what we were doing, and we would rather not take that money.

One woman collected welfare. One woman with a child received forty dollars a months from her estranged husband. During most of the commune's history they received "commodities," or surplus food, or food stamps from the Department of Agriculture's price-support program, but in their third year, because one member had a trust fund (discussed below), they were able to remove themselves from all government support (which several were opposed to on conscientious grounds). They took various odd jobs in the area—such as picking fruit, for which they got much fruit to store in their two freezers, as well as cash. One of their jobs, which they took on rotation, was on a bulb farm near the coast.

The growers used terrible chemicals that were dangerous to work with, the work was gruelling, the pay low, and the outhouses for the workers outrageous.

About a third of their food during this period came from government "commodities," about a third was grown in their bountiful garden, and about a third was "store-bought" organic food. A woman said:

Of course, we're not self-sufficient. Economic self-sufficiency is a myth. We just don't want to be trapped by a system that makes you try to meet a standard of living that's too high; makes you eat food that's too rich; live in a house that's over-heated in the winter and air-conditioned in the summer. I like to wear sweaters—this house stays around sixty with the cook-stove going. In the summer, it gets up to one hundred, but then you just take your clothes off. It doesn't cost anything.

The standard of living is comfortable, if not opulent. Unlike many such communes, they have electricity. The record player goes continuously—playing collections the members brought with them and some six or eight new albums per year that come on the flow. Cold running water comes via a hose from the spring in through the kitchen window. Keeping vehicles running is a major expense: at one point they had three trucks and one battery, which was shifted to whichever one was working best. Owner-ship of vehicles is the most persistent vestige of possessive-ness in the group, as when a woman attacked a man for taking the taillight off her car and not returning it. He said:

You get this straight. . . . As long as I'm in this commune, what you have is mine. You can't come in and dangle the keys over my head and say that as long as I'm a good boy you'll let me drive your car. I have every right to touch your car.

Other than vehicles, personal property of individuals is kept on a two-foot square of shelf space allotted to each. A large communal building has been under construction for a long time, but at last report was not completed, and work is not going very fast on it. The adults sleep in an A-frame some distance from the original house—a small building thirty by twenty-two feet "divided into four spaces: kitchen, living room, the 'kids' room,' and the small bedroom" where adults rotate sleeping with the chil-dren. Cooking is done on a wood stove. In the yard is an old wringer-washer, salvaged from the dump, and clothes

are sometimes dried in the sauna during the coastal rainy
season. (I haven't seen their sauna, but have seen saunas on
communes built for under ten dollars, heated by wood-
stoves.)

They don't work particularly hard. A visitor commented:

Suzy once remarked that the place was like a summer camp,
a brilliant description. I'm sure a lot of work got done in
planting and harvesting seasons, but while I was there [mid-
summer] very little occurred besides several wood runs to the
national forest, some progress on the communal building, and
a feast every night. Of these labors, women participated only
in the kitchen work. However, the . . . family appear to get
more reading done than at many places, and most of the couples were obviously "into each other," for which I give them
emotional work credits. There was a strong family feeling
among the members, but with most, couple-relationships
seemed to be given the most energy. The children [six, ages
three to eight] all spent a lot of time with their mothers. . . .
None of them had both parents at the farm, though the mothers . . . had all found new partners. However, all the adults
spent some time with the kids.

At a group meeting, one member suggested that they all
fast. The visitor commented:

Some liked the idea, some . . . said they wouldn't consider
going on a fast, and others suggested that it was a good winter idea, when there was less work to do (that must *really* be
something!).

One of the most industrious men said that some days he
doesn't feel like working:

But if I had a job in a factory and didn't show up one day,
they'd fire me. A lot fewer people would be dropping out of
the system if there were more jobs where you could work
your own hours. If you could work in one job for a week,

another the next week. If you could work a month and take off a month. But the system won't permit that kind of freedom. You're either in it all the way, nine to five, five days a week, fifty weeks a year, or you're a dropout.

Leisure increased markedly after they began receiving income from the trust fund mentioned above.

Around six months ago [before December 1971] we were having a meeting and two of the guys were talking about pinching pennies. "I go to every junk shop when I'm looking for a car part because I want to get that car part a dollar cheaper and it really wears me out." They were talking like this and one girl who had been living with us for six months said, "I want to mention that I have a trust fund from my father for a thousand dollars a month and I haven't taken this money from my father. I didn't want to, but I feel it would be all right to give it to the farm and I would like to do it." The two guys went on talking about whether you should save a dollar on junk cars for fifteen minutes before we got around to her thousand dollars. Everyone wanted to take the money except for the guy who was her lover. . . . When we need to make a decision and only one or two people disagree, they will agree to go along with a decision that they don't like. That's what happened with us with the money. He made it plain that he was not happy with it but agreed to go along with it for the sake of being able to do something. . . . So, since then we have been taking money from that source. Still it doesn't feel to us like what we really want. What we really want is to be making something and selling it for a fair price. What some of us want is to live in a world where everything is for free. The trouble is that we can't do that where we are the only ones who are doing that. We make a step in that direction when we give away some vegetables but that's only a token.

The woman with the trust fund has since left, and the commune again supports itself chiefly by taking occasional odd jobs in the area.

Some see subsidized living as paving the way for necessary, basic reforms, such as a guaranteed annual wage. Before they discontinued accepting government support a man said about the food stamp program:

I don't feel right about accepting commodities [but] . . . you think of all the surplus the government buys to keep prices up. We might as well nationalize agriculture. We've got to stop thinking of food and everything in terms of prices. It's like charging people to breathe the air. Why, the land doesn't really belong to the farmers. It belongs—to all of us, to God. The Indians didn't have any deeds. If we could do away with private ownership and charging money for food, why, we could cultivate enough land to produce enough food for everybody.

Even with the trust income, $12,000 per year for that number of people was far below the national average. The county sheriff and some other locals regard the many communes and hippie families in the area as parasitic, but they are, at worst, not expensive parasites, and a case could be made that they have increased cash flow and general prosperity in the area. Many farms such as this one would otherwise be abandoned. One of the members had hoped to farm on his own, but saw no possibility except as part of a commune:

Unless you have a lot of capital and know-how, it's almost impossible for an individual to operate a farm. You need more than a whole set of skills and a lot of money and labor. It takes a large family or a group like ours to run a farm.

Because a couple of the members happen to have income from home, and several would be able to earn professional salaries in the city, it should not be assumed that all were prosperous or able to be so. Some members are of working-class background; and modern communes, like the nineteenth century ones Ralph Albertson studied, "help a lot of stranded people." I will discuss later some of the ways such communes subsidize social functions; in this particular one, there was a policy of never turning people away. Acceptance of misfits and indigent people by the commune was at least relief to the outer society of economic burdens.

But the usual ways of thinking of profit and loss are inadequate for understanding communal economics. Talking about the work preserving food, a woman said:

It seemed like that's all we did during September and October. If you figured up the hours and multiplied our labor by a dollar-sixty an hour, I suppose that economically we didn't come out that far ahead of buying our food. But we're not living this way just to do things cheaply.

The savings are more complex than her comment implies. For example, the clothing, transportation, and housing that would be required by people living where they could earn regular wages add to the cost of the food they buy—not to speak of the cost to the planet of the mass production of agribusiness and of the whole system which delivers food "inexpensively" to supermarkets. Keeping life's transactions out of the cash nexus is an end in itself, as are the more ineffable satisfactions of an integrated life in which toil, learning, and pleasure are inseparable from one another. Preserving food becomes a social occasion, and the hours of labor are also hours of working in company with people one cares about, handling vegetables one has planted and weeded and harvested on land that is loved.

I've asked myself lots of times just what the hell it is that we're doing and I don't know. One way to look at what we are doing is that it's a school. I can recognize the stars now. I can recognize tomato plants. I know how plants look when they are growing. I know how to grow plants. I know what it feels

like to drink water from its basic sources. Those seem to me
important experiences, experiences which our culture has left
out.

The woman speaking recognizes that children growing up
with such experiences may well yearn for others, even
those of the city, and that she herself may "feel that I
have gotten enough of that and I need to do something
else." The time may come when she wants to split. Modern communes, like modern marriages, are not necessarily
life commitments. But counterbalancing the transitory
tendency in modern communes is a growing recognition
of the value of sticking. Many, this woman says, are
wandering in search of ecstasy (what an anthropologist has
called the "on-ramp syndrome" of hitchhikers). When
the newness of life in the commune wore off she was
strongly tempted to leave. But:

Many religious traditions talk about this problem that the
ecstasy comes and goes. What the Christian mystics said is:
have faith, hang on, don't hunt for it, don't worry about it.
Just hang on and keep relaxed; it'll appear again. The whole
nature of this thing that we're looking for is that the more you
hunt for it, the more uptight you get, the more you believe
that it's someplace else, the less it happens.

A new surge of ecstasy comes:

in getting to know the people that you're living with, the
people who stick. . . . I feel as if I didn't *know* anyone before. . . . We see people early in the morning, and you see
them when they're sick, and you see them when they're depressed, and you see them when they're happy, and you see
them when they're dealing with another person. You get a
chance to watch someone go through the same routine with
someone else that he goes through with you and you get to
know each other. That feels really, really, really wonderful.

Toward money as toward ecstasy there is a feeling of relaxed acceptance, of refusal to get uptight. "The saying around here is: money manifests." When one author visited, he made a contribution of thirty dollars in traveler's checks. A few hours later he sat through a meeting in which the members thrashed out their orders from the seed catalog.

In an hour, they'd completed their order of cool-weather crops for the year: broccoli, spinach, lettuce, peas, kohlrabi, and kale. Jack totaled it. "Comes to twenty-three dollars. Do we have any money?" Joe came in from the other room with the checkbook. "Robert gave us thirty dollars today which will cover it."

"That just makes it," said Jack, writing out the checks. Then, turning to me: "If you hadn't come along, we couldn't have got our seeds in on time. You see, you *do* fit into the flow."

One may doubt that such a commune as Enchanted Woods will ever get around to "making something and selling it for a fair price." More likely they will make do, as farm families have always done, going out for cash as needed to supplement their own productivity, and finding most of their satisfactions in the land and their life upon it, in one another, rather than in things that cash might buy.

"It was meant to be," "It will manifest itself," and "Praise the Lord" are not trivial exclamations in the new culture, but statements of faith. A visitor to a commune reports:

I mentioned to one woman that I desperately needed birth control pills; I'd run out and had discovered the day before that my prescription couldn't be filled in Canada. She said, Carol just threw out a six months' supply." . . . I fished the pills out of the trash pile and found they were the very type I'd used for years. I thought of offering to pay her for them, but decided that hippy ethics dictated against offering money for something that the Flow had obviously brought to me.

On a five-year-old Vermont commune a woman told me that she didn't remember once in all that time when money was a serious object of discussion, though they lived on almost nothing and had no dependable income. The deed to the farm was held by a member who had since left—and no one felt insecure. One of the men said:

The day we bought the farm Ray asked me if I had any money left. I told him I still had fifteen dollars, and he borrowed it. He took my money and some he had and bought himself a car. It so blew my mind that I've never worried about money since.

Outraged in this case triggered a kind of conversion. What is needed will come. Or we'll get it. But we will not let ourselves get hung-up on possession, acquisition, security. We will not, like nervous surfers, overcontrol. We must learn to relax and accept the power of the wave.

Confidence in chance comes easier if one has a safety net under him, whether he uses it or not, and many communards have rejected, but still have available, economic security waiting to sustain them, as do many who adopt voluntary poverty to join monasteries and convents. Their families might receive with glee any apostate who returned home. But synchronicity and synergy, as they operate in communal situations, make faith in the flow more practical than it at first seems. Sensitivity to the significance of chance readies the mind to take advantage of coincidences that otherwise might be disregarded. (Drugs sometimes enhance this sensitivity: trippers have remarkable success foraging.) Combined effort and a minimal standard of living are a natural formula for economic success, as the prosperity of nineteenth century communes illustrates. A group of fifteen in which individual fortunes are shared has fifteen birthdays (a quantitative increase in gifts, a

qualitative increase in festivities), fifteen times the chance
for receiving an inheritance, fifteen times the opportunity
to spot and procure useful items. (What might be called
syntropy also operates: the group is fifteen times as likely
to lose tools, have flat tires, catch and pass on colds.)
Group members feed one another creatively: there is more
than fifteen times the ability to hit on a profitable idea, to
carry out an idea when one occurs.

Every day on our farm tasks are performed (most
simply, lifting weights—as in building a log cabin) which
a private farmer would have to hire people or buy machinery to do. (A nearby farmer is nearing bankruptcy
because he cannot find dependable labor and so bought
heavy, uneconomical equipment—e.g., a $12,000 air-con-
ditioned tractor—to enable him to work alone.) It is more
likely, with greater numbers, that someone among us
will know at least a little about plumbing or preserving
vegetables or treating an illness or dealing with a legal
problem, or will meet someone who knows such things
and is willing to help. While it is certainly more likely
that one find birth control pills on the trash heap of a
commune in Canada than on one of a village in Nigeria
(or even in the slums of Toronto), it is also true that as
communes spread, the flow reaches many areas heretofore
stagnant.

But the basic economic discovery of the new culture
is not of means to increase prosperity, but to reassess needs.
I call it the revolution of alternative rewards: the point
is not to do without, but to learn to delight in making do.
Can sex become an automobile substitute? Can potatoes
replace potato chips? Renunciation is not much involved in
the voluntary poverty of the new culture, because few
of its adherents think of themselves as giving up anything.
Rather, they are moving gladly toward gratifications incalculable on the cash nexus. In fact, to get along without
much cash is itself one of those gratifications.

To understand this one need only go shopping with communards in a Goodwill Store. The pleasure with which they paw over and discover funky cast-off clothing, the pride they take in quarter purchases, are genuine satisfactions in the new economics. At a blow they are being creative, saving money, serving practical needs, and expressing aesthetic preferences—e.g., in the fine workmanship and durable materials of goods which have gone out of style. Compare such people to dour wives picking over garments in a tony department store. The communards are having fun, being endlessly social, whimsical, and functional at the same time, whereas the middle-class shopper may waste an afternoon of anxiety to end up with purchases which leave her still insecure, wondering how her taste will be judged, wishing she could afford something "better," and carrying home goods that are not really so practical, beautiful, or even stylish as their cost suggests they should be.

In the same Goodwill Store there may be shoppers who seem defeated and ashamed to be there. They would be in the department store if they could afford to be. For them making do is no delight. "Don't talk to me about the quality of life," a black man once said to me. "We're still worrying about the quantity." He was a well-paid professor, but he spoke for his race, or, rather, the social class to which most of his race is relegated. "Quantity" is associated with survival—though a good deal more than that is implied. The most pinching poverty is of acceptance, recognition, love, respect, status. If our society defines a man as still poor when he has two cars, he will want three, because "poor" is only partially an economic term. More critically, it is a class designation. When the poor shop at Goodwill it reminds them that they can survive, yes, but only by picking through the flotsam and jetsam of the more successful, by combing the surplus of our economy for scraps.

Though the communards may have less cash and live far below the poverty level, they are rightly distinguished from the "real" poor. This is not because they come from privileged backgrounds or have families willing to bail them out—though many do. It is because they are classless. They flaunt their freedom from respectability in the face of society, which uses such standards as a means of oppression. They have sorted out organic needs from socially imposed ones.

Do they have a plan which will provide a long-term solution? Will the real poor be eventually liberated from oppression by the new culture?

"Suppose everyone felt the way you do!" the judge thundered.

"Why then," the conscientious objector smiled, "there would be no problem."

In *The Coming Crisis in Western Sociology* Alvin Gouldner describes the emergence of a utilitarian praxis in bourgeois society which has had quite a pernicious impact on definition of self. When the definition of personal worth is limited to gainful employment, a neurotic sense of deprivation emerges:

In short, vast parts of any personality must be suppressed or repressed in the course of playing a role in industrial society. All that a man is that is not useful will somehow be excluded or at least not allowed to intrude, and he thereby becomes alienated or estranged from a large sector of his own interests, needs, and capacities. Thus, just as there is the unemployed man, there is also the unemployed *self*. Because of the exclusions and devaluations of self fostered by an industrial system oriented toward utility, many men develop a dim sense of loss; for the excluded self, although muffled, is not voiceless and makes its protest heard. They feel an intimation that something is being wasted, and this something may be nothing less than their lives.

The term *vocation* lost its holy cast. If one devoted his life to astronomy but happened to earn a living by selling insurance, he would be regarded as "really" an insurance agent, whose "hobby" happened to be astronomy. Some years ago I said in an essay:

This world tends to define people by occupations. When someone asks what you do for a living, you cannot answer, "Why, I eat and breathe and sleep. I think and talk and sing. I exercise and read books," although that sort of thing surely accounts for more of your life than your job. You are, however, expected to say where you work, where you draw your salary. If asked what you are, you do not say, "I am a biological miracle! I am an embodiment of a vital spirit and mind; I am a warm and loyal friend to many persons, a great observer of the night sky and lover of rainstorms, a wise and kind parent, a responsible citizen and wonderful guy to have at parties." No, you do not answer that way. Rather you say that you are an accountant or "I'm an English teacher." That is what I answer, though teaching and English seem to me the least significant things I do. I don't even dare answer, "I am a poet," for if my questioner were to discover that I also worked for a college, he would think, "Ah, he's *really* a teacher. He lied." *

As I became more professionally successful, more and more fully employed, our standard of living rising steadily, I felt more and more strongly that "dim sense of loss" Gouldner describes. In fact, what I was feeling was increasingly unemployed. The life-style demanded that I maintain a position in an organization, with healthy annual raises, and that I conform in order to provide. Nor was it merely a matter of working hard at a job to earn a living: I was required to define myself professionally. What I did

* "Letter to a College Freshman," *Orientation/66*, published by *motive* magazine, 1966, p. 16.

that advanced me professionally was "up time"—even if it meant reading a book or going to a movie or spending an evening at a dinner party with "important people." Whatever else I did was "down time," whether it was playing with the kids, making love, or working in the garden. Thus even enjoyments were inescapably corrupted: either they were "practical" or a "waste of time." I never found them simply and innately satisfying, unjudged. I even found myself playing cards with the family because I "ought" to do so, as though a handbook for success had recommended a certain number of hours per week devoted to such purposes, since a happy home was a necessary prerequisite to a rising career trajectory.

These days I like to rise before dawn and write; by midmorning I have put in a six-hour day of professional work. I happen to get paid for that—but would do it anyway. One day recently at noon, in the hot sun and high grass, black with grease, I was under a truck in a junk yard stripping a '51 Dodge truck of a master cylinder, drive shaft, hand-brake assembly, and other parts we needed to repair our own truck. In the afternoon I was fixing a rabbit hutch. Later my daughter and I were horseback riding in the woods. Other days I do KP or help with cooking, harvest the garden, put in plumbing, swing a pick fixing the road, cut dead wood for the fire with a chain saw, give and get nude massages, read, talk, carpenter, pour concrete, sit in the outhouse watching the sunset. Working out interpersonal difficulties and developing deeper relationships occupy great hunks of life. It is all up time—or down. I forget which. I have retired. I am fully employed.

I can't say that financial matters are of no concern. Much of the activity around the place has to do with setting up a new business, running around to earn money at odd jobs, and—above all—*saving* money, by tearing down a neighbor's old chicken houses for lumber, salvaging old stoves, repairing old machines. One of our young women hitchhiked or was driven back and forth to town, ten miles away, each day to earn fifty cents per hour plus tips as a waitress—a job which hardly paid for itself, but the only employment for wages available to an eighteen-year-old woman in this rural area. Several are on food stamps, until they can develop a means of earning some income otherwise. Eventually we hope to be almost entirely self-employed in activities which will not require our going away from the farm—and I think we have a better chance of that than most communes have. Like yellowing diplomas on the walls are the careers we have left behind, for most of those who have lived here were "former" somethings: a couple of professors, several schoolteachers, a mathematical psychologist, an educational media specialist, a computer-design engineer, and several young people, some with college degrees, who were never swept up into the career syndrome. Two moved away from the farm to earn money—as a college administrator and laborer in a lobster pound—hoping they can come back to stay awhile without income worries. There is a curious reversal in this life pattern in which the job, like a vacation in the old culture, is an interval that interrupts the serious business of living, working, being. Being. Together.

R. D. Laing talks of a kind of paranoia which is never diagnosed and has no name—the delusion that one is *not* persecuted, when, in fact he is. To overcome that delusion is to be bathed in the sudden light of sanity—at the same time that one recognizes his weaknesses and the extent to which society has painted him into a corner. It is as though one were suddenly able to see the world in colors, after many years of viewing it only in black and white. The new world revealed may be in many respects more ambiguous, more frightening, more insuperable. It is certainly more exhausting. But once one has tasted authenticity and wholeness, he is not likely to tolerate substitutes. He begins to trade dollars for sense.

5

The New Plenitude

Our dual revolution follows the pattern of what David Riesman (speaking of innovation in colleges) has called the S curve of a snake. Movement forward is a matter of tacking right and left in sinuous dialectic, with apparent parallels between elements of society at quite different stages of development (cf., the similarities between what Charles Reich calls Consciousness I and Consciousness III) and apparent contradictions between what seem logical allies (cf., the activist-hippie split in the new culture). Segments may quarrel among themselves about which direction the snake is moving and therefore who is in fact ahead. Choice and historical inevitability often seem at odds; it is unclear which provides the motive force. In the turmoil of cultural change such confusions and conflicts are usually impossible to resolve. But from time to time come moments of clarity when something like national purpose is felt and willingly responded to. Then the snake slithers forward with coordinated effort, free from paralyzing inner tensions. I have some hope we are entering such an era of agile progression.

In economic terms the dual revolution pertains to maximization and minimization of production of material goods, more particularly to entry into and rejection of an ever-expanding and ever more prosperous middle class. The dream of abundance evoked by the industrial era finds itself in conflict with a dream of plenitude, as defined by Lewis Mumford in *The Pentagon of Power*. "The tendency of the present power system," he says, "goes directly contrary to the ideal of plenitude," which would emphasize decentralization, autonomy, and the restoration of more and more human functions to conscious control. Primitive societies have often achieved a degree of such plenitude—relative leisure, variety, self-determination, integration and wholeness of personality—but only at the expense of "fossilization" and supine dependence upon natural windfall. Typically, the paradises of primitive culture are in tropical zones. "Plenitude on such a solitary, meager, unadventurous basis too easily sinks into torpid penury and stupefaction." Even Thoreau found his tenure at Walden Pond, after all, only a vacation from a life of fuller engagement.

It is not to go back toward such a primitive plenitude, but forward to a more generous regimen, far more generous than the most affluent society now affords, that the coming generations must lay their plans.

Two essential components of the new plenitude are a breakdown of specialization (elimination of the "division of labor" Emile Durkheim thought necessary to civilization) and correction of the economic model of unlimited growth by providing for (as Mumford says) "contraction as well as expansion, for restrictive discipline as well as liberation, for inhibition as well as expression, for continuity as well as change." From the point of view of the old culture, the new culture's emphasis upon diversity of activity seems to be dilettantism; its de-emphasis upon productivity seems regressive. But these are exactly the characteristics which may create the kind of economic objective toward which all contending factions of the body politic would be willing to strive.

Under a regime of plenitude abundance is permissive, not compulsive: it allows for extravagant expenditures to satisfy man's higher needs for knowledge, beauty, or love— . . . while it may exact the severest economy for less worthy purposes. . . .

This benign transformation can happen only on one condition, and that a hard one: namely that the life-negating ideals and methods of the power system be renounced, and that a conscious effort be made, at every level and in every kind of community, to live not for the sake of exalting power but for reclaiming this planet for life through mutual aid, loving association and biotechnic cultivation. . . . There is . . . little prospect of overcoming the defects of the power system by any attack that employs mass organizations and mass efforts at persuasion; for these mass methods support the very system they attack. The changes that have so far been effective, and that give promise of further success, are those that have been initiated by animated individual minds, small groups, and local communities nibbling at the edges of the power structure by breaking routines and defying regulations. Such an attack seeks, not to capture the citadel of power, but to withdraw from it and quietly paralyze it. Once such initiatives become widespread, as they at last show signs of becoming, it will restore power and confident authority to its proper source: the human personality and the small face-to-face community. . . .

For its effective salvation mankind will need to undergo something like a spontaneous religious conversion: one that will replace the mechanical world picture with an organic world picture, and give to the human personality, as the highest known manifestation of life, the precedence it now gives to its machines and computers . . . . such changes have repeatedly occurred all through history; and under catastrophic pressure they may occur again. Of only one thing we may be confident. If mankind is to escape its programmed self-extinction the God who saves us will not descend from the machine: he will rise up again in the human soul.

Above all, if our society is to cure itself of psychological impasse, to make its internal strains and tensions creative, there has to be a development toward seeing differences as complementary rather than mutually threatening, and, more specifically, seeing the new culture not as a refutation of the old, but an organic outgrowth from it. Though Mumford speaks in apocalyptic tones of what will happen if cultural change does not soon occur, he also recognizes the credit due for the processes which have brought us to a new point of reversal. "Precisely because of the productive technical advances made during the last two centuries," Mumford says, "the lifetime division of labor has become irrelevant." Similarly, as the new culture matures, it is able to move past rebellion toward the revolution which saves, rather than destroys, the culture which produced it.

The first surge of the contemporary commune movement (1965–68) was typically one of escape from the city. The dream seemed to involve an elitist search for bucolic leisure —not a particularly possible or even attractive one for the population generally. And descriptions of the new plenitude, including those of Mumford, often convey an air of aristocratic seclusion and retirement. But the principles of that plenitude can be applied in urban settings as well, as the phenomenon I will call UNITY illustrates.*

* UNITY is not exactly a commune, but I can think of no better word for it. It has been discussed in a book about communes, various newspaper and magazine accounts, and in a book by one of its members, written in fulfillment of doctoral requirements. This member was on the staff of this study and kept a detailed journal over a year's period, amplified in extensive correspondence with me. (I have also used another book-length journal of another member, also used in fulfillment of doctoral requirements.) I visited twice, for a period of about two weeks, and published a long account of the place and other living-learning communities in a journal of higher education. Four other members of the staff of this study visited and reported on it. But I have refrained from giving specific references to preserve the anonymity of the community.

Most members of UNITY have (like many in the new culture) reacted against the "whole hippy-trippy kind of reality that died not so many years ago." One wrote me:

One group of people also coming out of the Haight was [those who brought about] . . . the whole commercialization of that trip . . . hippy-trippy capitalism now talked about as the underground or the alternative society. But within that whole category of people there are those who have gone off into a kind of self-sacrificing masochistic survival trip on communes. There is a third group of people which is different from either of those. They are people who are essentially pragmatic, and realistic, and fairly broadly versed in real world machinations, able to select from among them those things that are important and tactically useful. They are not underground at this point. The underground has basically been co-opted by the capitalists with very few exceptions (or destroyed by the police). So what you see is a seed of something new and as yet undefined.

There is a note of self-justification in what he says; not all rural communes are "self-sacrificing masochistic survival trips." But Walden is where you find it.* Insofar as they are able to achieve greater personal integration, autonomy, and satisfactions outside the Megamachine, they represent a movement toward the new plenitude.

UNITY is a community located in 84,000 square feet of warehouse, rented in 1970 as five concrete floors of vacant space by a dozen artists, architects, and musicians looking for a place to start an urban experiment in living and working. About two hundred people work in the building, of which some seventy live there. The city had made an estimate of five hundred thousand dollars as the

---

* In fact at least two urban communes use that name. One in Providence, Rhode Island, is a highly sophisticated, behaviorist and technologically oriented group, one of several in the country distantly based upon ideas in B. F. Skinner's *Walden II*.

cost of rehabilitating the building, but the same work (minus air-conditioning) was done by members of UNITY for less than fifty thousand dollars. They are an unincorporated association—the form used by many private clubs and labor unions—governing themselves by consensus in weekly meetings. There is no boss, are no standing offices (though some individuals do accept responsibility for particular areas of concern), few assigned tasks (and these rotate). Members take turns collecting the $5,500 operating costs of the building (rent, utilities, maintenance supplies, insurance), according to a formula "based on the amount of floor space occupied, number of occupants and usage of utilities." Spaces have been demarcated (the word "room" is not used), walls built according to the building code (albeit the spaces are odd-shaped and some walls are built with great sloping curves), fire doors installed, along with wiring, plumbing, a heating system, and creative furnishings. Some thirty to fifty people were (at the time I visited) eating a communal dinner each evening on the top floor in a cafeteria run completely without paid staff. In a pamphlet they described themselves:

where do we come from?

Most of us were born between 1940 and 1950 . . . the end of industrialism and the beginning of an economy based on software rather than hardware. We were born at the beginning of the era of TV, computers, jet travel, nuclear physics. From the time we were born to the present the greatest economic growth has been in industry that produces software: information, research and development, electronic communications systems, media, education, the multiversity. . . . One of the corporate structure's concerns was to ensure that there would be an educated, highly skilled, specialized, and available working class to fill the software mills of the new technology. We were to become that working class. We grew up with the 'cold war,' the 'space race,' and the 'crisis in education'— all propaganda efforts designed to lure large numbers of young people into becoming teachers, engineers, scientists, media technicians, etc. We were fooled in the same way the Okies were lured to California by the growers. Five jobs were promised when there was only one job available. We were told that there would be an unlimited need for educated people—which was pure bullshit. . . . Whatever America creates, it always seems to create a glut of. . . . The ultimate triumph of industrialism was to apply the techniques of the assembly line to the production of a labor force for post-industrialism. . . . In 1960 the cold war was flourishing and no Ph.D. ever dreamed that 1970 would see Ph.D.s driving cabs and applying for welfare.

all dressed up and nowhere to go

So here we are. We can write dissertations, we can teach school, we can design bridges, program computers. We're doctors, and lawyers, sculptors and painters, film makers and urban planners, TV and film technicians, designers and architects, electronics experimenters, musicians, composers, and political organizers. And we're free. Free because we're irrelevant. We're the avant-garde of a tidal wave of surplus talent, training, and glorious expectations. A tidal wave that's just beginning to realize it's a tidal wave.

did someone say revolution?

It took us awhile, but we've done it. We've been shaken out of our little mental compartments of 'architect' or 'psychologist.' We've come together. And we've realized that we're either going to transform America or we're going to die with America. . . . We have seen our enemies and we're looking for our allies. We are no longer 'alienated' from our work because our work is the transformation of America.

The economy of the place is fairly simple in theory: in every way possible the cash nexus has been replaced with an energy nexus. People talk about "energy ripoffs," as, for example, when someone dominates a meeting with an ego-trip. When it is sensed that all of one's energy, or the group's energy, is flowing outward, with little coming back in, a rearrangement is called for so that a better balance and exchange can be maintained. It is common to refer to an individual or to a group project (or even a party) admiringly as having "so much energy!" One hears remarks such as "I didn't feel like putting energy into that relationship." A member says they "measure value in terms of the energy required to accomplish something rather than in terms of the cash price that something will bring in the marketplace." *

The approach to cash, by necessity, is in large part to learn to do without it, and to use what little is available for real needs that cannot otherwise be fulfilled. One hun-

---

* Problems arise when translation is attempted to cash value. The new culture seems to me quite different in its view of labor from that of Marx, where labor as "value added" is calculated in determining the cash reward due the laborer. Marx regards toil as an unpleasant burden. "Energy" in the new culture is on the one hand a value-free scientific concept, and, on the other, *élan vital*. There is no real distinction between energy put into productive work and that put into social pleasures and human relationships. A commune in Colorado has over a dozen buildings, each a work of art, the most expensive of which cost about two thousand dollars in cash outlay. That one, a highly crafted mountain chalet, would sell for at least thirty thousand dollars on the open market. Even though tax assessments are much lower than market values, they are much higher than cash costs. When the taxes were raised because of new assessments of the buildings, a member (who lives in an elegant, huge zome—i.e., an irregular dome—that cost him five hundred dollars in materials) complained: "You can't tax me for my own labor!" But the tax authorities could. There may be a perverse logic in this in a culture which assumes one should pay for joy, for the labor is a reward in itself. A woman in this commune said, "You can tell when the dope is running out, because the work slows down." She said that mescaline, especially, enhanced the fun of working on cliff structures at high altitudes on arduous, repetitive tasks; it sharpens perception and helps maintain a jolly work-bee atmosphere. In addition to manual labor, the buildings involve architectural designs requiring complex mathematical and other technical knowledge—all of which would add to monetary value in the old culture, but all contributed with delight by communards who approach their work as artists rather than businessmen.

dred and fifty dollars per person per month is considered an ample income for survival—less than two thousand dollars per year. Working for pay is kept to a minimum, freeing time for voluntary work. Most of the tasks around the building—putting up sheet-rock walls or carrying garbage cans or legal counseling or accounting—are contributed. A strong work ethic* has been established, but the bias against profit (or, more exactly, the bias in favor of the medieval concept of a "fair price") is as rigorous a discipline as the old culture's bias in its favor.

For example, I was sitting on the floor at the educational switchboard (an information service for the free school movement, conducted voluntarily), chatting with a lovely young woman (who happened to have been trained as a clinical psychologist), when a man came in to list his summer program. He had the hair, beard, and attire of the movement. He and some friends wanted to caravan to the Yukon in three vehicles, with about thirty kids, for eight weeks. "Far out," the woman said. She asked some questions about their plans and, when he responded, gave him supportive noises: "Outasight." Eventually she got around to asking what all this would cost the kids, and by now, knowing the question was coming, the man was squatting like a dejected Okie, looking out of his hair with guarded shame. "Well," he said softly, "we figure it'll cost about seven hundred dollars per child." The woman shook her head sadly, sympathetically, saying "Oh, wow!" as though he had told her of a death in the family or a tragic bust. "Why is it going to cost all that?" she asked, and he told her about insurance, supplies, repairs. She commiserated: "Oh, wow." But then she brightened a little. "Since most

---

* Not to be confused with the "Protestant work ethic," in which work is regarded as an onerous burden which must be borne in the name of heavenly rewards, social good, or, more materialistically, deferred benefits. The work ethic of the new culture is one in which work is valued for itself, indeed becomes a form of leisure.

of that stuff won't happen anyway," she said, "maybe you could divide up the money that's left over and give it back." "Yeah," he said shamefacedly. "We could talk about that. We never thought of that."

I thought of an applicant for a grant at a foundation—the subtle but heavy and determining pressure of the foundation on the applicant to bring his plans in line with the foundation's priorities. He needed the help of the switchboard in recruiting students. But if he thought that he and his friends were going to live through the winter on any rake-off from those kids, he'd better forget the whole thing. The "hipoisie" is as unpopular at UNITY as its straight counterpart.

That moral force pervades every meeting, every encounter; but one shouldn't get the impression that it is a negative or oppressive force. The point is replacement of one kind of gratification (profit) by another (love). A team from the radical medical group had just returned from visiting communes, a kind of traveling clinic, though they carefully avoided using that welfare-client term. One explained to me that there were three components in what they were doing: (1) they helped people in communes who had health problems; (2) they learned about medicine, particularly herbal medicine, from the communities they visited; and (3) they had a hell of a good time. For them the third reason was primary and upfront, and they had to be pressed to acknowledge the other two motives. The old culture would give these values exactly the reverse emphasis.

I felt that emphasis at work as we built the walls at UNITY. It was a Sunday afternoon, and it took about thirty minutes to round up tools and supplies from various spaces in the building—a very sociable half hour of interaction, information, and joking. Seven of us assembled where a door frame was supposed to be—two young men who knew how to do the job, a couple of boys (twelve or thirteen years old) from the free school in the building, a couple of young women, and myself. We were an awkward group at first, since only two could work. But after putting in a phillips screw with the gun, one of our teachers handed the heavy screw gun to a boy and patiently waited while he struggled to get the screw started. Within an hour we were two teams, working in two places, the knowledge and skill somewhat distributed. Again, there are three components in this experience: (1) necessary work was getting done; (2) skills were being spread—so that they would be harder to stamp out, easier to duplicate; and (3) we enjoyed ourselves, as we now had a way of relating which we lacked at the beginning. We became buddies very rapidly, and when we stopped working a couple of hours later, the afternoon blended into the evening's festivities without a seam.

A member writes:

The business world measures value primarily in terms of efficiency and productivity. At UNITY, value is also measured in terms of strengthening the cohesiveness and vitality of the community, improving interpersonal relationships, enhancing individuals' well-being, and ecological concerns such as reusing and sharing resources. Whenever possible, we use energy as the medium of exchange, trading our labor and ideas, rather than using money—which is in continual short supply.

The external economic world has fixed demands, to which UNITY has learned painfully to adapt:

If a person or group is more than one month behind in their rent and utilities payments they are asked to leave unless someone—or the entire community—agrees to cover their share.

That principle—which seems simply common sense to the world outside—took sixteen months to be learned at UNITY, where the community is reluctant to become rigid and hardheaded regarding its own, particularly over finances. (Compare this to the vast tolerance and forgiveness needed in a family. At what point do parents kick out their children—or even cousins, aunts, uncles, or grandparents—for nonpayment of bills?)

As in most communes, there is an acceptance of the need of "shit jobs" for survival. In my own generation young people in high school or during breaks from college took such jobs as interludes on a career trajectory; but it was generally assumed that as soon as possible, one should decide what he wanted to "be" when he grew up, and start becoming that—which meant finding a means of lasting employment. It is increasingly true today, however, that people make a clear separation between what they do for pay and the way they define themselves. Each graduation time the newspapers carry stories of young men leaving elite colleges to tend bar or work as laborers—not merely because of the scarcity of jobs. Nor is this merely a phenomenon of youth: the average age of the members of UNITY is probably in the late twenties and quite a few members are in their thirties and forties. Some few are employed at what they consider to be their professions (e.g., an accountant, a lawyer, a psychological therapist). More typically, they disregard employment in self-definition:

A young woman film maker worked for several months in a local chain restaurant and then as a saleslady in a clothing shop. Several artists paint houses by day and canvases by night. Another painter in the building drove a cab for several months. An urban planner works half-time on government Model Cities programs, training evaluators. A woman on the ECOS and Fort Help staffs [ECOS is a foundation for ecological and urban planning; Fort Help is a therapeutic center] works about three hours a day washing glassware in a laboratory at a local hospital to earn enough to live on. While she had gone to Washington for two weeks to organize a conference on environmental education, two other people in the building did her job for her, getting the money for themselves. The Alternative Employment office in UNITY is trying to set up other such job-sharing opportunities so several people can hold a single job. One regular nine-to-five job can provide enough income for several people's subsistence needs.

There is no question that the film maker is a film maker— even if she is not making films. One such young woman finally found herself "employed" by a film company making radical documentaries. But they had no money to pay her, so her "salary" was theoretical. At the time I spoke with her she was tremendously excited about this career opportunity, worked many hours overtime in the company's office and cutting room, and ungrudgingly continued working part-time as a waitress for income.

Also, as in most communes, many draw food stamps, welfare, or assistance for dependent children or disability, "but find it a real hassle to play the bureaucratic game that is necessary." Attitudes toward accepting government support vary from guilt to a sense that "their work is legitimate and ought to be supported by the state." Terms such as "instant socialism" or "midnight shopping" are commonly used, reflecting a pleasant cynicism concerning scavenging or appropriation of loose bits of city surplus. (I am reminded of World War II soldiers who spoke of "liberating" wine, food, or women in occupied towns.)

In the building are a number of self-employed people working for profit (a painter, a masseur, an engraver— whose machinery, installed in his living space, supports him and another man). There is a film-processing laboratory, a woodshop, an electronics firm.

The Ecology Center Press [since closed] is barely making enough money to pay subsistence salaries ($100 to $150 per month) to three people. They are trying to keep their prices low for poor groups which have purposes similar to ours, while charging higher rates for more established customers who have more money to spend on printing. They often give away extra materials which they could sell.

There was considerable community resistance to allowing profit-making businesses in the building at all. At one community meeting guidelines were proposed and discussed:

(1) individuals' incomes should be limited to reasonable subsistence with excess income going into the building or other useful projects; (2) they shouldn't get locked into employer-employee relationships that are authoritarian, exploitative, and divisive; (3) they should provide access to their tools and equipment by other people in the building; (4) they should, when possible, employ people from the building.

But consensus was never reached. A member comments, "Listing guidelines destroys the organic possibility of guidelines establishing themselves as they are necessary and appropriate."

Though there do not exist hierarchies, offices, or leadership structures in UNITY (or in most enclaves of the new culture), there invariably are "heavies" who have been around longer, are more intimately involved with the ideological purposes as well as the practical working of the group, whose skills and personalities are of central importance, or who are older or more experienced than most members. This is not a role always of their choosing; people often "lay a leadership trip" on those who appear to be strong, bringing questions and problems to them for decision, so that inescapably they have more knowledge of the inner workings of the community, and their voices, whether they like it or not, become more decisive. The most effective kind of leadership in communal situations is that which evokes leadership in others, a progressive and perpetual withdrawal from responsibility as new potential leaders are able to assume it.

Influence from the heavies radiates outward in educational rings, as more and more are able to take over and—most importantly of all—as they internalize the unarticulated philosophy and ethics of UNITY.* Those who remain indifferent or exploitative vibe themselves out or are vibed out by the group; occasionally they are explicitly "offed," or asked to leave, by community consensus. There is an awareness that knowledge and commitment must be spread for survival, that fibers of belief and ability and affection must do the job that more mechanistic organizational forms do elsewhere in society.

There is a surprising degree (considering its size and turnover of membership) of close family feeling at UNITY, particularly among those who live in the building. It is a home, in no way like an apartment house or dormitory.

Distinctions between work and play break down as children run through an office, issues are argued as people paint a wall, or a visitor is invited to help prepare and eat a meal. The fun and stimulation that come from friends working together to paint a hallway or write a proposal often makes it seem as much like play as work.

Being together with the same group of people twenty-four hours a day, seven days a week, makes the life-style very intense and, often, very fast-paced. This is particularly true since most people strive to operate on a norm of personal openness and readiness to confront interpersonal problems as they occur. . . . When two people get turned on to each other as they work, they may go and make love immediately without waiting for evening. . . .

The frequency and spontaneity with which people come

---

* A member protests, "Philosophy and ethics are mental institutions which defy growth and change. UNITY is too fluid to say it has a philosophy." While there is certainly constant change—and this portrait is very specifically limited to the second year of UNITY's existence—I believe outsiders are often able to delineate "the philosophy and ethics" of a group more clearly than can those who have lived through its evolution.

and leave and change their activities and interests make it necessary for folks to adjust to living without the certainty of long-term, secure relationships. People are learning to draw their personal security from inner resources rather than depending on friends to the extent that has become so common in "other-directed" American society. Paradoxically, this seems to make interpersonal relations deeper and more open for some. People are learning to live with transformation and in fact begin to find security in the process of continual change which provides ways to meet one's ever-changing personal needs and interests.

The population of UNITY is basically made up of people from three backgrounds: former hippies, former activists (who have developed "a desire to create alternatives born of their frustration with protest as a tactic for social and political change"), and those who have left behind "regular nine-to-five jobs as laborers, craftspeople, professionals, because they had become alienated and dissatisfied with the illusions and role-playing of the traditional working world as well as the divisive separation of work from living." They recognize among their motives "at least four basic desires": economic (cutting rent and living expenses, sharing tools), communal (relating to others, belonging, loving and being loved), educational (getting stimulation, knowledge, and energy from a diverse group), and the desire for autonomy (gaining more control over their lives). The atmosphere is the opposite of what one normally associates with indolence and ease; but it fulfills rather exactly that described by Mumford as the new plenitude.

I am amused to remember how dazed and disoriented I was when I first visited. After being shown through the maze of the building, introduced to many of the people at work and play, witnessing a multiscreen slide show with rock accompaniment, and mellowed by a shared joint, I was shown to a "space," and left on my own for the

evening. Toilet kit in hand I went down to the bathroom
—which has a door with glass panes revealing sink, stool,
and shower to the hallway. Does one knock? Does one
wait? What does one do? Invited by phone to a com-
paratively straight middle-class home for the night, I fled
—in gratitude. I was not ready for the new world.

The next day I went to an inner-city free church, with
a rock service and squirming lights and overlapping slides
flashing on the sanctuary, a black, bearded preacher in
bellbottoms and pulsing pelvis evoking joyous dancing in
the aisles. The place was packed, and only a large minority
were long-hairs; there were obviously straight, middle- and
lower-class blacks and whites, teenagers, and children—
including the children playing around the feet of the
preacher as he read out "Quotations from Chairman Jesus."
The message was not to resist the spirit, to let it happen,
and a black middle-class matron next to me grabbed me in
bosomy embrace. The message spoke to my condition.
Never before had I attended a church service with which
I could so totally identify. In the basement were pressure
tables for a wide range of radical causes and organizations.
As I went back to UNITY with *The Big Rock Candy
Mountain* (a new-culture magazine) tucked under my
arm, I was prepared to stay a few days.

Monday morning, however, the shower-room was awash
with an inch of water, and the mop was missing. So was
toilet paper—from every john in the building. The halls
were littered with paper, butts, cans, drab in the dim lights
from ceiling bulbs (many missing). Ah well, I sighed, I
somehow knew it would never work. It was not a bust
from the outside they need fear: the place would collapse
in its own stew of filth and disease and unpaid bills eventually. I spent the morning visiting the free school, where
youngsters drifted in as they pleased, jumped on the water
bed, bummed cigarets, read comics. Who needs it? I

thought. That old world out there may be meaningless and suicidal, but at least it's tidy. It may give me ulcers, but it's not a bore.

But by afternoon volunteers were sweeping the halls, cleaning and supplying the johns. The switchboard and reception desk were manned steadily by volunteers. News hummed through the halls. Sheetrock was being unloaded at the dock in the basement, and the community truck was grinding its ancient gears in busy errands. A gang was heading off gaily for a demonstration (in which several were to be arrested). The press was churning out pamphlets to save the earth. Who needed it? I needed it. I was ready. The mop was replaced. I never showered alone.

It has chiefly been since 1968 that the new culture turned the corner from withdrawal and rebellion and aching disillusion to creating more deeply rooted enclaves and a network of communication and cooperation sufficient to sustain its life. The mood has been one of peacefully ignoring the system in order to work on concrete building of alternatives—decentralized, relatively closer to the land, non-authoritarian, non-profit-oriented, based on "soft" technology (called by Mumford "biotechnics"—i.e., ecologically sound and emphasizing self-sufficiency of relatively small communities).

For example, a Michigan urban commune which has persisted since 1964 with a remarkably consistent membership of nineteen adults and three children recognized a transformation in its focus in 1970:

All these things . . . pushed our whole approach farther and farther to the left, toward the general hysteria and frenzy which was driving the former civil rights/peace movement into the streets with rocks and bottles instead of protest signs after the Chicago stomp scene. The problem with this approach, which soon overshadowed the constructive work we

had been doing, was that it was mounted out of simple frus-
tion and rage without much thought for its consequences. We
had been pushed to the point where we just *reacted* against the
forces that were messing us over. . . . We started threatening
the government with all kinds of ridiculous militant rhetoric
which we could not possibly back up, and the government of
course took us at our word . . . and moved in ways that
would insure our elimination. . . . The total *senselessness* of
what had happened was what hit us the hardest—it began to
dawn on all of us that we had just been stumbling along doing
whatever popped into our heads without regard for either the
personal or political consequences of our actions, and that
something had to be done about it *immediately* if we wanted
to have any future effectiveness, let alone survive. . . . We
really learned that we could solve our problems by discussing
them openly. . . . It blew our minds!

They came to understand, "We were not revolutionaries;
we were only rebels." By 1972 they had brought together
a Tribal Council in their city, a "shadow government"
composed of local groups concerned with food, health,
community activities, education, transportation, housing,
and defense. With the help of a grant from HEW and
rental by the city of two huge buildings, they set up a
permanent headquarters for a whole range of health and
educational services—drug help, food co-op, people's defense, finance, artists' workshops, music, a ballroom, and
community gardening. They had suffered through the
changes from a sometimes sullen, sometimes manic militancy to a joyful, regenerative, open spirit.*

---

* For example, the group had been active in efforts to legalize marijuana,
when, according to a woman member, "A group of state legislators
came around to find out what pot looked like. We poured out a pile
of it on the table, showed them pipes, how to roll joints, how to
hold roaches. Then we insisted they should try a little so they'd know
what they were dealing with. We turned all of them on, except one
black dude who went in the other room. He said he knew very well
what it was like to smoke it—but he didn't want to get caught."

Before 1968 there were many stories in the papers of harassment of communes, but these have largely disappeared.* Good relations with neighbors are a high priority for communards who are more dedicated than desperate in their efforts to change society. "They think we're crazy, but they love us," is a typical comment from a rural commune in New England. Neighbors learn to respect the capacity of rural communards for hard work, their interest in traditional wisdom and skills, and their willingness to help others. On the other hand the neighbors have learned to tolerate (and in some cases to enjoy) a certain amount of nude farming, pot smoking, and blurring of sex roles as women show up to help on the hay wagon, leaving men to tend the babies.

As each new commune forms it typically sends out tentacles of association with other freaks in the area—or around the country. Many new communes (if they have access to ditto or mimeograph machines) start newsletters

---

* At least from the papers, but legal harassment of communes continues. After several years of severe financial and emotional strain in legal battles with public authorities, a well-known open-land commune in California finally had its access road virtually closed in 1972. "When it finally happened, we welcomed it as a good change," they reported, as visitors were forced to hike in through a canyon, and the result was much more community serenity and stability. Nonetheless, the case represents a constitutional setback for the new culture. Typically, cases involving communes illustrate unequal enforcement of laws, but it is extremely difficult to establish that persons in the new culture are being discriminated against as a group (as can more easily be established pertaining to members of a religious sect or ethnic minority). For a discussion of several classic cases and the constitutional questions involved, see Jonathan Shor, "*All* in the 'Family': Legal Problems of Communes," *Harvard Civil Rights/Civil Liberties Law Review*, vol. 7, no. 2 (March 1972), pp. 393–441. There are occasional victories. Two members of a Cambridge, Massachusetts, commune successfully defended themselves against the charge of "open and gross lewdness and lascivious behavior," and the amusing and enlightening transcript of their trial is printed in *Lewd: The Inquisition of Seth and Carolyn*, Beacon, 1972.

resembling the Christmas letters straight families sometimes circulate among their friends and acquaintances. Most of these are abortive: the buoyant expectations of the first issue soon grind on the rocks of personal dissension, membership turnover, daily work demands, and other hard conditions of communal survival. Within a few months I heard of half-a-dozen groups which hoped to establish commune clearinghouses—e.g., for people seeking to join communes, communes seeking members, goods to exchange, and other news relative to the movement. These, too, generally disappear, though a few in urban areas persist. One in Boston reported twice-weekly meetings (attendance ranging sixty to eighty per meeting) for people interested in meeting others in communes or hoping to start new ones, a referral service handling some forty people per week, involving over a hundred and thirty-five communes in a four-month period. They offer life-style counseling, facilitation for problem-solving in communes, legal assistance, a food co-op involving some fifty communes, an urban/rural network, "consciousness raising data collection," and assistance in finding and acquiring real estate.

In the San Francisco Bay area a private commune newsletter circulates among over three hundred communes. Each issue is hand-lettered, hand-bound, tied with thread, illustrated. Each copy is a work of art, hand-delivered to communes on its circulation list (which is carefully limited —especially to exclude mass media and researchers). It contains want ads, tidbits of personal news, and survival lore (e.g., a recipe for kitten soup, prefaced by the statement that cats rip off affection that should go to human beings). An organization of Vermont communes maintains not only a newsletter, but provides a whole range of cooperative services from food buying to childcare. One year children from the communes in this group formed their own children's collective, a kind of free school (with some adult participation), in which children substantially ran their own lives on their own farm.

Like educational conferences in the straight world, there are numerous, periodic conferences held around the country on communal living, alternative life-styles, consciousness raising, free clinics, organic gardening, inexpensive building, folk music, and other topics of interest to the new culture. I attended one such (on education) in which some eighty people packed together in a five-room farmhouse for a winter weekend in upper New York State. In better weather, the communards and the curious are likely to gather, like Okies along Highway 66, in battered VW vans and Econolines adapted for camp-style living, on a farm. Many of these conferences are sponsored by universities; one was sponsored by the National Institute of Mental Health; but most are called by individual communes as a public service.

Some organizations formed for other purposes (e.g., associations of organic farmers, peace groups, small foundations) have, in effect, been taken over by new-culture people, and their meetings become virtual conferences on communalism. Similarly, some periodicals (such as *Mother Earth News*) have gradually moved toward becoming journals and exchange media for communards. One (*The Modern Utopian*—now defunct) began with a broad range of interests (religion, the peace movement, sexual liberation, etc.) and moved toward almost exclusive concern with communes (finally resulting in a series of books on communes by its editor, Richard Fairfield, and melding its magazine function with several other commune magazines to produce a national periodical, *Communities*, beginning publication in November 1972). A number of more general publications (*Win, Rolling Stone, Organic Gardening, Quicksilver Times, L.A. Free Press*) devote space to communal matters. *Workforce*, a magazine (and publisher of pamphlets and leaflets) aimed at helping people find socially significant employment and living opportunities, is itself produced by a commune and has increasingly concerned itself with the spread of communalism. *Black Bart Brigade* is aimed specifically at middle-aged people seeking creative alternatives.

Beneath the clutter of newsletters, food conspiracies, free clinics, free stores, free schools, free churches, legal aid groups (e.g., the Counterculture Law Project in Chicago—and law communes and collectives in most major cities), conferences, journals, and other appurtenances of a growing web of political-economic services and communications, the basic medium by which the new culture grows and develops is personal contact. There is a huge network of trust spread across the nation among friends and friends of friends. If I know a hundred people you don't know—people to whom I would, for instance, gladly extend the hospitality of a meal and floorspace for the night, people to whom I would lend my car—and you know a hundred people in that category whom I don't know, and we trust one another's judgment enough to extend trust to one another's friends, our orbit includes some two hundred people. If we feel the same way about our friends as we do about one another, the progression is exponential: ten thousand are included in this relationship. As for chain letters and other such devices, there are natural limits restricting the unlimited spread of the web, but there are surely some hundreds of thousands of freaks by now who might, if they compared notes, find that they were at least the friend of a friend of a friend, and such relationships have a meaning and function in the new culture which they have not in the old. The web of trust developed primarily as a result of the extralegal planning and collaboration in the civil rights movement and then the drug culture, when secure credentials on the basis of personal testimony became critical, and written credentials, positions, and formal affiliations were suspect. "He's cool" was an assurance that could pass from person to person at least three or four removes from the original basis of inter-personal trust.

At one point an unscrupulous entrepreneur put some LSD of poor quality (i.e., laced with strychnine) on the streets. Immediately those who call themselves "the people" responded to the threat. Those dealing in "good" stuff gave it away. If someone tried to sell acid, the prospective customer could be fairly certain it was bad. Bad stuff was cleared off the market in a matter of weeks. That phenomenon could occur only under conditions in which personal trust had a functional meaning in a coherent culture.

Given the distinctive garb and hair styles of the new culture, even indirect personal knowledge is usually unneccessary. When we bought a farm to start our own commune, I opened a personal checking account in the local bank with a $1,000 check. But I needed cash that day, and the bank refused to cash a check until my deposit was cleared. I offered to pay for a call to the bank on which the check was drawn, but that was insufficient guarantee. I gave them the names of local merchants where I had opened accounts, but these were too recent for the comfort of the bank officials. From there I went to the supermarket and happened to strike up a conversation in the aisle with an identifiable freak—a long-hair mechanic who had operated a garage in the town for over a year. When I mentioned my difficulties with the bank, he immediately offered to countersign the check, though I had met him five minutes before. He went along to the bank with another long-hair —a member of our commune. By chance they got the same teller I had dealt with, and she, remembering my name, was now faced by two freaks, with my check for $100. "Do you know these people?" she asked the mechanic—who had an account at the bank. "I just met them," he said—but she had no choice but to cash the check his account covered.*

I do not mean to imply that such trust is always warranted. Any long-hair has stories of being ripped off by long-hairs, even those they regard as close friends. Sometimes such experiences embitter the victims. In "resigning" from the movement, Abbie Hoffman wrote:

The movement to me now is a little group of vultures from Ithaca that broke into WPAX (we were making tapes for Radio Hanoi) and stole all the equipment they needed because "Hoffman's rich anyway." . . . I know one thing. I don't use the phrase "brothers and sisters" much anymore, except among real close friends and you'll never hear me use the word "movement" except in a sarcastic sense.

But the web of trust is sustaining enough for most purposes. Most new culture people haven't enough possessions to be much concerned about ripoffs. Even if the mechanic's $100 in the bank had been his last, it mattered less to him than $100 meant to the banker; he wanted to keep his income down to avoid paying taxes and was ridding himself of possessions to which he felt he had an unhealthy attachment.

Without that element of relinquishment of material goods, the new culture might be a kind of Mafia, in which

---

* In spite of this apparent conflict, the ethics of the new culture are very much like those of rural America. That same bank makes loans and does business primarily on the basis of informal personal knowledge and trust. After a few months in the area, any member of our commune could make deposits or transfers of money from one account to another, including personal accounts, at the same bank, without signatures of the parties involved. This could even be done by phone: we can call up and ask for $100 to be transferred from Joseph's account to the farm's account, for example, and the transaction will take place without so much as a deposit or withdrawal slip being signed.

bonds of the "family" are inviolable, based on personal contact and affection, communication is instantaneous, the mes-
sages classically brief and pungent, and outside the family is
a vast, valueless jungle in which anything goes. Ma Bell,
for instance, is fair game to many in the new culture. An
article in *Quicksilver Times* signed by "The People's Operators" gave inside information on telephone credit cards,
advising readers to switch to phony special billing numbers,
which (as of March 1972) had not been programmed into
the computers that check credit cards. "Give the largest
pig monopoly in the world another big headache," the people's operators advised. Thus it seemed not only convenient,
but a matter of principle, to cheat the corporation.

But communards generally have little interest in playing
games with corporations. More common are the attitudes
expressed by a member of a farm commune in Pennsylvania:

I just don't trust a ripoff mentality. It's like what mothers used
to say about the cookie jar. Once a guy starts ripping off the
phone company, or welfare, or a foundation, or a supermar-
ket, he kind of gets the habit, and he'll be ripping you off next
thing you know.

Though this man technically qualified for welfare, he did
not apply for it. "I don't really need it," he said. He took
pride in living on almost no money at all and believed that
if he had more cash he would "live soft" and be less able to
cope. "I want welfare to be there when I really need it," he
said. He did use food stamps, however—a price support
program which he thought served the interests of farmers
(though in fact it serves primarily the agribusiness which
destroys small farmers) as well as providing needed food
he could not raise himself.

Traveling and visiting are much more important means
of communication in the new culture than are telephones

or publications. Some make a career of visiting—e.g., a young man who figures horoscopes in exchange for hospitality. His dharma, he says, is to go from commune to commune bearing the news. An expert on organic gardening, massage, and yoga, in his fifties, was present in the early days of such well-known communes as the Lama Foundation, Morningstar, Olompali, and the Hog Farm. Wherever he goes he is welcomed and loved; he helps out on the garden and sometimes acts (like an encounter group leader) as an outside consultant on interpersonal problems. Lucy Horton reports:

While I was staying at Breadloaf in New Mexico, the Pride Family arrived in a gaily painted delivery van, with their tipi poles on top. Remnant of a commune in California that had broken up when the owner of the house they occupied raised the rent, the five had crossed and recrossed the country in the last few months. First they had gone up to Atlantis in Oregon and planted the garden that I had later admired. Then they headed across the Midwest, stopping over at the Foundlings in Iowa and the farm in Wawa, Minnesota. By the time I got back to Vermont, I was no longer capable of much surprise at learning that Sue, who was visiting my friends there, had lived with the Pride Family in California for seven months. I was glad to be able to tell her that although they had planned to winter in Arizona, Breadloaf's subtle magic had appealed to them and they had pitched their tipi out behind the pueblo.*

Information is power. A hitchhiker trudges down the drive to crash for the night, and likely as not he is bearing news of scattered friends. Dropping in on a commune in Vermont, my wife and I left bearing an invitation to a Thanksgiving feast for a commune in New Hampshire. Beyond personal news, visitors also carry skills and data,

---

* Commune names are fictional. Incidentally, the California landlord is a wealthy man who started two communes in Vermont and still lives in one of them.

from wiring and composting to advice on income taxes. Since visitors are frequent and unannounced, communards are not likely to take time off to entertain them. Rather, the visitor fits in to whatever is going on—from weeding squash to joining in an encounter meeting. The members of one commune had succeeded in disassembling a tractor and locating a broken bearing, but didn't know what to do next, when a visitor happened along who knew how to get a replacement part and reassemble the machine. A woman there was going through mail on the dinner table. "We never send for anything," she said. "If it is important, it will come to us." The next thing I heard from her was "Far out!" A book had arrived, addressed to someone who had left, written by one of the woman's friends. She drifted off toward the outhouse thumbing through it, and I heard her murmuring "Far *out!*" through the open kitchen window. Though few communes have television or even radio or subscribe to other than local newspapers (e.g., for ads about jobs and auctions), they seem mysteriously to keep abreast of current events, largely as carried in the heads of visitors. Organic food stores, record and book shops, and other new-culture businesses are, like seventeenth century coffeehouses in London, or the salons and cafés of Paris which generated the French Revolution, media of information exchange.

Growth and strength begin inward, with the individual, and radiate outward to the group, the local community, the far-flung tribe of the new culture, and last of all to the larger political and economic system. Diet and health are major topics of communication, closely followed by mental health, interpersonal relations, and questions of leadership, organization, property ownership, and sharing. Next come economic and practical concerns such as work schedules, tools, supplies, marketing, buying and bartering, mechanics, cooking and baking, farming and forestry, local politics. Here communication begins to fan out to neighbors and the surrounding community. As communes and communards grow more mature, they have more energy to spend on larger social concerns.

For example, thirty-year-old Koinonia, in Georgia, now conducts an impressive range of national charitable enterprises involving hundreds of thousands of dollars. Four-year-old Twin Oaks, in Virginia, spent most of its first years preoccupied with internal matters; its members are noticing now that they have energy to spare for setting up wider communications, attending to political developments in their region, fostering the kinds of economic growth and cooperation they approve of. Urban groups are more likely to have an outreach of social concern from the beginning; indeed many are formed explicitly for social action. Reporting on communes in the Berkeley area, Steven V. Roberts says:

A whole range of new institutions has sprung up: medical clinics, schools, law firms, churches, businesses, and, most importantly, living groups. Taken together these institutions are beginning to amount to a distinct alternative society . . . something is happening here. It's very tentative, and very fluid, but quite real.*

These new developments are quite in contrast to the years of protest that ushered out the sixties. There is a new patience and historical sense, perhaps derived in part from Maoism and Oriental philosophy, Roberts notes.

Communal living helps overcome the contradiction between their life and their work. Life and work are integrated into a "whole," another key word in the movement. . . . "There's a lot of knowledge here and people share things. There's also a lot of support for what you're doing, and that's very important." . . . "Here there is always dinner at 6:30, and usually

* "Halfway Between Dropping Out and Dropping In," *New York Times Magazine*, Sept. 12, 1971, pp. 45 ff.

there are ten or twelve people around. It's good companion-
ship." A girl in another commune explained how they had
started: "We got arrested together and no one wanted to go
home alone anymore." . . . "More and more people in the
movement are saying, 'Which collective—not which individual
—will take care of thus and so.' I really like that. I like that form
of identity. It's a place to belong." Home, family, belonging—
the words tell a lot about the yearnings of the young. Collective living is also an economic necessity. Since many people in
the alternative society have given up the idea of a "career" in
the traditional sense, and do not want to work full time, the
struggle for solvency is constant. . . . Many communes cannot afford even meat loaf. But there is a pervasive feeling in the
movement that people do not want material rewards, except
perhaps a good stereo and the chance to travel. "Things seem
to come along and we're able to make enough," said Barbara.
"I guess one of the distinguishing facts of our generation is
that we never really think about money."

City communes are living bases for people engaged in quite
diverse activities—both for subsistence and political action
—during the day and through frequent evening meetings.
Though there is general agreement on political direction,
the hassles about fine points of ideology or life-style are
apt to be even more disruptive than would be arguments
among people with more extreme differences of point of
view. But for all their tensions, urban communes are
hotbeds of information and collaboration. Like rural communes, they are likely to send their energy out in widen-
ing rings, first attending to individual growth, better
functioning of the group itself, improvement of the neighborhood, local elections and issues, and last of all national
or international politics.

"Family" membership is not necessarily limited to those
present at any given time in a commune. A communard
from Berkeley told me their group had a number of members in, and regular traffic between, related communes in

Amherst (Massachusetts), the Taos area, northern Ohio, and New Haven. On the road, a member of one was a member of any of the others as long as he chose to stay. A large religious commune in Oregon considers itself to have over a hundred and fifty members, all in a group marriage. Only about fifty at a time are actually living at the Oregon site, but like cousins abroad, the others are still part of the family. A group marriage near Pittsburgh has entirely dispersed except for one man and two women. The man defined them as "a family without the disadvantage of blood relationship." Someday they might live together again, but maybe not. It didn't affect their sense of belonging to one another.

Such seething activity as characterizes the new culture in the seventies is a far cry from the indolence the popular mind associates with dropping out, or the leisurely connotations of the new plenitude. Mumford sees "a slowdown, sometimes even a stoppage" in productivity as essential for many reasons, including the need for leisure to foster "more intimate human relations"—e.g., for physicians to take time to know patients as persons. He quotes Thoreau's *Journal* approvingly:

The really efficient laborer will be found not to crowd his day with work, but will saunter to his task surrounded by a wide halo of ease and leisure.

But "ease and leisure" need not mean luxury and idleness. A cultural winter is a season of passivity and inaction, except for the glacial movements of the corporate tide. Spring brings bewildering, spontaneous busyness (a kind of opposite of business)—chirping and squirming and tangling of tentacles, with sometimes absurd and tender forms of life pulsing toward dominance, spreading in wild, benign redundancy. Nature's plenitude encroaches on the old economy like moss upon a rock.

6

Yin and Yang

A ruling class, to survive, must propose a Law: a law to work
must have a hook into the social psyche—and the most effective way to achieve this is to make people doubt their natural
worth and instincts, especially sexual. To make "human nature" suspect is also to make Nature—the wilderness—the adversary. Hence the ecological crisis of today.*

GARY SNYDER

Most experienced communards would probably laugh
sadly at this definition of a commune by the British psy-
chiatrist David Cooper (italics his):

A commune is a microsocial structure that achieves a viable
dialectic between solitude and being-with-others; it implies
either a common residence for the members, or at least a
common work and experience area, around which residential
situations may spread out peripherally; it means that love relationships become diffused between members of the commune
network far more than is the case with the family system, and
this means, of course, that sexual relationships are not restricted
to some socially approved two-person, man-woman arrange-

* *Earth House Hold: Technical Notes & Queries To Fellow Dharma
Revolutionaries,* New Directions, 1969, p. 115.

ment; above all, because this strikes most centrally at repression, it means that children should have totally free access to adults beyond their biological parental couple. These definitional elements point to an ideological *prise de position* that one may state thus: *making love is good in itself, and the more it happens in any way possible or conceivable between as many people as possible the better.**

In one sense, however, Cooper's definition expresses what might be regarded as an ideal of communal living in regard to sexuality. "Making love" need not refer to orgasmic, genital sexual activity. The idea is not orgy, but an ambience of loving, and, indeed, erotic interpersonal contact among a variety of unrelated people. But that ambience is only intermittently and tentatively attained in this early stage of the movement.

The ideal is confusing because it implies a difference of quality as well as of quantity in sexual relations, a quality which infuses yang with yin. The key word in Cooper's statement is *diffused*. In communes sexual energy tends to be released to spread and mingle, to work into the fabric of life. Perhaps the word should be spelled *defused*. An even better word might be *disseminated*, with its reference to the sowing of seed, an image of gentle, benign, unclimactic fertility, quite in contrast to the pattern of constraint and focus and forceful ejaculation, followed by a slump of ennui or guilt, which is the common mode of sexual experience in our society.

Western civilization depends to a large extent upon the bottling up and channeling and selective explosion of sexual energy. Like the fossil fuels pressed and stored under the mantle of earth, the erotic drive is buried under strata of custom and contempt and (ironically) idealization. It is dark, subterranean, rather smelly, and immensely volatile. It is capable of miracles. It generates cathedrals like ossi-

* *The Death of the Family*, Random House, 1970, p. 44.

fied fountains; it tunnels under cities, propels the engines of commerce, and crochets the intricate lace of computation and calculation and rhetorical justification. A great metropolis is a throbbing, towering concentration of diverted, sublimated, refined, pressurized libido, frozen potential (capital) draining in glandular dusk the energies of the region to maintain a quivering salute to a Heaven of transcendental yang. Imagine now a great wilting, as of the Empire State Building, not as an aftermath of the ferocious discharge of war, but yet in orgasmic melding, a tantric flowing of one into another, in which the urban yang is relieved of its intolerable tension and the fallow yin of the countryside is charged and renewed.

I do not mean to imply a dichotomy; it is not a matter of either/or. I am not suggesting that in a communal future everyone will move to the country and practice Tantric yoga. If we have overemphasized domination, rationality, individualism, order, the correction is not an overemphasis on submission, emotion, collectivism, and spontaneity. There need not be a battle between the poles. The search is for integration and complementarity. Discussing the yin-yang as a symbol of "complement dualism," Wilfred Cantwell Smith says:

We in the West are familiar with another type of dualism, which we may call conflict dualism. In this, two basic forces are in collision, as opposites that struggle and clash: good and evil, right and wrong, black and white, true and false. This type of dualism seems to have its origin about the middle of the first millenium B.C. in the Tigris-Euphrates valley or in Iran. . . . It found its way into the Jewish, Christian, and the Islamic traditions, and has been vigorously resuscitated in recent times on a world scale by Marxism.*

The conflict model of dualism may be associated with original sin in the Edenic myth; "knowledge," or discrimination

* *The Faith of Other Men*, Mentor, 1965, pp. 67–68.

of Good and Evil, is specifically that which separates humanity from integration with nature. A view of life in which opposites (man-woman, heaven-earth, hot-cold, dry-moist, active-passive) are seen as harmonious and necessary complements of one another prevails in Eastern thought and, as has been frequently observed, is increasingly characteristic of Western science (e.g., in the wave-quantum theories of light, the principle of complementarity in physics, theories of matter and antimatter, and acceptance of all fact statements as probabilistic rather than absolute).

Like *synergy* and *synchronicity*, *complement duality* is not a term one hears bandied about in the communal kitchen or bedroom, but the concept is nonetheless important for understanding communal phenomena. "Tolerance of ambiguity" is another expression for the quality cultivated by the intimacy of communal life. In the yin-yang symbol, that circle combining tears of black and red nestled softly together, there is a spot of red in the bulge of the black, a spot of black in the bulge of the red. Women are not yin, only more yin than yang, and men are more yang than yin, but never absolutely yang. The emphasis is upon common humanity rather than sexual difference.

"Unisex" was a mass-media label for the emerging mode, but it implied a mod style of colorless compromise obliterating differences. The hard-bitten, masculinized, blue-jeaned chick of the New Left (especially in urban scenes) and the soft young men with ornate clothing and flowing shoulder-length hair were momentary stereotypes of rebellion against traditional sex roles, but these were not, I think, indicative of anything permanent about the new culture. The heroes of that culture, such as Mick Jagger, often were blatantly androgynous and highly erotic: not neuter, but forces deriving their overwhelming dynamism from complementarity. Janis Joplin may have had the muscular drive of a trucker, but contained within her the serene sensuality of yin. It is more that kind of vitality that feeds on its own use which characterizes sexuality of the new age, something motile, powerful, various. Especially on rural communes one finds a profound womanliness and manliness emerging —Mother Earth and Father Sun, peasantlike clothing without peasant oppression and rigid patterning, women who swing axes and men who bake bread and tend babies, but with deep mutual respect for sexual distinction. "Unisex" did not liberate so much as it shaped people into even more procrustean expectations. The yin-yang vision is quite otherwise, as it encourages the full flowering of difference without anxiety when these overlap. But people who move into communes carry with them the rooted conditioning of the old culture, much of which takes place in infancy and is all but irradicable in most mature adults.

It is difficult to explain to an outsider how much and, in a sense, how little sexuality characterizes communal life. It is now 8:30 on a freezing October morning. My wife and a teenaged daughter are standing by the fire in the living room as I write, talking with an eighteen-year-old woman, whom I will call Sally. Sally is nude. She and Alex slept last night in a bedroll beside the fire. When I built up the fire at 5:30, I was stepping over Alex's outstretched arm. Later, when I came in from feeding the horses, they were awake, and I plunged my cold hands between their nude bodies to warm them. Sally and I kissed. She and I have had intercourse often, most recently with Alex sleeping (I think) in the bed alongside us. This morning I kissed Alex on his bare shoulder. As an adult I have never had an erotic relationship with a man, nor do I feel inclined to, though the thought is not repulsive, and my love for Alex encompasses intimate, physical affection. Can a reader believe that whether or not we have closer erotic experiences is simply not a matter of concern for either of us?

When I next enter the living room Claude and Stephanie have come in to use the basin in the bathroom adjoining the living room. The door is open as they wash and brush their teeth. Alex is now sitting on the couch with a lolling erection, and the discussion among the four of them is about why his large penis curves to the left. He jokingly attributes it to masturbation. Claude thinks it is gravity. Claude and Stephanie are monogamous; so far as I know, no one in the commune has had any sexual contact with either beyond a hug and peck, and so far as I know, no one would have the least inclination to intrude on the exclusiveness of their relationship, though they are attractive (in their early twenties) and warmly loved.

Is this morning typical—for us, or for many communes? It is, at least, not surprising. A reader not familiar with such life might get the impression of obsession with or flaunting of sexuality, but from inside the opposite seems to be the case. During this period, the normal morning activities of the farm were taking place. Did the plants in the greenhouse freeze? Who wants what for breakfast? We need another load of hardwood for the fire. The dynamics of communal life force an immersion in and transcendence of sexual preoccupation. There is no way we could live together comfortably in such close quarters without overcoming embarrassment and squeamishness—and, most importantly, lustfulness and possessiveness in regard to sex.

Sally's experience illustrates patterns that are increasingly common among the young. She ran away from home at fifteen. By the time she was sixteen she was living in an urban commune with her divorced mother's knowledge and consent. "I didn't want to live alone," she said. "I wanted to be with people who loved me." The love she sought was not primarily erotic, but familial, though erotic relationships were very important in the commune's life.

That commune had begun (before Sally joined) as the aftermath of an encounter group. The participants decided that they wanted to live in deliberate openness together, and rented a three-story house. During the nine months

Sally lived there, the commune had usually about nine members ranging in age from Sally at sixteen to a man of thirty. Several were involved in GI counseling and the peace movement, and AWOL servicemen were sometimes given space on the third floor of the house. "They were sometimes pretty freaked out by the commune," Sally said. "By the sex, the nudity, the openness. One guy wouldn't come downstairs except sometimes for meals."

They had come together as singles, and pair-bonds began forming within the commune or between members and outsiders. Often these outside attachments became members in time. Then within the commune new pair-bonds formed, simultaneous with the original ones. Sally might be sleeping regularly with Henry. Then occasionally with George—with Henry's knowledge. (Secrecy about such matters is nearly impossible in communes.) Occasionally, after awhile, she might sleep with both. If any sexual activity took place in such threesomes, it was between one of the men and the woman, the other man more-or-less pretending to ignore what was going on. One man had a gay friend he sometimes slept with, and sometimes was with that man and a woman, but on these occasions there was no sexual activity between any of the three.

Each person had a private room, and there was an important tent—first in the dining room and afterward in the basement. It was in the tent that pair-bonding gave way to group sexual activity. Five of them were in there one evening, stoned, listening to music, when they began making love, first to one, then to another. Even then and in the group experiences which followed (fairly commonly), sexual relations were between individual men and women. Sally, who enjoys making love to women, too, was frustrated because the other women in the commune were "uptight" about contact in the presence of men. (Her experience with other women has always been outside the commune, alone with a woman who was bisexual or gay.)

At least in this commune, group sex was essentially heterosexual pairing, stimulated by the presence of and casual
contact with other bodies. "Would you ever have gotten
into it if you hadn't been stoned?" I asked. "For sure." She
regarded the breakdown of pair-bonding as an inevitable
and natural result of group living.

One woman in the group was distant and restrained.
Sally hadn't realized—for months—that she was "moving
in on like a monogamous thing" between this woman and
the man Sally first coupled with. The woman was even
then pregnant, and in Sally's opinion didn't get the kind of
support she needed from the men. The man involved between them was himself, in Sally's opinion, culpably detached. He left for Arizona when he learned the woman
was pregnant—running away, "for sure." When he returned, he was the one man in the commune who did not
become involved in group sex. Except for this man and
woman, Sally said that everyone related to someone, or
several, sexually, with deep emotional ties. "It was definitely
not a matter of kicks." The commune implied a way of life
in which personal caring and understanding were central,
including but not limited to sexual contact. And no one
was left out.

A critical example was David, who had been crippled by
polio as a child and was, at about twenty, "really skinny,
hunchbacked," with a deformed leg and shoulder. A test
of the success of a commune might be whether all members
are able to make a satisfactory (if not satisfying) sexual
adjustment. Before joining the commune David had had
no sex life (with other people) at all. He had never felt
free with his body. Sally said:

For a long time David was playing this game with himself, putting a lot of sexual pressure on the women, saying, "I'm horny;
why don't you make love to me?" He acted like he was
some kind of playboy. We had several group meetings with

David about himself, but nothing much changed until Martha made love with him. She really cared for him, and this overcame her reactions to his body. David just changed. He cooled down in his demands and stopped the games. When we could honestly include him, because we loved him, he became someone we liked to be with.

Loved, he became lovable. Many of the interpersonal problems communes have result from their inability to break the pattern in which a rejected person behaves in such a way as to perpetuate rejection. A rural communard said:

If a strange dog came down the road, we'd feed him. Yet night after night around here couples go off to their monogamous beds and leave some guy to jack off on the shitter or some woman making love to her fingers.

Orgasmic gratification is not the primary need, but is a recourse of loneliness, a mechanical, minimal substitute for what the excluded person really wants—intimacy, acceptance, and some degree of snuggling sensuality.

Some elements of communal living help to relieve and some exacerbate such problems. The new culture has decidedly broken the John Wayne–Marilyn Monroe syndrome in which human worth is judged in terms of stereotyped physical attractiveness. Blue-jeaned and unbarbered styles democratize personal appearance and minimize both machismo and femininity. The close day-to-day living in communes (as in marriage) dispels glamour and replaces it with appreciation of (and sometimes contempt for) a wide range of human qualities inalterable by style. But though it is breaking down, there is a bias toward youth in the new culture: the middle-aged and elderly both have more old-culture conditioning, or hang-ups, to overcome and are more likely to encounter prejudice from the young adults they find themselves among than younger people, many of whom have gone or are going through phases of rejection of parental and authority figures. Moreover the openness of communal life, in which nudity and erotic behavior are apparent all around one, can provide painfully fruitless stimulation for anyone who is not a full participant.

Weight is one of the most intractable obstacles to sexual acceptance in communes as elsewhere. A new member of our commune was chronically frustrated in his relations with women and ashamed of his overweight body. To be nude in public was a courageous and difficult step for him. The open-door policy in the bathroom sometimes caused embarrassment for him in masturbation (which he discussed rather freely). He was thirty, a graduate student who had poured his considerable intelligence and energy into scholarship, business, and organizational management through much of his mature life, avoiding those situations which might test and expose his weaknesses in physical application. For example, he had vast book knowledge of such things as forestry, organic gardening, goat breeding, and automobile mechanics, yet, in a context in which such activities were going on all around him continually, was rarely in the woods or the garden or the goat stalls or under the trucks. Predictably, he collected and consumed pornography to fill the great void of his sexual practice.

Living in the commune, he enjoyed seeing other people nude, but long tended to hide himself. *Playboy* no longer was enough for his fantasies with the sounds of lovemaking coming through the thin walls of his room. He would hang around nervously, making loud, distracting, and studiously casual conversation while others were engaged in massage, but it was a couple of months before he submitted himself to the experience. One of the women asked him to give *her* a massage. Alone with her in her room, both of them nude, he became intolerably excited and left miserably. Because of his fear and expectation of rejection, he could not bring himself to move toward intercourse; and because she surely felt his demanding needs, she would probably, indeed, have refused.

A woman commented, comparing this man to another overweight man in the group:

Ralph's problem was deeper than just needing a good (or even a bad) fuck. It was in part his sureness of his own undesirability. Mike is to me as *physically* unattractive as is Ralph, yet has something in his *head* that says he has overcome (if he ever had) his lack of satisfaction with his body. He's therefore *far* more sexually attractive than Ralph for that reason. I don't think any woman could give Ralph the confidence he needs just by fucking him or even by loving him alone. He has to overcome (somehow) his problem with himself first—something we can't cure for him easily if at all. We may have failed him, but not because we couldn't or wouldn't give him sex. He would probably have found some way to discount a sexual experience with any of us as giving him a present because we felt sorry for him. He would have thought it an act of pity and it might have been more harmful to him than not having the experience.

As when a wheel begins to yaw, each turn takes it further and further from equilibrium, such a life pattern more and more easily fulfills its own dire prophecies. Larding such a person (the phrase seems painfully apt) with reassurance only increases his insecurity, for whenever we embraced him and told him we loved him (which we increasingly did as we knew him and understood him better) he was unavoidably reminded of a huge *except* standing between brotherhood and total acceptance. Finally he left to work in the city, hoping to return—but only if and when he could bring a woman with him. A commune functioning effectively would find some human resources to accommodate such basic needs in one another—but it is clearly not so simple a matter as providing sexual partners.

The new culture has been called *cool*, but as McLuhan uses the term, that does not mean indifferent, reserved, self-contained, but involved and involving. A lecher is hot, wanting gratification specifically *without* involvement and relationship. The most common forms of swinging in the straight world are hot in these terms, because they are specifically devices for taking the pressure off marriages by introducing relatively anonymous and temporary sexual partners. Communal sensuality is of the opposite nature: it cools by saturation.

A somewhat extreme example is that of a commune in California which was also a growth center. It was remarkable for what a member called its "raw sexuality": continual nudity, group bathing, massage, public lovemaking, Tai-Chi (a form of meditative exercise which, when done nude, blatantly exposes genitalia—along with everything else). One foursome on a whim went from room to room performing intercourse in each. The Zen master, an elderly Chinese, often prescribed for others "a good free fuck," and vigorously took that medicine himself often and with sundry.

There was a continual flow of visitors and transients, but, a member explained:

We vibed them out instantly if they were the wrong kind. You know, the ones who come panting, glittery-eyed, asking if they can get a massage. We had one of those every day or so—and three or four phone calls from such people daily. But the amazing thing is how quickly everyone could sense the bad vibes and deal with them. Even people who had been there a short time could get rid of the lechers in a few minutes.

One young man came as a temporary resident who was a classic example of an uptight, rigid, and extremely lustful product of our society. He described himself as one who habitually stripped in his imagination every woman who passed him on the street. His effeminate manner and dread of contact with males suggested a deep-seated inclination toward and fear of homosexuality.

One might predict that such conscious and perpetual

exposure to sex would increase the man's neuroses. On the contrary, he began to relax, to cool. When everyone is nude, mental stripping is impossible. He even became able to massage and embrace other men without panic. Sex became something he could take or leave. Probably only through total immersion was it possible to achieve the sexual balance and adjustment that enabled him to become more tranquil and likable in other aspects of his personality. Of course some who have successfully armored their neuroses —to the point that they can function, albeit unhappily, in the straight world—do freak out or break down under such shock treatment, and it is an open question whether they are better off with their sickness hidden or exposed.

In communal situations, familial continuity and support are usually available for members undergoing traumatic change. Group health takes precedence over individual health, so that some cases might call for expulsion of a disturbing member as the body rejects an alien element; but more likely there will be a recognition that the welfare of the group depends upon the welfare of individuals, and thus there is a strong motivation toward patience, understanding, and compassionate intervention.

Individuality and group fulfillment are encouraged in communes, but subgroups, most notably couples, are likely to encounter some resistance, though coupling remains the standard pattern of sexual relationship. There is a built-in antagonism between the family and the commune. Charles Lane, of Brook Farm, wrote:

We must either serve the universal (God), or the individual (Mammon). Both we cannot serve. Now marriage, as at present constituted is most decidedly an individual, and not a universal act. It is an individual act, too, of a depreciated and selfish kind.*

* Quoted in John Humphrey Noyes, *Strange Cults and Utopias of 19th Century America* [History of American Socialisms], Dover, 1966, p. 520.

That antagonism is reinforced today by a general stance in the new culture against one person's possession of another. Women's liberation has stressed the actualization of the individual as more important than perpetuation of heterosexual relationships. And the practical dynamics of communal life often make coupling at least an inconvenience for the group and for the couple itself. Nonetheless, in spite of a good deal of rhetorical opposition to the nuclear family and monogamy, most communes are monogamous to a degree that single people, even those without such severe problems as the overweight man I have discussed, are likely to find them frustrating places to live.

A pathetic letter in *Commune-ication*, a newspaper for communes in Boston, tells the story of a young man who never found "her" all the way through high school, college, and subsequent travels:

Lately, I've come to believe that I'm just *not* going to be comfortable as part of a monogamous couple. . . . So the question raises its ugly head, "Is there an alternative to monogamy?"

He thought communes might be just that:

This was ideal: a synthesized family of people who were interested in redefining sex roles and who were obviously comfortable with their own sexuality and sufficiently secure in themselves as to be ready to transcend "pair-bonded" relationships.

So I set out to find me a commune.

In the intervening year and a half, I must have stayed with, spoken with, eaten with, and slept in over forty communes. With the exception of only one that stands out in my mind, they were all essentially clumps of people who were either couples or "singles" (who I would define as people who are not *yet*, for whatever reason, couples). In most communes, it is considered O.K. to have "casual" relationships with people outside of the commune family, but in almost none of them is it considered O.K. to do the same thing *inside* the commune family.*

Our evidence does not indicate a widespread prohibition (stated or unstated) of relationships within the commune, but these do threaten to upset the delicate equilibrium of a group. The degree of freedom of internal relationships described by Sally in that urban commune is probably achieved only when the members are fairly close in age—and the median is young, and when none of the couples look forward to a life together.

Rampant sexual sharing is a can of worms most communes seem unwilling to open. And when they do try it, often their fears are justified. At one rural commune, after about a year of uneasy stability, individuals in the four couples, one after another, began what they significantly called "affairs" with other members. These were teachers and professional people in their early thirties who had gotten a good start on conventional, nuclear family life (there were nine children, all under six, in the group) before attempting communalism. Within a few months the commune had disbanded in great bitterness, one man (who had the largest investment) calling the police and having other members forcibly removed from the premises (a more extreme response than we have heard of in any other commune). I asked whether the sexual experimentation had caused the breakup; and a woman told me:

No, I don't think so. I know our own marriage certainly grew and benefitted from it. But it was as though sex was the *only* thing that could break down the silences between us—all the things we hadn't discussed and hoped would take care of themselves, such as different attitudes toward work, toward the business [they operated a large orchard], toward educa-

* *Commune-ication*, New Community Projects, 302 Berkeley St., Boston, vol. 1, no. 1 (April 17, 1972), pp. 1–2.

tion and child-rearing. I would say the sex made an inevitable breakup come earlier, because it opened up so much we had been avoiding and hiding.

From another rural commune, started as a school for problem children, came this letter indicating they had weathered a similar storm:

Ha, I bet you thought that we went the way of so many other hippie communes and dissolved back into the middle-class woodwork after a few months of sexanddope in the country.

We are, on the contrary, alive and well and changing. We've got a commercial rabbitry going and a medium-sized herd of beef cattle and a sawmill and we're still tryin' to look after a few family and school reject teenagers.

We got into some typical middle-class commune sexual experimentation with triangles, and rectangles and hexagons and parallelograms, which resulted in one gal splitting and her former mate living here with the other vertex. . . .

And so on. A very high percentage of the couples who go into communes either split up or leave, and often couples which form within communes leave—perhaps to escape recent sexual history, perhaps because there is tacit pressure in communes against exclusive relationships (and even communards are likely to want a little privacy and exclusivity in the early stages of romance).

One commune was started by five families that wanted private dwellings, each out of sight of the others. Within four years every one of the original five couples had broken up. In some cases the partners realigned with others in the group; in some cases one or both left. The members ascribe the present solidarity and maturity of the commune to two Thanksgiving orgies in which the tight bindings of coupledom were finally broken down; they got past evaluative, finite love and developed a much more nearly unconditional commitment to one another. Though new couple-

relationships formed, and most live in primarily monogamous pairs, they joy in their tendency to mix things up a
bit. In fact, there is a commune on the commune where
two or three singles live most of the time and others go for
periods of days or weeks for a change of pattern.

Nonmonogamy is the evolutionary direction of communal living, though rarely the reality. Ironically, many
couple relationships are strengthened in communes. A psychologist writes me:

Dori and I had lived together before the commune started and
had broken up over various incompatibilities, though we still
felt affection. When the commune was forming, we got involved independently of each other and came together again
as a result. We lived together there for four months, going
through various quarrels and crises, with much help and support from other members in working them out. Our relationship ended when Dori decided to leave the commune. I think
it would have ended soon in any case—but we had a longer
and better time together than we would have had without the
commune and learned some useful things (about how we tor-
tured each other).

Compared with the divorce rate (not to speak of countless
instances of unmarried couples breaking up) in outer society, particularly among people under thirty, the record of
communes for maintaining relatively stable, monogamous
relationships may be very good. For one thing, a certain
amount of sexual freedom relieves pressure that would
otherwise drive a couple apart. When couples do split up
in communes the break is not likely to be surrounded by
the bitterness and hostility often characterizing such breaks
in society. Nor is it likely to be so final. Often separated
couples remain amicably in the commune, with new partners or alone, so that they can go on seeing one another,
are not separated from their children, and can easily re-
unite as a couple if they are so moved. The most signifi-

cant breakthrough in regard to variations on monogamy seems to be for divorced women or women with children but no mates. The alternatives for such women in outer society (get a job, find a man, farm out the kids, etc.) are so unappealing to many that an ambiguous status as a "single" in a commune is rewarding: adult company, some sexual relationships, and help with childcare are more available in these settings than elsewhere.

But it would be a mistake to apply conventional values in assessing these phenomena. In the old culture, exclusive relationships (in rhetoric if not in practice) are the goal to which we are taught to aspire. If a couple breaks up it is assumed that something has gone "wrong," and there is likely to be a good deal of mutual accusation and suffering of guilt. Communes do not idealize exclusiveness, and, when necessary, recognize the need of cracking some eggs to make an omelet. Separations can be liberating—if there is relief from loneliness and children can be absorbed in the evolving life pattern with minimal insecurity and rancor. A number of communes (usually with disastrous results) have insisted on complete sexual sharing. Threesomes, foursomes, and larger groupings are tried—even to theoretical group marriages involving very large communes (e.g., over seventy adults living in a four-room house, the children in a trailer outside). But the utopian tendency to project an ideal into an absolute is generally not characteristic of the new culture. To require by social pressure that one have a dozen mates would be a dozen times more oppressive, and no more in key with new consciousness, than to require that one sleep always with one.*

---

* At times communal pressures do seem intrusive to those used to privatism. Charles Nordhoff, visiting Oneida in the 1870s, was perturbed to witness a "mutual criticism" session in which a pair of young lovers were being discouraged from keeping such constant company with one another. A couple in a Michigan commune was planning to have a baby, but some members objected. One of the women told me: "They say it is their own business, but I say bullshit. We are

Coupling patterns in general, however, have much less to do with communal sex life than one might expect because of a prevailing yin-like de-emphasis upon genital, orgasmic experiences. An attractive young woman hitchhiked around the country to dozens of rural communes, and I admired her pluck—traveling alone into situations which might be sexually threatening. She said, "One reason I like to visit communes is that the men don't flirt." The very word *flirt* sounded quaintly out of place as I thought of my own experience in communes. I asked whether she didn't encounter men who wanted to go to bed with her. "Sure, sometimes," she said, "but they usually don't bring it up unless they are pretty sure I want it, too." This was not often; she had difficulty achieving orgasm in intercourse and tended to shy away from sleeping with men for that reason. The few exceptions to her generalization occurred under unusual circumstances, as when, arriving late at a commune, she was directed to what the members thought was an empty bed. She found it occupied by a sleeping man, who woke up when she entered. She asked whether there was room for her, and he moved over for her to lay out her sleeping bag. She had dropped off, when she was awakened by the lunge of his body on top of hers. But when she explained that she wasn't in the mood, he

---

very choosy about taking in new members, even about pets. A new baby rips off a lot more attention and support than a new adult member or a dog or cat." Romance drains energy, as when couples want to spend long hours together away from the group—and from work. And the bad vibes from quarreling lovers bring everyone down. I walked in on an encounter at a commune in New England in which a man was saying, "I'm not fucking Sarah. And since I've been at this place, I haven't fucked anybody else." He wanted the group to help him resolve the differences between Sarah and himself, but in this case the group was reluctant to be involved—perhaps because the discussion itself was such a drain on time and energy, or perhaps (though no one said this) because of a feeling that his problem had less to do with working out a relationship with Sarah than with overcoming his exclusive concentration on her. Monogamy may be tolerable, but not if it is laid on the group as a problem.

rolled back and went to sleep and didn't bother her further. Such an incident hardly falls under the classification of flirting.

It is amazing, if not unbelievable, to many in the straight world that in the new culture strangers often sleep together without any more overt sexual activities than snuggling. A man with whom I was discussing this protested that it wasn't natural. "To sleep with a woman without having intercourse is as bad, if not worse, than having intercourse," he said—a classic instance of damned-if-you-do-damned-if-you-don't. I asked whether he considered it normal or abnormal for mature people to sleep alone. One of the problems that communes deal with are the obsessions of visitors with scoring. Communal resistance to such urgency is not a tribal or familial protectiveness: on most communes there are unattached men and women, and it is in everyone's interest that sexual partners happen by. But the need to make out is itself a kind of rape that undermines rather than enhances gratification. A visitor who is cool in the new-culture sense can be absorbed into the sexual life of the commune without tension.

For example, at one of our group meetings I was openly nuzzling a woman of our group who was sitting at my feet. A visitor who had not even conversed with her beyond introduction (he had arrived that day) leaned over and asked her quietly (but by no means secretly), "Would there be any space in your room for me to sleep tonight?" She thought about it—then said, "Sure." I was amused and pleased, and I am confident that there was no thought on his part or mine that he was moving in competitively. As it happens, they did not have intercourse, that night or the next two he stayed there. The visitor mentioned to my wife that "nothing happened," but he enjoyed getting to know her, cuddling, sharing a bed. (How persistent are the prejudices buried in our language: even for him, that was "nothing.") Their brief relationship was agreeable, sensual, involved. In such situations intercourse can be eminently desirable, but not required, not urgent. Only when it is clear that no points are scored either way can genuine relationship be developed. Minimally, human company and contact are often preferable to loneliness: it would be absurd for a man to sleep on a couch in the common room when he prefers company and a woman has space and wants to share her bed. Before she said "Sure," the woman had to judge whether the visitor would hassle her, whether his expectations were going to confound spontaneity. The wording of his request was all the reassurance she had— or needed—to be comfortable. Whether they were turned on by one another was not at that point relevant: they'd find out later. In any case, without cultural blinders, there is an ease in nestling the yin with the yang.

What has happened in recent years concerning nude (or "total") massage illustrates the problem. At one time massage took place primarily in such places as locker rooms, reducing salons, and chiropractors' offices. It was a rubdown, with alcohol, for specific therapeutic purposes, characteristically muscular, hard, accompanied by slapping and pounding and digging into flesh like kneading dough. The first new-age massage I experienced was from a woman who had just returned from Esalen in 1969. First we bathed together, washing each part delicately. Then I lay on a table in darkness while she, still nude, went over my body with touches like butterfly wings, spending about forty-five minutes on a side. Seasoned as I was in the old culture, I took all this as preface to going to bed and was astonished to realize, as I lay there relaxed, that she was quietly dressing and leaving the room. I bounded up to "finish" what I thought had begun, and she tolerated my amorousness for awhile, then insisted on leaving. Intercourse was simply not what she had in mind.

What, then, was the purpose—of the intimacy, the incense, the scented oil, the deliberate arousal? My mind was filled with clichés—that she was a tease, a hypocrite, that I was somehow entitled to orgasm, to closure. This was a confusion of immediate and larger purposes. As I have come since to learn, sensory awakening, tenderness, even conscious erotic stimulation can be in a sense ends in themselves, contained within the larger purpose of spiritual communion. That does not mean that intercourse never occurs in the context of such massage, which may flow into conversation, sleep, lovemaking, or other activities. But to view the massage itself as some kind of elaborate foreplay is to miss the point. A communard said, "If you massage a woman when you really want to fuck her, the vibes go right through your fingers." He was not implying that one should not want intercourse, but that the massage itself should be a meditative experience, like Tantric yoga, a suspension of desire. Nor did he mean that one should be free of erotic response. Erection, for example, often occurs when a male is massaging or being massaged, by a male or female. But that sensation is divorced from the urge to ejaculation, even from focus on the other person. The "friends," as a popular book on massage refers to the participants, come together on a plane of heightened awareness which is both sensory and spiritual, their minds in that blank peace attained through meditation. More immediate objectives than such communion merely distract one from that more profound satisfaction, a kind of mystical exchange of energy in mutual melding.

At such moments constraint and freedom lose their meaning, for both words represent partial and pragmatic views. Freedom from what and for what? Constrained from what and why? In one sense excruciating discipline is required, but it is the discipline of the artist which is so intricately part of the satisfaction sought that it does not seem to require effort at all. Using massage as a means of getting to intercourse or orgasm, my lady friend might have told me when she introduced me to its mysteries, is like a concert violinist rushing through his performance so he can get home to dinner.

I have deliberately refrained, so far, from talking about love. Modern acceptance of the sexual revolution often takes the form of sentiments to the effect that it doesn't matter whether they are married or not, so long as they love each other. This seems to me a liberal evasion. One of the principles of sexual revolution is to establish the premise that sexuality is a primal force in nature and human nature. As Gary Snyder put it, it is that wilderness which we will no longer make the adversary. It doesn't matter whether they are married or not, or love each other, or even know each other. It doesn't matter whether they are of opposite sexes or of mating age or fit the accepted styles of physical attractiveness. Indeed, it doesn't matter whether another person is involved at all.

I remember looking out the window on a hot July morning. The earth was still soft from last evening's rain, and the naked farmers (including my wife and six-year-old son) were knee-deep in the straw mulch, weeding the beans and beets. I was reminded of spreading the bales. After the first itchy resistance of my citified body, I found the sharp crush of the straw against my nude flesh sensually arousing, as was the aroma of dusty straw and sweat, the moist film of dirt on face and thighs. It was a sensuality which evoked a tingling liveliness of the groin and skin all over, a distributed erotic energy reaching each pore. That night some of us, along with friends from a neighboring commune and from town, gathered in the living room for a poetry reading. I wanted to share, like a religious text, Robert Frost's "To Earthward," which compares the sensuality of youth to that of maturity. As a young man, Frost says, "Love at the lips was touch/ As sweet as I could bear; . . ."

I craved strong sweets, but those
Seemed strong when I was young;
The petal of the rose
It was that stung.

Now no joy but lacks salt
That is not dashed with pain
And weariness and fault;
I crave the stain

Of tears, the aftermark
Of almost too much love,

and he wishes he had the weight and strength to press his
whole length of body against the earth with the force he
could exert leaning hard on a single palm.

Pain and joy, yin and yang, become inseparable. The
shallowness from which sexuality needs to be retrieved is
that of seeing the wilderness only from marked paths and
enclosed vehicles. In the old culture it is shallow to seek
pleasure; but the point of the sexual revolution, however
imperfectly it is achieved in the new culture, is to find pleasure abundantly everywhere, and to have the wisdom to
dwell in its moment.

Nonetheless it is true that sensual and psychic gratification alone are insufficient foundation to build a culture on,
and when the old culture asks for "love," it makes a valid—
though often misinterpreted—demand for commitment to
something beyond the moment. Indeed, that commitment
is insufficient if it is to individuals. Even in conventional
understanding of marriage there is recognition that it is not
enough that two people love one another. They must also,
in a sense, love marriage. Their commitment to building a
relationship that is "bigger than both" must be strong
enough to tide them over the vicissitudes of personal
change, moods, sickness, hardship, aging, and decline of
physical beauty and strength and coping ability. In communal life, that commitment is to the group—not to a specific set of individuals, for these may change—but to the
ideal of communalism. Somehow it has to be important
enough to the members of a commune that the group go

on (whomever it may be made up of month to month, year to year), that they can endure periods in which they do not much like one another, much less turn one another on sexually.

Arthur Gladstone, a psychologist with much communal experience writes me:

Confusion about love and loving is so endemic in and characteristic of our culture that we are all bound to be affected, communards included. The "love" that most people speak of and long for is illusory—it represents a longing to be compensated for the wounds and disappointments which our way of life inflicts on people, which we vaguely realize are worse than they really have to be, especially the wounds to our pride and self-esteem, since we specialize in putting one another down—our child-rearing and education especially are full of put-downs and rejections. So we long for the opposite, which we imagine as some kind of total acceptance. At the same time, we ourselves, longing for acceptance, do not accept others—we criticize other people, situations, groups, withholding our full approval and acceptance from all, for all fall short in one way or another. The leap of "I-death" is the abandonment of this critical, uncommitted stance. But when this comes, or when somebody else accepts us, it doesn't take the form of unconditional love that we've been expecting—we don't live happily ever after—there is still plenty of struggle and criticism and anger—but it is within a context of belonging—we belong to each other, despite differences and disappointments and disagreements—we are committed to each other and to whatever working out is necessary. And then perhaps we can understand that love is a way of being, not something bestowed on especially attractive or deserving people, and that the crucial thing is to unlock and develop our own capacities for loving and for perceiving and responding to love.

The communal ideal is not one of eternal eroticism nor of a valueless ambience of acceptance (where anything goes). On the one hand there is continual striving for total acceptance, as illustrated by this statement from a Vermont communard:

WHAT THE COMMUNITY NEEDS

The community needs trust beyond reason. Trust with reason is good enough for neighbors, but not for lovers. One must refuse to believe the worst of his brothers in the face of conclusive damning evidence. Incidents or remarks which might be insulting or hurtful among ordinary citizens must be suffered and forgiven within the community.*

On the other hand, not only are communards already conditioned by (and made insecure by) life in outer society, but they live under conditions in which intimacy and practical needs make unjudgmental acceptance of one another very difficult indeed. Commitment to communalism implies a commitment to personal growth and change, not a sinking back into a bed of mutual indulgence. Love in this context means, indeed, that one trusts and forgives beyond reason—but it is acompanied by an expectation of effort, that one help others and himself enlarge potential and dedicate much of it to welfare of the common enterprise.

In trying to understand the relationship between communal form and its human content I think of an ocean wave. The individual particles of water are not carried along, but rotate, doing their own thing, remaining in approximately the same area of the sea. The wave rolls on, distinct, a conception of almost pure form, though not a rigid form, but one which is always changing to accommodate conditions of bottom and wind and tide as well as immediate constituency, infinitely various, quite individual, yet, withal, resembling generally the countless waves before and after. The particles affected by the passing wave have neither a random and promiscuous relationship to one

---

* Marty Jezer, *Win*, August 1970, p. 4.

another, nor are they linked inseparably, being swept up together in the purposive energy of the wave, which passes through them as uniting spirit. But, of course, human beings in communes are not passive particles, though to some degree they are sucked into historical and environmental currents beyond their control. Powerful as these may be, human beings individually and in chosen combinations consciously and voluntarily participate in their destiny. And they seek not only erotic gratification and individual recognition, but social forms that provide for the nurture of children, accommodation of the old and infirm, security and continuation of self and others. The life-force does not merely bump them round in helpless rotation, but thrills them and inspires their reverence. If it is true that waves are made up of them, it is also true that they make waves.

I had first seen Fellini's film *8½* in a theater in the Virgin Islands and had not liked it, had not understood it. But shortly after four other adults and a child had moved into our home in Columbia, Maryland, and we had launched ourselves into communal life, I happened to catch it again on the late show, intending to watch only a few minutes of it before going to sleep, and sat captured throughout—at first in deep embarrassment. The story concerns the professional paralysis of a film maker, who is clearly Fellini, and is set off against two flashbacks and a dream fantasy of what seemed to me at that hour and in that situation a kind of subterranean exploration of communalism.

In the first flashback we see the director as a child of about four in an orphanage, a convent, being bathed and swaddled and carried to a dormitory with other little boys and girls, kissed, and tucked away. The atmosphere is joyous, warm, polymorphously sexual, though there are no men. The nuns sing as they mop the floors, bathe the children, joke and giggle and wink. In the second flashback the boy is about twelve. He and some other boys from the orphanage, now a monastery, are caught by one of the monks as they are watching a fat, whorish woman doing a lewd dance on the beach. In the world of men, the architectural lines are severe, behavior disciplined and stiff, chastisement for the erotic incident strict and uncompromising. Toward the end of the film the director has a dream of himself, now a mature man, back in the convent, surrounded by the women in his life and fantasy. They bathe the man in a huge tub, wrap him in a huge towel, carry him off to bed as the nuns carried the little boy.

My embarrassment came from my recognition of the source of my own communal motivation. My memories of childhood are filled with images of a household of women —my grandmother, mother, aunts, cousins—in which I seemed to be the only male. (The men, when they rarely came on scene, meant trouble, full of drink, admonishment, business, and practical demands.) My women sang and read to me, taught me verses, played games, fed, bathed, and bedded me, swept me into domestic activities having to do with cleaning and cooking good things, feathering the nest, spilling their bounty of affection and delight on the world. Even I remember that it was not quite like that, really, but that is the fantasy, as distilled by the years.

I asked myself whether what I really wanted was, as in the director's mature dream, a bordello of women to serve me, in which I could be the male martinet, carried off in a giant towel still wearing my bowler. As erotic fantasies go, that indeed is an attractive one. But it does not touch the core of my response to the film. In that fantasy the yin and yang are too much at war, yang like a cocky boat conquering and supported by the sea of yin. It is not that the nuns were women, the monks men, that is important, but that they represent the sexual stereotypes of our culture. Sexuality is a whorish temptation to be repressed and dominated by austere virtue. In that context, men indulge in sexuality only in the way they engage in business, with rules and power and perverse demands. Left alone, women and children create an ambience of affection and tactile gratification. Sexuality permeates life rather than being confined to private, intense moments of passionate urgency. It is much broader and more inclusive than the drive to procreation: it is the emotional sustenance needed constantly as air or water or food, lest deprivation warp the spirit.

What Fellini seems to want, what I want, what I believe most of us want, is an ambience in which yin and yang are unselfconsciously combined; and the nearest we can approximate that in our imaginations is through idealized memory of preadolescent sexuality, an Edenic time when boys and girls and young and old cozily bedded together. The nuclear family of parents and young children (itself a recent and local anomaly in human culture) seems a conscious device to frustrate such dreams. The extended family, such as I knew as a child, provides such an ambience for children, but incest taboos and the tradition of repression of adult eroticism drive many from its smothering, sexless embrace. The intentional family, at least potentially, creates a similar ambience, but without the restrictions and repressions implied by blood relationships. It is only regrettable that those creating such new models are themselves products of conditioning that makes it difficult for them to break free into a richer and more sustaining sexual life.

Since the disease of parental attitudes toward sex is communicated so many years before its symptoms become evident, it is almost impossible to eradicate it in one or two generations. But as I watch my own children develop, with sexuality flowering within them and around them, in the house as well as in the woods and barnyard, the odds seem good that a healthy life-force can assert itself and that they will not suffer the obsessions and fears and self-hatred which hounded me and most of my generation as we tiptoed through the wilderness we had learned was our adversary.

7

I-Death

What is decisive is whether the spirit—the You-saying, responding spirit—remains alive and actual; whether what remains of it in communal human life continues to be subjected to the state and the economy or whether it becomes independently active; whether what abides of it in individual human life incorporates itself again in communal life.

MARTIN BUBER *

Most of us who sought communalism in the 1960s and 70s were in search of a more satisfying, fulfilling, and productive personal and interpersonal life than seemed possible in society at large and in the private bourgeois family. Whatever value communes may have as political or economic endeavors, their primary function is to strengthen and enrich spiritual and personal growth and the quality of human contact. But the experience of most who enter communes is that they find themselves in what seems—especially at first—a snake pit of interpersonal tensions and insecurities immensely more terrifying and punishing than anything they experienced in their lives in outer society, at the same time that they find in communes much more pro-

* *I and Thou*, tr. Walter Kaufman, Scribners, 1970.

found and supportive relationships, something much more nearly approaching an ambience of love, than is possible in other settings. To live with others transparently, with no holds barred, is both a dream and a nightmare for most of us. That paradox is the painful interface of ideal and reality, as groups more and more closely approximate the communal model of human association.

The paradox can best be understood if one keeps in mind a whole range of paradoxes in human behavior typified by Leslie H. Farber's discussion of two realms of the will in *The Ways of the Will*. To achieve some of those things we most deeply want (which we seek in will of the first realm), we must surrender control of other activities which are subsumed under will of the second realm:

Obviously, life contains a vast variety of getting, achieving, winning, possessing, doing, and owning that is responsive to this will. Some of these objectives, when reached, may turn out to have little utility, while direction of the will of the first realm may have great utility, though utility is neither its motive nor its purpose.

As Farber points out, we are continually trapped in confusions of the two realms in what he calls our "century of disordered will."

The problem of will lies in our recurring temptation to apply the will of the second realm to those portions of life that not only will not comply, but that will become distorted under such coercion. Let me give a few examples: I can will knowledge, but not wisdom; going to bed, but not sleeping; eating, but not hunger; meekness, but not humility; scrupulosity, but not virtue; self-assertion or bravado, but not courage; lust, but not love; commiseration, but not sympathy; congratulations, but not admiration; religiosity, but not faith; reading, but not understanding.

In the terms of this book, one can will utopia, but not Eden. The most graphic example Farber uses of the frustrating intrusion of will of the second realm into an area in which will of the first realm can alone have dominion is that of orgasm, especially simultaneous orgasm, discussed in a chapter amusingly titled, "I'm Sorry, Dear":

Although normally truthful people, our lovers are continually tempted by deception and simulation: he may try to conceal his moment, she to simulate hers—as they stalk their equalitarian ideal. . . . And, always lying between them will be the premise borrowed from romanticism: if they *really* loved each other, it would work.

The very mental set they take to bed with them makes naturally occurring mutual satisfaction impossible.

To leap from orgasm to politics, we can see that achievement of larger aims can be frustrated by concentration on more limited ones—in what Murray Bookchin, in *Post-Scarcity Anarchism*, calls the realm of Need:

But the revolution can no longer be imprisoned in the realm of Need. It can no longer be satisfied merely with the prose of political economy. The task of the Marxian critique has been completed and must be transcended.

Bookchin, of course, does not mean that the problems of poverty, racism, injustice, and war have been solved, but that we cannot deal with those problems without some vision based on a transcendent range of values. The just society is a goal in the realm of Need, and it is related to the goals of communalism as the Old Testament to the New, as Newtonian to Einsteinian physics. Transcendence does not mean invalidation of needs in the practical realm. Love does not require renunciation of orgasm. But the more finite concerns are encompassed in the infinite range. To achieve what will of the second realm, or action in the realm of Need, so busily seeks, one must pass through a terrifying phase of relinquishment, must take a leap of faith. And that, by definition, is a leap one cannot decide consciously and rationally to take. Most of the interpersonal problems in communal living, involving the contradiction between the ideal and the actual, pertain to hesitation on the brink, the futile, desperate exercise of control where only surrender can succeed.

When our family moved to our communal farm, one of many loads was a twenty-foot U-Haul truck packed with tons of middle-class debris. That symbolizes very concretely the problem of ego most of us bring into communes. I do not mean egotism; quite the opposite. It is the deeply planted sense of unworthiness in most of us which makes us desperate to establish some—any—claim on community love. Had we greater ego strength we would find it easier to cast off ego, and the scrabbling for security, self-righteousness, judgmentalism, perfectionism, and self-indulgence it fosters in us.

For example, a particularly helpless woman persistently manipulated others to drive her into town, to help her build her A-frame, to score dope, to tend her children, even to amuse her at card games after dinner. If someone resisted, she was likely to say, "That's not very communal." She insisted that she would help other people if she could, but somehow she never developed the skill or initiative or insight to put into the community the amount of energy she drained. Even her gifts could be burdens—for example, an elaborate feast she prepared at great expense and inconvenience to the commune, creating a situation in which people felt pressed to express gratitude for something they would rather not have had at all. Her inept efforts to be helpful or even cheerful (involving neurotic telling of jokes, punning) were more an encumbrance than a benefit. She had so little faith she was valuable to the group that she either failed to see how she could make positive contributions or made them with self-defeating awkwardness. Moreover, she had continually to test the love of others. If she got their help she had a momentary assurance of acceptance (more needed, probably, than the practical assistance itself); but if they resisted, she fed herself the news that she was not really liked. This is, of course, a self-fulfilling prophecy. In such cases the other commune members (if they are to endure her at all) have to exercise a very finely discriminating "hard love," withholding that kind of attention and compliance which only feeds the neurosis and yet conveying the reassurance which can help her develop the ego strength to cure herself.

The task at times seems insuperable. In *The Joyful Community*, comparing the Bruderhof to contemporary communes, Benjamin Zablocki describes in detail the factors peculiar to family patterns in our society which breed "anti-communal character traits." For example, a strong emphasis on deferred rewards, especially sexual, creates

alienation from here-and-now reality, a skill at going out of contact with the world and retreating inward. This leads to the numbness to stimuli which . . . is an important survival technique in the post-industrial city.

Not only the city. A boy of nine from an isolated rural commune went to a village school for the first time. "What are you learning at school?" a man asked him, after he had been in classes a few weeks. "I'm learning to space out," the boy said. "I'm getting into myself a lot." He was learning not to listen, one of the required courses in the unacknowledged curriculum.

If one's rewards are in the future, he is subject to threats of their loss, hence inordinately subject to manipulation. He is also, as was the woman discussed above, manipulative. Zablocki says:

The isolated nuclear family is quite unstable and thus breeds emotional insecurity. It is plausible that this combination fosters

the need for continual reaffirmation of love which is so characteristic of our society . . . [and] this need for love continually reaffirmed naturally creates a need to manipulate others. . . .

Ironically, some of the same factors which make it difficult
for the post-industrial child to enter into communal relationships also create in him an unusually strong need for community. . . . This cool, detached, sensually and sexually dull,
manipulating, and manipulative individual earnestly desires
community and involvement.

Such momentous needs create a population ripe for fanatic
commitment to mass political and religious movements. The
communal alternative, responding to the same needs, is an
infinitely more difficult means of absorbing the mutilated
self, yet, *unlike* the mass movements, offers a real opportunity for—in fact demands—full development of personal
potential.

If a person has thought of his life as a career, has tenaciously maintained some status or label in the meritocracy, he or she feels desperately vulnerable without it.
The very concept of the "drop out" (I prefer the term
"peak out") implies that valuation by society: a person
who refuses to play the game disappears into a kind of
limbo (wherein also float many of our elderly and retired,
many of our young yet unbaptized into social identities,
many minority group members who never achieved specific
vocations, many females who have drifted from girlhood to
womanhood without acquiring a label more specific than
"student" or "housewife"). Having relinquished the only
security they have in a society which associates worth with
labeled functions, many find it almost impossible to live
merely as people, to accept love which is not attached to
merit or function.

A professor who has joined the commune cannot stop
professing. Insecure himself, he thinks he is contributing
his "best" to the group by sharing his learning. But the

group intuitively rejects that best because the members want contact with the nonprofessional self within. (His problem is compounded because so many communards have also rejected, or had serious problems with, father-figures, older people in general, academia, or any person who can be stereotyped as representing the establishment.) Despairing of being accepted for his strengths, he then hopes to be loved for his weaknesses. In a world in which slobs apparently are loved, he becomes the king of slobs—another weird twist on the meritocracy.

A woman with a few specific skills believes that she must "earn" her way by hard work in the kitchen or garden. But the more she labors, the more distance develops between her and the group; her very efforts to justify her existence seem to put others down, to support a hated Protestant ethic, and her labor becomes an obstacle to basic communication and affection.

In his first days in the group a young man gets pegged as a doper. In order to live up to his reputation, he talks dope, takes dope, gives dope to others. Dope symbolizes his insecurity; it is the token by which he is recognized, he believes, even when he senses that others actually *dislike* him for his preoccupation, and he clings to it with suicidal pride because it is the only identification he has. If someone tries to get him to cool it, saying, "Relax, just be yourself," he may become defensive: "That *is* myself. Love me, love my dope. If you reject that, you have rejected the only me there is."

And since the unemployed self—the professor without his professing, the hard worker without her work, the doper without his dope—is buried from the sight even of its owner, a paralysis sets in. Noncommunication. How can we get to know one another if each piece of behavior is seen as a disguise of, rather than a revelation of, true self? How can we ever prove to one another and ourselves that we are worthy of love? And how can we get *past* judgments of worthiness to the belief that as brothers and sisters we are automatically worthy?

Trapped in these mazes of paradox, communards behave with much the same desperation as children do who doubt their parents' love. Testing behavior is often described as a search for limits; it seems to me better understood as a search for love (for response). Of course you love me, the child unconsciously reasons, if I behave well. Who needs that? I can put on a superficial, conforming, sweet exterior whenever I want; but what I need is assurance that you love me *in spite of* what I do, that you love me *with* my faults. As he behaves more and more recklessly, he finally finds a limit and earns a rebuke, which confirms his central doubt that he is lovable for "himself." An alcoholic similarly tests and tests again the limits of love until he "proves" that he is accepted only on condition of merit or good behavior. Brilliant people or those of high achievement (such as often appear on communes, having peaked out of other life situations) are especially susceptible to this pattern. Like poor little rich girls, they can never be sure that they would be loved at all if they stopped achieving or showing off.

Frequently a commune reinforces such personal doubt. Most communes begin under conditions of financial and physical hardship; they do, indeed, find it hard to support persons who cannot pull their own weight in the collective effort. In rural communes especially there is a high priority on evoking energy and skills—in gardening, plumbing, electricity, building, and so on—which enable the commune to become relatively self-sufficient. But even when a group recognizes that it is slipping too heavily into modes of evaluative love, it may be paralyzed in its efforts to save a member from self-destruction. As in the case of a child who is testing love, tolerance or feigned indifference only makes the testing become more extravagant. The group may recognize that one of its members needs strokes of affection and reassurance, but people with such needs are often insatiable, partly because they rightly sense that the strokes are being rendered deliberately and condescendingly. The insecure person does not believe the attention he is getting is authentic; he gobbles through it as through cotton candy, sticky with sweetness, and finds his craving unsatisfied. There is really little a group can do for a person in this situation except to say, "If thine ego offend thee, cast it out," and stand ready to support him after that operation.

The need for composting the ego, or I-death, has been written about by a number of analysts of community. It is dramatized by the question of membership. Is one or is one not "in"? Typically, a visitor shows up in some rather vague state of search. He likes the place, the people, what he takes to be the ideals and objectives, and asks whether he can stay longer, then longer. How does one join? A few communes have specific, stated policies for this process, but most, like families, grow through an undefined movement toward love and mutual acceptance. For the newcomer, conditioned by preconceptions based on qualifying for organizations and institutions, this can be a Kafkaesque nightmare. What are the rules? What is expected of me? What positions need filling?

For the most part, there are no satisfactory answers to such questions. There is resistance both on the part of the commune and of the prospective member to using or being used, to relationships based on defined roles. A member of one of the older communes comments:

Every single time we admitted anyone because of a special skill, that person refused to use the skill once admitted. Say a guy was a mechanic: he would just refuse to go near the truck. Or a woman was a cook, but then wouldn't sign up for kitchen duties.

Once the melding has taken place, these skills may again be liberated. But there is a kind of paralysis until the sense of membership is secure.

As the visitor hangs on he perceives that there are degrees of being "in," and yet a very distinct difference between all gradations of indecision and a core membership (perhaps half-a-dozen to a dozen adults) which bears the major responsibilities of the place. Visitors and fringe members are hardly aware of the ongoing processes of cleaning house, shopping, laundry, turning compost, weeding the garden, ordering materials, repairing vehicles, answering mail, paying bills, keeping accounts, though they are happy to pitch in when asked. A family member simply knows what has to be done and does it (as an experienced parent picks up toys while passing through a room without expectation of credit or acknowledgment), maintaining some sense of perspective and priorities along with sensitivity to other members' strengths, weaknesses, and needs, an organ in an organism. Being part of the family is a condition which those on the periphery can hardly grasp.

Joining that inner core is a subtle but definitive step. It is not a matter of time or seniority. Some take it instantaneously. Others put their physical and economic all into the community (which they can do by will of the second realm), but not their psychic all. Gradually it dawns on the prospective member that the question of whether or not he is acceptable is entirely misplaced. Perhaps the most surprising discovery one can make about communal living is that joining is more an initiative of the newcomer than a decision of the group. The so-called intentional family does not, finally, choose its own membership. Of course there is a tacit process of judgment on both sides, and the group response can discourage a person from joining, but in such cases there is clearly no question of membership. More commonly, there is stasis while a person hesitates, like an inexperienced diver at the end of the three-meter board,

wanting to jump, yet fearful of doing so. He has to believe
that he will be accepted—not *because* he is a doctor or
gardener or even simply good company, in fact almost in
spite of such qualifications. He stands there quavering,
knowing absolutely that those people down there have no
reason whatever to accept him. Yet he must trust and jump.
In the pool, the rest wait impatiently for the miracle. There
is no question of there being enough water to share, and
that everyone's life will be easier once he is in.

Imagery of the leap pervades both written and oral discussion of the phenomenon. For example, a middle-aged
man joined a commune after a life of high adventure. He
had been a mercenary soldier in several wars, an international dealer in drugs and currency, a minor movie actor,
an owner of a notorious bar and restaurant, a gambler. In
the commune his prodigious strength and energy and buoyant sociability were fully engaged during building operations and the formative period. But as the excitement and
challenge paled, he began to be increasingly domineering
toward other members. They "called" him on that tendency, telling him to lay off. He took to the bottle, and for
a couple of months hounded the commune in a stuporous,
morose, self-pitying condition. Finally he decided that he
had to leave, at least for awhile, to pull himself together.
His friends felt that if he went off to the city, as he planned,
he would be lured back into the very life he hoped to leave
behind. A member said:

We told him not to go. He was halfway to safety. It was like
all he had to do was jump and believe we would catch him.
"Just give it up," I told him. "Let go." He had to believe we
loved him, but he couldn't do that.

The demand was frightening, for he knew it meant stripping himself of those manifestations of ego which gave him

security. He dominated others as might a rapist, getting what passed for love the only way he knew how, knowing all the while he was destroying the possibility of real love, like a drowning man convulsively breathing water, unable to wait a panicky moment until he can breathe air. Stop bullying. Jump. We'll catch you. Who, tottering on that cliff, can quite believe the promise? Don't believe. Jump. It is an act very much like suicide.

Ray Mungo in *Total Loss Farm* describes what he calls *ideath* as it occurred to one after another member of his commune during a Vermont winter:

It starts with crying and shaking all over and kneeling to god Ashley for comfort which it cannot give; it continues into distrust of words and incomprehension of their meanings and wondering if any person any place could understand; it goes on into helpless surrender before the demons of darkness and the waves which vibrate around our heads; it ends wtih a kiss. We die.

Each of us has built a store of ego which must be cracked and spilled, some particular way in which we must fall upon the rock. For Ray himself the armor to be broken was his security in writing:

The words have built up over the many years until they strangle us. Raymond chokes and gags on his own words: where is the fool who allowed such words to accumulate so, what of those who have been listening and suffering the unending flow of words from his foul mouth, why is there so little wisdom and so much pride in those words? See Raymond wildly stuffing his back pages, correspondence, manuscripts into the Ashley and warming chill bones over their fire. For a moment's quiet warmth, were they worth all the arrogance and temporal braying? Raymond, the anal-retentive filing-cabinet mentality, is at last forced to chop off his head in order to clear his throat.

That does not mean, of course, that the skill is abandoned. Judged by *Total Loss Farm*, in comparison with his earlier book, *Famous Long Ago*, ideath must have opened springs of lyricism and insight which ego had buried.

Discussing this phenomenon in regard to the Bruderhof, Zablocki uses the term "world-view resocialization."

Change of world-view is possible, although rare and difficult. It can occur in a religious conversion and in psychoanalysis. Both of these processes are undergone voluntarily. Classic thought reform, on the other hand, is an involuntary method of changing a person's world-view.

Zablocki compares in detail the conversion process in the Bruderhof community with that of brainwashing, as studied by Robert Lifton in *Thought Reform and the Psychology of Totalism*. The steps by which ego is systematically destroyed and a new ego, or new world-view, is implanted have an apparent structural similarity whether the process is voluntarily or involuntarily undergone. In the desperate final stages of conversion such as Mungo describes, the imagery is again that of the leap (cf., quantum jump). One of Zablocki's informants described it this way:

The metaphor or simile or whatever you want to call it that came to me was, can I jump over this cliff? I said to the Servant, that he was over here and I was over there. I had to jump over this cliff and there was this chasm to get to where the people in the Bruderhof were. And I couldn't jump. I absolutely couldn't. Or into the chasm. Anyway, I had to jump over a separation, over the chasm or whatever you want to say. And I couldn't. I couldn't let go. I said to myself, "What the hell am I holding on to? I'm holding on to this stupid, impoverished ego." I knew it, and I still couldn't do it. So there you are. To be able to let go, this is called faith—to believe in the impossible, to go ahead.

A woman describing the failure of a commune puts it this way:

We had plowed and begun to plant the earth, but we had not pierced our own ego skins. Decay, stagnation had already set in. I went into the woods to meditate. The woods explained: it was high time we plowed the earth of this community. We must apply the blade to ourselves and cut back the outer skin to expose the pulsating flesh. And then we must harrow and pulverize the outer skin and use our egos for compost. Then, in the new flesh, we must plant the seeds of the people we wish to become.

Similar imagery, as used by Ray Mungo, is given poignancy by the suicide of Marshall Bloom (whose name is used as a pun in the passage to follow). Bloom and Mungo founded Liberation News Service, then left political engagement in disillusionment and moved into communal life. Quite literally, Bloom's brilliant ego was sacrificed in the rebirth process:

The seed has built up unspent until it burns us out. The sap has been tapped into buckets—books, poetry, bread, carpentry, academe, pen-and-ink, post-offices, autos, hospitals, cows, roads, gardens—until it no longer reached the limbs of the tree. The tree was dead and fit for chopping and burning in the long night. But hold: see patience and healing and grafting and fucking try, slowly but surely, to make it Bloom again. See touching and reaching and hugging and kissing and five long bodies all evening on the floor in a quivering wondering mass. See Wrongness and Weirdness and Mustn't and Shame crumble in the face of the emergency at hand. Stamp out Couples! Admit it, propose it, then do it! . . . We die and rise the same.

That last sentence, from John Donne's "The Canonization," celebrates the mystery of transcendent love with a pun on *die*, which had a secondary meaning of orgasm in the seventeenth century. Death of ego is quite literally and figuratively comparable to that "shudder in the loins" (to quote another poet) which intention only frustrates and delays, which comes as a spasmodic leap from the secure cliff of individuality and reason.

This is not as extreme an experience as the ego death of mysticism; it is much more like achieving the commitment in marriage in which partners at some point stop wondering whether they belong together or should stay together. In another respect, however, the dynamics are the opposite of those of other alliances, such as political parties, religious sects, society at large, and marriage. The need for predictability in these arrangements encourages perpetuation of self-image and resists profound personal change. The leap into communal membership is not to a specific destination, not even to a specific group of people, but a leap into the truly unknown, with unknown behavioral consequences for the person involved. There is nothing one is supposed to become. A clinical example, given by David Cooper, illustrates the emergence of will of the whole person, of his gestalt, over his finite, conscious will, of the orgasm of meaning as opposed to that of mere genital release, and the difficulty of absorbing such personal change in a marital relationship:

A man in his late thirties, married with four childen, once told me this story. One night, not having taken alcohol or any other drug, he awakened at 3 A.M. He had been in a dreamless sleep until he suddenly awakened to a startling realization about what he thought to be the meaning of his whole life. At first it seemed very gentle, a gradual silting up of the blood in the small vessels at the extremities of his body. It started under his fingernails and toenails and in the lobes of his ears and the tip of his nose. Then it spread as an ominous clotting through all the major blood vessels of his body. At each moment he felt he might cancel out the experience by disappearing—flying off from his fingertips, dropping off from the tip of his nose. The capillaries in his brain filled with coagulating blood, and one by one his cortical neurons died; just enough were left for a consciousness of his heart. Then his coronary

arteries clotted up, until his heart stopped, died, and then
burst into a huge galactic ejaculation that spread throughout
the cosmos. In that moment of universal dissemination, he experienced a melting away of every bit of anger and resentment to anyone that he had ever experienced. It was all pure
love and beyond love, compassion, until he told his wife of
the experience later in the morning. He had been through a
death-and-rebirth experience, he knew at last the meaning of
compassion, there need no longer be any problems that really
mattered between them.

But how she hated him for that. And how right she was.
The social collective exists, after all, and as long as we need
it to exist as a collective, we will need families that define love
as subversive to security and normality.*

The term "galactic" was used with reference to orgasm by
a woman from a commune in a story that makes an interesting contrast to the above. She is describing her experience on an acid trip at a festival where a number of communes were gathered. This woman does not often have
orgasms in sexual intercourse, but in this case the occasion
—probably as much as the drug—opened her to spiritual
involvement:

I started to dance, and then the music took possession of me.
I became part of its will. My body moved wildly, with perfect
freedom, absolute abandon. . . . Suddenly I felt the acid vibrations from everyone, a hundred people dancing and tripping to irresistibly driving music, in the world under the
stars. I began to have orgasms all over my body, which felt
feather-light and totally one with the music. Then I suddenly
knew the meaning of life. Everyone else already knew it, and
now was my moment to be initiated. The universe was having
a giant orgasm and I was its medium. I totally lost my awareness of anything outside myself except for the music, which I
realized I was generating. I saw glorious colors and my body
shook with the tremendous orgasm I was spontaneously hav-

* *The Death of the Family*, Pantheon, 1970, pp. 40–41.

ing. I heard someone's voice say, "Are you all right?" I was on the ground. I gasped, "I'm fine! I'm having orgasms all over my body!" It seemed to me that people were talking to me, saying something about how you didn't see this very often. I was quite beyond speech—I was in paradise, I was God, universal salvation was being attained through me. I can remember only palely the inconceivable glory of the experience, and my memories are tainted by my picture of what I must have looked like; but it was the peak moment of my entire experience. Then someone was making love to me. Then I was being taken to a car by people I knew. . . . I felt an enormous love; everyone was included in the salvation that I embodied. . . .

In the house at breakfast, Fred said to me, "Congratulations! You were as freaked out last night as I've always wanted to be." Later, alone with Mandy, I asked her what I had done the night before. "Well, you were dancing wildly, and then you suddenly fell over," she said.

"How did my panties get down around my ankle?"

She hesitated. "Well . . . you went off into the woods with someone. We didn't mean to drag you away, but you didn't really seem aware of anything outside yourself. So we looked all over for you, and when we finally found you we brought you with us to the car. Your eyes were shooting sparks, and you were super-enthusiastic about the whole thing. You kept saying things like, 'Acid forever!'"

Cooper argues that the family (like the institutions of society—which all replicate family structure) is essentially a repressive force, particularly of sexuality. The contrast is quite sharp when we see that the woman's friends in the commune were intuitively delighted by and supportive of her in her experience, acknowledging their identification with her joy ("as freaked out . . . as I've always wanted to be"). It is hard to imagine any other response in a communal situation. The living structure is one in which predictability and mutual utility are somewhat less critical factors in human relations than they are in society generally. Thus a person has relatively less need of remaining in the tight control of will of the second realm. There is relatively more freedom to respond to the promptings of that larger will which directs one's whole being and discovers more profound purposes. To use Buber's terms, one escapes his fate for a while in order to achieve his destiny.

The problem is thus not that of the group to tolerate diversity or strong individuality, but (generally) the fear of the individual to relinquish the controls which hold him together in the outer society. A buried insecurity in one member is likely to hurt the group eventually. In purely practical terms, the incompletely fulfilled person is less valuable to the group. There will be bad vibes from someone whose life is pinched off or espaliered on the trellis of rigid role definition. The woman who thinks she is "perfectly happy in the kitchen" may—if she is mistaken about herself—become bitter, cynical, judgmental, morose, unless she takes the leap and allows the group to catch her. One of the most dangerous emotions for a commune to endure is envy or jealousy, which is most likely to erupt from persons who have defined their security in such a way that the behavior of others, as well as of themselves, is constrained. Communal pressure to change such self-definition is the organism's need to maintain its own smooth, effective operation.

In community, as opposed to society, it is unthinkable (as Menenius Agrippa points out in Shakespeare's *Coriolanus*) for the hand or leg or brain to rebel against the belly, or to demand quantitative equality, or to try to take over the function of another organ. Obviously, the pressure is not for all parts to be the same, to be interchangeable, but for each to be as fully itself as possible (and not bound by specialization—as it is possible to drag oneself on one's hands when legs are broken). Moreover, we are likely to confuse the injunction to be ourselves with aimless freedom, as though, having stepped outside society for a moment, we find ourselves at loose ends, on vacation. An arm must be free of constraint, of course, to do its job— and in one sense that is freedom. But it is also part of a larger necessity, for if it doesn't, once free, begin function- ing as an arm, the whole organism suffers, including the arm itself, which can only be healthy if the other organs are healthy, too. Far from providing empty freedom, a commune demands an overwhelming discipline. A new member may have a momentary sense that now he can re- lax, as he sees himself liberated from the many restraints which kept him from fully functioning before he joined. But that sense soon passes: he may next find himself over- whelmed and even anguished by the requirements and ex- pectations of the organism of which he is a part, as a leg newly out of a cast is not yet ready to bear the weight the body puts on it. You call this freedom? the leg might justly complain. You call this not being used? The difference, of course, the body must explain to the leg, is that once you develop the strength you need to function, we will all be healthier—and freer within our encompassing discipline.

And the right hand always knows what the left hand is doing. Part of the pain and eventually the primary comfort of communal living is the transparency of the medium, the clear air. A communard remarked of a fellow member:

Whatever weakness he has, he tries to lay it on the group by pretending to seek our help. Like he says he wants to stop smoking, and whenever he's around someone smoking, he asks for a drag or bums a cigaret. Pretty soon the message comes through that *he* can't stop smoking until *everyone* stops smok- ing. Pretty soon he's got everyone uptight about their own smoking, and he hasn't even seriously cut down. Or he starts accusing people of being judgmental. I mean like *judging* them, to the point we all get this feeling we have to live up to his expectations of not judging. Not judging *him*—that's what he wants. It's a joke. It's so transparent! Even Polly sees through it!

Polly is thirteen. Once the defenses are penetrated, and the offender knows they are useless, they will be abandoned. The therapeutic effect of group living grows out of the conditions themselves. Rhetoric, consciousness-raising, leadership, moralism, rules, no form of directiveness is as effective as the organic development of group interaction as the commune seeks its own health.

"A narc would never make it in a commune," a communard once remarked. This may not be literally true, but if a commune is functioning well, disguise is ineffective. After a point one gives up trying to have private conversations or secrets. A resolve not to talk behind people's backs is a good ethical directive for a commune, but in time it becomes unnecessary, because not only talk but even private thoughts become public. To attempt to hide a mood would be like attempting to hold a polite grin on one's face in sleep. On the other hand, indulgence in mood is equally impossible. After an angry exchange, a member goes out banging a door. The gesture was intended to get attention, to make others think about the angry person, to make them feel sorry or anxious, or to provoke a discussion about his behavior: in other words, manipulation. But another member simply yells after him, "Oh, get off it!" This is not insensitivity, but a refusal to play games. Real communication will begin more quickly when such stratagems are abandoned. A sulky man announces in the kitchen, "I'm going up to my room and close the door and send out such bad vibes no one will bother me." Laughter. The mood is punctured.

One commune calls itself ZBS, for zero bullshit. The new culture is apt at penetrating hypocrisy and games—as when someone is putting another on, or laying his trip on others. But transparency is not merely a matter of seeing through, of heightened cynicism. If one communard asks another, "How are you?" he is likely to be answered in considerable detail. A bore has been defined as someone who, when you ask how he is, tells you. In a society in which such questions are hypocritical, the answer is either superficial or tedious. In an atmosphere of caring, the substance of life is knowledge of one another's activities, thoughts, and emotional states.

And it needn't be all talk. A young woman in a commune said lovingly of her mate, "When he's in a room with me it's like no one is there." She could be herself. Transparency was relief. Ironically, the quality of a relationship is not so much to be judged by the conversation that takes place as by the quality of its silences. Coordination of organs within the organism is a frictionless, unconscious process. As one gets in touch with his own body, becomes at ease nude, familiar with its burps and kinks and depressions and elations, so the commune brings each in touch with the other. Nude. At home. One no longer doubts his membership. He is home. One quickly becomes addicted to such an ambience. No one wants to get dressed to go outside.

8

I-Thou, and Them

Martin Buber's *I and Thou* defines the sacred I-Thou relationship sought between person and person, person and God, person and the inanimate world, a kind of wordless fusion of consciousness in which the identity of each is absorbed in and revered by the other. Without some such spiritual dimension society is a machine. Buber also talks about the It, which inescapably surrounds us and must be agreeably accepted and incorporated in our lives. In terms of the new culture, there is a rewarding but sometimes dangerous sense of brother and sisterhood, of belonging, that could not exist without the coexistence of an out-group, a Them. Analysts of the new culture have noted its tendency to distinguish the saved and the damned, a characteristic associated with apocalyptic thought. There seems to be little rational mediation between the groups, no set of processes or steps by which one moves from one group to another. Eldridge Cleaver's statement that we are either part of the problem or part of the solution is a stark delineation of this point of view. As I have said in regard to membership in a commune, there is a conversion process involved with, at its apex, a moment of emotional surrender, of buckling, at which point there seems to be a kind of instantaneous resocialization to the viewpoint of the in-group. Similarly, for the new culture generally, dropping out becomes dropping in, a shift of loyalties and values reminiscent of the words of Jesus in the Book of Luke, "If any one comes to me and does not hate his own father and mother and wife and children and brothers and sisters, yes, and even his own life, he cannot be my disciple." Salvation implies commitment to a transcendent purpose which makes irrelevant merely private and materialistic concerns.

One of the functions of communes is to serve as induction centers to the new culture. The intimacy that is essential to communal life is subject to constant traffic with outsiders. If a commune is in some respects a family, it is inescapably to some degree an institution. Most communes have names (a practical necessity, if not for legal corporate identity, for providing some way of avoiding implications of ownership or personal domination—e.g., "Henry's farm"). Many willingly or against their will get listed in one of many commune directories or published accounts. Once a place has a name and has been publicly called a commune, it may expect a stream of uninvited guests. No private family is so besieged: strangers do not show up at the door hoping or even expecting to be accommodated for a few hours, overnight, or a few days; people do not show up hoping to join; families do not have to cope with reporters, sociologists, vacationists looking for inexpensive ways to see the country, crashers, runaways, fugitives, and public officials—e.g., police—who feel they are entitled or even obliged to drop in and look around.

Imagine the reaction of any private farm to this kind of incident:

But the real trip is with the other kind of visitors. A week ago, we were all out here working in the late afternoon, and up drives this baby-blue Cadillac with Texas plates and an "I belong to the Silent Majority" sticker on the bumper, out on a little side trip to see the crazy freak farmers. The husband and wife in the front seat, two little kids in the back. It must have taken them hours to find the place, and I'm surprised that they could get their Cad over the stream at the bottom of the property, but here they were pretending that they had just lost their way en route to Las Vegas or something. They approached very slowly, the man and his wife doing this insane evasive thing, looking and not looking at the same time. The kids had their noses pressed to the windows, which were completely closed, of course. Got to be careful, it might be catching. Then one of the kids snuck the V-sign to Tom out in the fields here, and Tom flashed back a smile and held up two fingers in return, and it just made the kids' day. But what do you think the parents did? Did they stop and talk with us? They did not. They turned around in the courtyard and headed back where they came from. It's just too much. And they think *we*'re on some strange trip.*

Again and again communes have learned that visitors can literally destroy them. Media coverage is like an attack of a dread disease. An Oregon commune was photographed by *Life* in 1968 and written up very favorably, but its name and location were not revealed. Nonetheless, the word was out, and the commune since then has had over two thousand visitors each year. In this case the commune has remained stable and strong, though their gentle and accepting ethos makes it difficult for them to enforce their visitor policy (one stated visiting day per week, no one permitted to stay more than one night unless invited). Others have collapsed under the burden. After several years in one of the most widely publicized communes, a member reports:

I wake up one morning naked in bed with my old lady and look around and see strange faces at every window in the

* Keith Melville, *Communes in the Counter Culture: Origins, Theories, Styles of Life*, Morrow, 1972, pp. 149–50.

dome, and I decide it's just too much. We've got to get out of here.

He and others abandoned that commune, which became and has remained a crash-pad with nothing but transient members, to start another with a strong emphasis upon isolation and exclusiveness.

Some communes have made a business of accepting paying guests, deriving a good deal of their cash income from this source. The guests at such places are likely to find themselves mingling only with other guests, as the permanent members, fed up with the transience, the perpetual explaining, the demand for surface pleasantness, have a way of making themselves scarce. (I am reminded of the titled families in Europe who open their estates and castles to tourists and may have tea or dinner with groups for special fees.) Guests are usually expected to bring gifts and, especially, to pitch in on any work project underway. Urban communes, which have relatively few projects except the dishes available for casual labor, find themselves bogged down in heavy rapping into the night, some members burrowing in their rooms more privately than bourgeois newlyweds.

The real drain is on the energy and attention which are needed to develop familial relationships within the commune. "Oh, we don't have any visitor problem," said one communard; "if we get someone we don't like, he leaves in a couple of hours." But bad vibing a person out has repercussions in internal life. The rude and aggressive manner of this commune is notorious—and many who have lived there report that it is nearly as intolerable for members as for visitors. One woman wrote of it:

The major problems of the commune were male chauvinism, insensitivity, and stagnation. New ideas met with incredible resistance. In order that people notice that you were upset about something it was necessary to do a total freak-out scene. New suggestions met with laughter and ridicule. It is impossible to live in such conditions. When I saw Lottie freak out precisely over the unwillingness of people to change I saw her old man hit her in the face so badly that she was blinded for two weeks. She and I were called the "dykes" because we were so uppity. Only she was braver and so paid a higher price.*

In one three-week summer period in our own commune (which was then only a few months old and had not appeared in any public listing), I counted over ninety visitors, most staying overnight or longer—an average of over four relative strangers per day (strange, at least, to most members, though many were close friends or family of individuals), to be ingested to some degree, to be dealt with. Sorting them roughly by categories, I came out with this approximation:

relatives of members	5
friends from precommunal life	21
members or former members of communes	34
freaks (new culture, but not communal)	10
officials (school board, health department, post-office, police)	5
prospective members	4
local friends and neighbors	8
commune researchers (and those visiting communes out of curiosity)	5
searchers (people in personal transition)	6

There were sixteen members during this period, ranging in age from five to forty-seven. While the buildings and grounds have plenty of space in summertime for people

* Vivian Estellachild, "2 Hip Communes: A Personal Experience," *Utopia, USA*, Alternatives Foundation, 1972, p. 190.

to bed down, we were then using the small (seven-room) farmhouse for primary social space and were cooking in a kitchen designed for a nuclear family. Needless to say, both our psychic and physical resources sometimes were strained.

But inconvenience is a misleading side of the ledger. It would be impossible to summarize the benefits ranging from good company and wisdom to useful skills, hard labor, and gifts we derived from the flow of guests. Especially in the vague area of "prospective members," there is a kind of life-blood of new relationships and deepening experiences. The ambiguous status of communes somewhere between being private homes and public institutions may be an important element of their vitality and viability. They are forced by circumstances to be in continual encounter with the world; there is no way they can maintain the seclusion of the private home or apartment. On the other hand, because they are, after all, primarily homes, they are not likely to petrify into impersonal institutionalization. Like sessile forms of life (such as oysters), they thrive on the flow, with an evolving ability to select and absorb nurture from what appears to be empty air or water.

A sharper division than that between communes and visitors is that between communes (or the brother and sisterhood of the new culture) and "straight" society. We may dream of some millennium in which society is transformed into communal life, but it has not come and does not seem imminent. Meanwhile, commune and society, like yin and yang, define, supplement, and complete one another. That is not to say their relationship is without conflict. What is surprising is that in recent years relations have improved so markedly. For one thing, society has become more accustomed to communes. They don't make such good copy anymore and so are being mercifully ignored, except when there are middle-aged, middle-class people involved in well-organized, productive communes, and newspapers report them sympathetically.* The commune movement is no longer a youth phenomenon. Also, especially since 1968, there has been a new tone of seriousness in the movement, with less emphasis upon flagrant display of opposition to the system and more upon quiet, constructive efforts to build a new culture.

* For example, an unintentionally amusing pair of articles appeared in *Wall Street Journal* in 1971: Lewis M. Andrews and Miles Schlossberg, "Contemporary Communes, Con and Pro," May 17; and Barry Newman, "What's This? Distasteful as It Is, Many Communes Turn To Business Techniques," Dec. 22. The articles are amusing because they incongruously project the values of the business world on the communes they report. For the most part, the *Journal* says, communes are "dreary, disharmonious places" inhabited by "confused, listless and quite helpless people." The "communal fiction is dangerous" because it attracts runaways. (Most communes will not accept runaways—finding it too risky to do so.) But the *Journal* finds some redeeming value in their performing a "psychiatric function," e.g., in rehabilitating "an ABC network executive." Some new communes are "distinctly materialistic" and find in communalism "economic efficiency." Moreover, there are many "work communes" which are professional groups (e.g., the Pacific Dome Institute, the Ant Farm, the Portola Institute—which published the fabulously successful *Whole Earth Catalog*)- providing a new blend of practicality and idealism, with a "high regard for technology." The business soundness of the huge, messianic commune Brotherhood of the Spirit (now Metelica's Aquarian Concept, Inc.) is praised; the group has a business manager with "UCLA degrees in finance and quantitative methods and . . . two years of experience as a systems analyst." All this distorts the main point. The Brotherhood, for instance, seems to me financially to be somewhere between chaos and racket, but it throbs with a vitality and joy that makes its material arrangements insignificant. Its economic value to society is not its productivity as a source of apple pickers or rock music, but its function in saving and giving meaning to the lives of nearly three hundred people, many of whom would have been alcoholics, suicides, drug addicts, criminals, or chronic welfare cases without it. I met a paraplegic in his thirties there, confined to a wheelchair. He was unable to feed himself, and could converse only by pointing out letters on an alphabet board with a device strapped to his forehead. He was surrounded by love and attention; and I shudder to think what institutional alternatives were open to him outside the Brotherhood. Insofar as such publicity as that in the *Journal* is favorable to communes, it is like praising churches for their Bingo games.

Culture implies an ethos, a set of values and beliefs, a style of behavior, of ritual, of aesthetics, an intellectual ferment productive of creative effort, a way of understanding and dealing with self and others, a sense of the spiritual and of human relationship to the universe, indeed, as the word implies, a cultivation of life, to which communalism is profoundly relevant. Inescapably, however, the new culture will require embodiment in a new *society* as well, and there are evident approaches to law, politics, science, economics, technology, medicine, institutional structure, and other social arrangements which can support and be supported by communal living. This is the It, the objective reality outside of the I-Thou relation. It is the inorganic world in which the organic must thrive. And I believe we are already at the point of evolution in which beneficial or, at worst, neutral relationships can be developed between communes and society.

The process of renewal is from the inside out, the transformation of self, then of close relationships, then of larger groups such as communes, and, like spreading rings of inclusion, of neighbors, regions, the nation, the world. But the process is not so simple as that model of gradualism implies, for each unit in the series defines itself through relation to the other units. I can hardly renew myself without you, you without me, we without the rest of us, and so on. The I-Thou requires a Them, or an It, as yin requires yang or darkness light. Growth requires opposition, as a stream requires banks in order not to be a swamp.

There is no question that communes derive a great deal of their inner strength from exclusiveness. Any experienced communard will advise those starting a new commune, "Be selective." Like lovers in their minute polarity, they spin in a universe of others, clinging together in their opposition so as not to lose one another in the surrounding entropy. The commune enlarges that dyad to include a wider range of reference and more complex dynamics, still with a mu-

tual attraction and dependency and a clear line of definition between the inner group and outer world. And so on,
ever drawing more and more of the scattered and external
world into the orbit of love.

As I understand it, this is the life-force, this process of
organ-izing, incorporating, embodying, vivifying. It is not
without its edge of destructiveness at the interface. The
animal sees a leafy plant which is very much an It. The
animal eats and contains and converts. In some sense the
animal loves the plant and, in digesting, mingles its life
with its own. The human animal goes so far as to store
seeds and prepare soil and weed out competition to perpetuate the life of the plant he loves, and will eat.

Understanding this paradox seems to me to be the key
to developing compatible relations between organic communes and inorganic society. To love is to celebrate innate
opposition, to recognize that without what the existential-
ists call *engagement*, one would be dead. As a couple becomes part of a commune it goes through something like
that same experience an individual does in learning to love
another, to see that the "others" are in fact essential (or at
least marvelously enriching) to life. In their rebellious, ini-
tial phases, communes are likely to see all outsiders as the
enemy, or as things (objectified people) to be used. The
step out of that finite state is to recognize in them (by steps
—first members of other communes, other freaks, then
neighbors, then the wider straighter world) a needed opposition, to recognize, as well, dependency in which other-
ness is an innate and valued characteristic.

The result need not be a vapid, homogenized universal
love in which one forgets and forgives all differences.
New-culture opposition to such tendencies of the old culture as competitiveness, acquisitiveness, hypocrisy, and aggression is deeply and rightly engrained. But to move from
a state of mind which sees only in black and white to one
of natural growth is to recognize the possibility of colors

yet unrealized, to discover not the gray of compromise but the rainbow of pluralism. The Movement, or counter-culture, began in a spirit of sick defiance, and affronted society responded with blind prejudice. On both sides it was we against them. A healthy revolutionary state will be one of lively engagement, free of destructiveness, but vigorous and charged with emotional heat. It is possible for people to oppose one another and to use one another, and yet retain for one another a vivid love.

From the point of view of the new culture there has to be a valuation of outer society not (or not merely) for its food stamps and electric power and hitchhiking opportunities, but for its profound questioning of the very premises of the new culture itself. Indeed, can free-form, organic, voluntary modes of human association adequately perform the functions of providing security, health, education, and nurture such as society relegates to institutions and enforces by laws? The new culture will have to look to society not for answers to such questions, but for doubts, inquiries, challenges, and for examples of other ways of life dramatized by everything from armies to small towns to suburbs and metropolitan Playboy Clubs, which may lure one away from communalism, for instance, or strengthen his commitment to it.

On the other hand, society has, similarly, to recognize the value of the new culture. A civilization, it has often been noted, needs both its rabbis and prophets. Without the conservative rabbinical element there will be chaos; but without a prophetic element there will be stagnation. Society has to recognize its own tendency to die within. At some point organ-ization becomes organization, incorporation leads to corporations, and organic matter solidifies into indigestible lumps within, as much "other" as the It without.

At this point in history the mechanical efficiencies of our civilization have to some extent undermined its overall efficiency in sustaining meaningful life. Alan Watts says, "The paradox of civilization is that the more one is anxious to survive, the less survival is worth the trouble." * The new culture is green growth in society's petrified inner parts. It is a revivifying force, but we can anticipate that the sodden sleeper will at first resist with sluggishness or fury all agitation to awake and love. The next phase— which I believe we have entered—is one in which there can be willing and alert interaction.

In one sense we have an innate desire to be perceived as individuals—a desire strongly emphasized in Western civilization. Simultaneously, however, we yearn to break out of the finite bounds of selfhood into anonymity.** A woman on an Oregon commune said:

It felt as if we were all vegetables cooking together in a pot, only each of us could jump out whenever we wanted to, and each of us could stick out our tongue and taste the developing broth. Like that. I kind of liked the flavor of us.

As in a good vegetable stew, there is some individual flavor of each ingredient, yet a broth which synergetically develops a flavor of its own, of all and of none.

That sustaining awareness of group oneness is a sense of communion, which Zablocki defines in *The Joyful Community*:

---

* *The Two Hands of God*, Collier, 1969, p. 9. Watts points out that the Hebrew words in the Eden myth for good and evil mean precisely the useful and useless. The Fall is associated with "obsessive and continuous preoccupation with survival."

** Anonymity is an almost terrifying word for Westerners. The most beautiful use of the word I have encountered is in an anecdote about the Indian poet Tagore. Walking along a country road one evening he heard an ox-cart driver singing a song using the words of one of Tagore's poems. "This is the greatest reward a poet can have," he said later, "to have achieved anonymity in my own lifetime."

Communion is based on emotional feelings; for example, a friendship is a communion relationship. Communion differs from society in that the members are committed to one another as a whole people. Utilitarian considerations, if present, are always secondary. Also, people are important to each other in a communion for what they are, rather than what they can do.

The difference between communion and community is less easy to see. In fact, since communion formation is often accompanied by the desire for community, the one is often mistaken for the other. For instance, many hippie communes are thought of by their members as communities although they are actually communions.

In what Zablocki calls "true community," such as the Bruderhof, communion is a recurrent experience of intense joy. This is not to be confused with happiness, a distinction explained by David Cooper in *The Death of the Family*:

The most liberating thing is always the most joyful, but we must understand joy here as clearly distinct from happiness (which always devolves onto security in some form, that is to say, a deceptively comfortable restriction of one's possibilities). Joy comprehends despair, running through an end point of pain into joy again. Whereas happiness is a unitary feeling tone issuing from security, joy is the full, simultaneous expression of a spectrum: joy at one end, despair in the middle, and then joy again at the other end.

Life in the Bruderhof, as described by Zablocki, is, indeed, colored by "lows" of crisis and "highs" of joy which seem almost deliberately engineered in the group's political life. Part of the preciousness of joy, as of the bloom of the rose, arises from our awareness of its insecurity and transience. Zablocki says:

This emotion is rarely light-headed or light-hearted, and often not even exuberant. As one member put it: ". . . the joy can be solemn. It's definitely not just happiness. You could feel it inside, the welling of the greatness of things."

There is a certain reductionism in Zablocki's term, "emotional feelings," which avoids the spiritual dimension of communion. What does it mean to be committed to "whole people," for them to be important "for what they are"? To some extent such language refers to individual uniqueness, to the iceberg of unemployed self floating beneath the social waters. More deeply still, however, these terms refer to a sense of union, of commonality. If friendship is "a communion relationship," it is based not merely upon acceptance of one another as whole individuals, but also on a sense of oneness.

When members of a commune (as is very common) hold hands together in silence before a meal, they lose selfhood in a group spirit which links them not only with one another as individuals, but with the cosmos. Meditation reaches for a thought-free state of mind, a kind of neutral plane of awareness beyond individuality. Chanting *Om* or a mantra in a group, each person blends his voice with others. (A good singer may be a distraction in a chant, as the individual voice cannot easily be lost in the group sound.) If community consists of people who know one another personally, phenomena such as Woodstock—an instance of mass communion—are the antithesis of community: the whole point is that the people did *not* know one another; the joy was in the discovery by strangers that they were *like* one another. In each of these cases there is willing suspension of self accompanied by heightened awareness of common spirit. Communion is a mystic experience.

Insofar as we are conditioned by strong social values of individuality and rationality, such experiences convey to us a set of connotations ranging from mindlessness to orgy. Drug experiences, especially group acid trips, have been important binding forces for many communes, particularly in formative stages, and, indeed, sexual orgy has often served the same purpose for groups. While most of us have deep fears of the reign of unreason, there is, as Pierre Teilhard de Chardin says in *Human Energy*, some cause to regard mass communion as a possible step in human evolution:

Communism, Fascism, Nazism, etc., . . . all the major currents into which the multiplicity of sporting, educational and social groups eventually coalesce, are often condemned as a return to primitive gregariousness. Mistakenly. Life has never known, and has hitherto been incapable of knowing, anything comparable to these mass movements which require for their production a homogenous layer of consciousness and an extreme rapidity of communication. . . . Today, for the first time in the history of the world, the possibility of *reflective masses* has made its appearance.

He argues that it may be precisely through some form of collectivization that we free ourselves from the oppressive, mechanistic forms of collective life (the city, the factory, the organization) which characterize modern society:

If in truth the social unification of the earth is the state towards which evolution is drawing us, this transformation cannot contradict the results most clearly achieved by this same evolution in the course of the ages—that is to say the increase of conscious and individual freedom. Like any other union the collectivization of the earth, rightly conducted, should "super-animate" us in a common soul.

Psychic communication and other extrasensory phenomena (not to speak of mystic experiences) are more common in communes than elsewhere in society.* In what

* Considerable work in this area has been done by Stanley Krippner and Don Fersh: "Spontaneous Paranormal Experience Among Members

sometimes seems the pressure-cooker atmosphere of communal life there may be conditions in which unpredictable developments in human potential for communication with one another and for creative participation in evolution are particularly fostered by frequent, and sometimes ritualistic, experiences of oneness. A woman with long experience in communes said:

A commune can't survive without some kind of spiritual center. Otherwise, people get freaked out by the psychic events. Like, all these weird things are happening, and unless you have a frame of reverence (I meant to say *reference*, but *reverence* will do), like somewhere to file them, you know, a way to understand, you wig out.

The gregarious appetite is in some ways a search for a deeper level of reality. Living with other people in a specific place under conditions of greater than normal intimacy, one is forced to heightened awareness of what Steve Diamond calls "Real Life" in *What the Trees Said*:

The difference between the commune and the family has always been obvious: The commune is a *place*, an "alternative institution," which must of necessity give way to a more important and absolutely intrinsic social structure based in *individual people* and their relationships to each other, The Family. Place must always be secondary in priority to the people, otherwise the magic stops. For many kids who came to the farm during its early days this was but a way station, a passing phase. It is no longer that way. For the members of the family, this is It, Real Life, there is where the stand is being made; which accounts for the demonic intensity of the players.

In the midst of societal maya, "Real Life" must be deliberately created. The biological family seems to under-

of Intentional Communities," *The Journal of Psychedelic Drugs*, vol. 3, no. 1 (Sept. 1970); and "Psychic Happenings in Hippie Communes," *Psychic*, vol. 3, no. 2 (Sept.–Oct. 1971), pp. 40–45.

mine the ambience of love, commitment, and sense of reality communards seek. Frequently they signalize their membership in the adopted family by taking on a new identity —a new garb or name (such as Rabbit or Flower or Ulysses S. Grant). Membership is conceived to be absolute, retained even when one travels or takes up residence elsewhere. But it is inconceivable that one be a member of a commune without having lived there—in a specific place, usually under the same roof. Communes are not clubs one may join by mail.

Solitude and privacy are always possible (indeed, are highly valued). But in noncommunal life one is alone unless he chooses to be with others: people get together by invitation or in clearly defined public places. In communal life this norm is reversed. People are together unless they choose (and take steps) to be alone. Life is to a large extent public—the "public" including not only other members but also the continual flow of visitors and transients. Gregariousness is not only accepted, but valued as an end in itself.

Communion is forced sometimes in deliberate ways (such as the decision that all adults will sleep together in an open loft) and sometimes accidentally, as when a natural disaster such as a flood brings a community together. An Oregon commune intended for its members to spend their first winter on the land in separate tipis; but it was one of the hardest winters in the history of the region, and they were forced to live (some thirty adults and ten children) in a large one-room cabin for over three months. Some were driven away by the forced intimacy, but those that remained became open and mutually accepting to a degree that other communes have striven for years to achieve. Critically, for example, they became unembarrassed about the sights and sounds of lovemaking. Most communes have open-door policies toward bathrooms and outhouses; in fact the "shitter" at many—often without walls or even roof—is a place of sociable gathering, often of great architectural originality. A commune in Boston has a bathroom adjoining the kitchen with a glass door, presumably to separate vision from odor.

Nudity is casual, indoors or out. When the dust of an automobile approaches many a rural commune there may be another cloud of dust in the fields as people scurry for clothing—not that the communards are embarrassed about being seen, but they have learned that nudity and dope are the two things which cause uneasy relations with local neighbors.* Nudity and lack of privacy are not to be confused with deliberate primitivism: primitive people are more concerned with what they regard as propriety, decency, and tradition. When one considers the lengths to which our society goes to insure privacy of toilet and bedroom and to avoid public nudity, he understands how central such exposure is in the conscious pursuit of gregariousness.

If there is, as Diamond says, a "demonic intensity" about that pursuit, it is nonetheless a search for serenity and peace. For home. Rooted in the communion experience is profound assurance that one belongs, not on sufferance, not on the basis of qualification, but unjudged, unconditionally, without condescension or even concession. The substratum of mutual human love and acceptance is separable from coddling, affection, praise, or even attention. It may even exist without approval, for one may disapprove strongly of another's behavior or his attitudes without bringing into question his basic right to be there, the only glue which holds communes together. For some at least,

---

* One quickly learns to distinguish in the distance cars of friends from those of the straight world (the latter being called "booger cars" in New England communes). Many communes have parking lots at some distance from the buildings. People who go to the trouble to park and walk in may usually be assumed either to be hip or accepting of what they find.

a core group, the commune has to become as home was described in Robert Frost's "Death of the Hired Man." In that poem Warren and Mary see opposite sides of the same phenomenon. Warren stresses obligation: "Home is the place where, when you have to go there,/ They have to take you in." Mary sees it as reward unearned, as grace: "Something you somehow haven't to deserve." Such a bond is inarguable as weather, be it drab and demanding or radiating sunny beneficence. We can hope it changes, but we can hardly hope it goes away. It is there. It is all we have.

Some have the vision of the earth as home to all humankind, a pervasive, abiding joy (which, as Cooper says, "comprehends despair"). For scraps of such vision we build our various domestic nests, hoping at least to create a nodule of warmth in the irredeemable void. It should be ours by birthright, as a friend of mine described his membership in the Yugoslavian village where he was born. He came to the United States as a refugee during World War II, but knew that if he went home he would be accepted, along with any family he might have acquired, even if he returned as an invalid or derelict. He could be sure of care. It should be ours as members of blood families, the least intentional of human groupings, in which mythically Mother's love is not a matter of evaluation, in which Mother-in-law may be detested, as in the comic strips, but is inescapably part of the family, and her visits may be postponed but not ultimately prevented. That classic line of nineteenth century melodrama (from *Rip Van Winkle*, the play that held the boards longer than any other in American history), in which Father says to Daughter, "Never darken my door again," is, like a negative form of incest, a primal horror, the depth of perversion and villainy. In some sense all of us need a psychological insurance policy, an unshakable confidence that there is somewhere we will be taken in by human beings who care about us and are somehow bound to us (i.e., who are not merely institutional functionaries), some place, some basic reference group, in which we need not measure up or meet terms. It is an experience that requires almost daily renewal—to come in the door and kick off one's shoes. To be home.

But we do not have such villages, nor even such blood families. In our society pressures for individual achievement cause parents to make children feel at very young ages that unless they mind their manners, do their homework, behave in public, some vague threat of expulsion hangs over them. The school system implants the notion that acceptance in the human community is (a tragic double-bind) simultaneously compulsory and a matter of qualification, a cattle prod behind and an endless succession of hurdles ahead. The worst punishment in school is expulsion from the place one is required to be. (Compare this with ancient ostracism.) Indeed, in schools, some are more equal than others.

And the dread that one will somehow fail to qualify extends even to the home. I have heard mothers speak proudly of children under ten in such a way as to imply credentials for family membership: "This is Beth, our dancer," when the talent of the child was less evident than the need of the parent to find a label. Compare that statement with this drivel from a commune's newsletter, stammering to describe members in terms of qualifications:

George is our clown, but he also keeps the truck running and the taps from dripping. Marj honchos the canning operation that is keeping us so busy these days. Bill and Jan have a special thing with the animals, and the animals with them. And Suzy. . . . What would we do without Suzy? She's just a wonderful human being and we love her dearly.

Poor Suzy. Perhaps she does give out good vibes, and communes are likely to value a person for simple radiance, warmth, and sweetness: such people linger like incense and

grace the house. No commune is without its component of
people who have little identifiable skill and little motivation or ability to acquire any. As for wit or charm or lov-
ableness or even agreeableness, however, the Suzies know
they have no corner on the market. Often they are there
for lack of anywhere else to be.

Not even in communes is the prevailing meritocracy
escaped. Pity poor George who must always be clowning
and mechanicking, or Marj always honchoing or Bill and
Jan always communing with the beasts, each trapped into
maintaining an uncertain status, or freaking out in anti-
social behavior that will blow their cover and force the
community to confirm the suspicion each carries of his own
unworthiness. Fortunately one may read between the lines
of such newsletters and know that they do not actually
describe the way people live with and relate to one another
in the commune. The language represents the residue of
attitudes from bourgeois life, in which each is responsible
for his own salvation, and since there is no God to answer
to, salvation equals one's image in society, the lonely crowd.
The economic extension of this attitude is that each must
earn a living, or must perform a recognized function. Such
newsletters come from minds conditioned by living in suburban rows like children at school desks, occasionally steal-
ing a peek to right and left, not to cheat, but to reassure
themselves that they are correct in what they are doing
(when shall the lawn be mowed, the shades drawn, the
piano played, what shall be worn indoors and out, what
food served, what furniture purchased, what magazines
displayed?). People with such conditioning relate less to
one another than to the right answers, which only the
teacher, or the system, knows.

And they come together as near-strangers to form a
commune, to escape all that, to build among themselves
the home society did not provide. (It is fascinating that
so many young people in this country today feel it is

necessary to *leave* home and community—especially when community means a plastic suburb—in order to find themselves.) They are an out-group hoping to create an in-group. Momentarily, as they discover one another, they experience that orgasmic opening of self into communion. As a student demonstrator once said, after a violent confrontation with police, "while we were in there together, we were beautiful!" Many communes grow out of such desperate experiences and resulting desire to live the vision, to retain the passion and joy of belonging in daily life. Always to be home.

As you may have suspected, it is not all that easy.

While I have been writing and revising this chapter, our own commune has been undergoing traumatic change. Of twenty members, seven (six adults—including two of the original members—and a baby) moved out together. The morning after their announcement and departure I was going through papers on my desk and came across a flyer from *Win* magazine, which said in part:

Last October when we packed up and moved out of New York City to come to live in Rifton we thought that we were going to make a new start. Well, we didn't quite realize what a *real* difference the move would make until quite a while later. For example, we never imagined that communal living would get to be so high pressure and so relationship-altering that half of our group would wind up leaving. And the intense hostility that was generated left us all uptight and paranoid beyond anything that we'd experienced before. We'd read about these things—we'd even published articles about them in *Win*—yet it all came as a shock. I guess that's what happens when you go from theory to practice.

Now, as I look back on that period, it seems to me that the wonder of it is that we survived at all through a situation which has wiped out many other good communes. In a very real way we came out of that experience reborn and with new determination to struggle to create what A. J. used to call the "beloved community."

It has been chastening to review the concepts in this chapter—which I had read and written about before, now under the fire of agonizing, present experience—an experience that nearly every commune has undergone once or several times.

All I can say, rather weakly now, is that it is all true. We had gathered as near-strangers, accretion taking place casually, as people happened to hear about us and drift down the drive and attach themselves—without taking the leap. Reading what I had written about I-death, psychologist Arthur Gladstone commented:

Crucially important!!! This is what makes the difference between a bunch of people living together and a commune. This is what most city "communes" lack. It was also the essential thing lacking at the Ark [a rural commune he had been a member of]—most of us never took the leap. I realized this about myself when an outside therapist came and worked with us for a weekend on problems we were having among ourselves. When I was able to admit to myself that I'd been keeping myself aloof and that I was unwilling to make the leap *with this group*, I knew it was time for me to leave.

In our case, it is impossible to say who was unable to leap to whom. Those that left planned to stay together as a commune (they didn't). Those that remain were as unable to leap to them as they to us. The polarization was mysterious, and I will not attempt to give a one-sided analysis here; but it prevented the emergence of transparency, which might have held us together, of communion, of glad gregariousness. Some in both groups (possibly all of us) were unable finally to surrender the security blankets of their egos. Some held pathetically to roles. Some kept their unemployed selves submerged. Some tried vainly to make will of the second realm achieve what only will of the first realm could command. We were unable to develop commitment—but that makes it sound as though the failure is moral, that it is a matter of choice. On each side (probably —though naturally I see this more clearly in the Others) there was insufficient belief in self, insufficient confidence that there was *enough* (water in the pool, space, love, tolerance, understanding, generosity) to accommodate them. They left and we stayed because of a mechanical and external consideration: my wife and I owned the land at that time. But they could have stayed on the land. There is plenty of land. The separation, so crosshatched with affection and bitterness and shared experience and silences and secrets and exposures, demanded distance. An uprooting. As the *Win* editors put it, a rebirth.

Zest on the farm soared after they left—the morning after and in the days to follow. There was freedom of breath, joy, communion—and astonishing industry as we threw ourselves, with our depleted numbers, into the tasks of readying for winter. Crisis engenders closeness and almost manic energy—which, indeed, may wane along with the crisis. An almost guilty sense of relief wells up after any instance of psychic surgery: a divorce, leaving home (or seeing others leave home), even the death of a loved one. That does not mean that redemption has been achieved, that we have learned. We probably have not learned at all.

Typically (so far as any evidence we have about communes will substantiate) the external form of our differences was expressed in envy (of life-style, of privilege), guilt, and blame (allegations, real or imagined, that someone was not doing his part, was goofing off, was self-indulgent—and the defensiveness such allegations invariably evoke). The issue of membership was the symbolic battleground. What must one do to qualify? How much is enough? Must I measure up to your expectations? One

way communes deal with such questions is to spell out
work loads, financial expectations, rules of conduct. At
least, they reason, one will know where one stands—and
escape the nightmare in which qualification is on ineffable
grounds, requirements unspecified, but fiercely enforced.
At least one commune—and one of the most successful—
has been able to maintain a high degree of stability, and
freedom from guilt and envy, by explicit structure: Twin
Oaks, in Virginia, which employs the behaviorist techniques of control and positive reinforcement such as suggested by B. F. Skinner's utopian novel, *Walden II*. But in
most communes efforts to rationalize structure and make it
explicit seem to be evasions of more profound personal
issues which eventually erupt through the organized overlay.

Ambiguity is a nightmare, of course, only if the people
involved are desperately dependent upon the relationship
continuing. Part of the experience of separation may be
relief from that burden. At one point in my quarter-
century of marriage I thought I was reassuring my wife
when I said, "If you were to leave me, I would die." It
took some difficult learning for me to see what a burden
this attitude was on her. Until I was able not only to say,
but to believe, "If you were to leave, I could get along,"
could she and I both feel liberated and grow as individuals.
That understanding, of course, proved to be a new basis for
stability. The threat removed, there was no need to test it
or suffer it in the night.

It may be exactly that liberation which communes en-
during mitosis require. We come together with such urgency, with such overwhelming sense of alienation from
the outer society, we are likely to feel that we have no
options anywhere except for one another. That mind-set
is crippling for individuals and a burden for others, each
in a group feeling both dependent (and resentful of those
upon whom he is dependent) and exploited, needing to

establish for himself that he has choices, that he has strength enough to get along without the others as a prerequisite for living with them. With such weakness at the foundations, a group may fall into sullen noncommunication, with patterns of politeness and liberal accommodation replacing authentic interaction. Each grows armor. No one is at home.

Considering the odds against achievement of satisfying interpersonal relationships, it is astonishing that again and again communards emerge from crises, as we did and as did the editors of *Win*, with renewed commitment. One hears often of people leaving communes to join others, of groups splitting off, of communes folding and dispersing, but very rarely of anyone going back into private life after living in a commune, almost never (I know of one case) of a person resuming a role in the straight world after being inducted into the new culture.

Certainly that is what we feel here now on the farm. In a process in which personal, loving absorption is (as in impregnation) the means of growing, in which the life within swells beyond the tolerance of skin, and there is a breaking forth of new life, there is also severance of tissue. But that, too, is the life-force.

9

Intelligence at the Tiller

Pitched on this sea
                    (expansive canvas straining/
the rigging taut/
                  laboring tonnage of hull/
the bulging current
                     breaking like bombs at the bow/
the empty air
               pouring its power upon us)
who are we?
              (riding this weight
                      in violent weather)
but a whisper of intelligence at the tiller
our quarter inch of leverage
                    telling whether
we head up
         into failure
             or fall off
leaning the fast and easy way to waste.

                         RUMORS (6) of Change

We came to feel that ANY school AS SUCH—at any level
and no matter how "free"—cannot be as natural, spontaneous,
organic and life-intergrative as we want our lives to be. Sev-

eral of us have gone on to join with still others in founding in intentional community, hopeful that it will prove a better alternative for us.

"Beyond Free Schools: Community!" *

The terms "intentional community" and "intentional family" are oxymorons: the adjective *intentional* contradicts the very nature of community and family, which are essentially spontaneous and traditional forms of human association. Dissatisfaction with stultifying traditional forms and, especially, the artifices and regulations imposed upon them by the larger society impels some of us to attempt to create intentionally what we envision to be, ironically, a more "natural" way of life.

This paradox pervades discussion of education and therapy in communes. In our present society one finds education and therapy treated as commodities supplied by schools and other institutions. As one goes to the store for bread, he goes to school for education, to specialists for treatment of disorders, to hospitals for healing. In communes there is a disposition to let children grow and the "sick" heal themselves, to let nature take its course as much as possible. Nonetheless there is a good deal of conscious intervention in the process, a whisper of intelligence at the tiller. On the one hand there is freedom and opportunity; on the other there is neglect and evasion of responsibility. Problems arise in determining the line between these, in discovering how to minimize coercion on the individual and yet to create facilitative structures that make community itself an educational force.

A woman speaking to a college audience about life on her country commune was asked whether the children

---

* The first passage is from an unpublished poem of my own. The second is from an article by Jerry Friedberg in *Mother Earth News*, no. 6 (November 1970), p. 82.

raised there might not rebel and want to live in the city. "We're either going to make the mistakes with our children that our parents made with us," she answered, "or we'll make other mistakes. But as long as we have children, we'll make mistakes."

This new-culture response is quite in contrast to the attitude of utopian communities, old and new, which classically develop theories of child-rearing and therapy and create formal structures for carrying them out. In these there is a felt need to separate children, to some degree, from parental influence and consciously to orient the young toward group loyalty and group goals. In such diverse contemporary groups as the Hutterites, the Bruderhof, the kibbutzim, Synanon, and Twin Oaks, children tend to be removed from the home or parents' quarters, at least for substantial portions of their lives, and to be indoctrinated according to group policy. Most modern communes, however, have no such theory or practice. Those that begin with ideological positions and educational structures are likely to evolve away from them, tending more and more to let things happen, and to accept the inevitability that there will be mistakes and changes; but they prefer to rely on the Flow than to impose controls which may prove to be more destructive than helpful in the long run.

But as youngsters in free schools have sometimes perceived, lack of control may amount to indifference, or lack of love. On the one hand is the danger of manipulation and limitation of a natural process, on the other that of callous *laissez-faire*. Daily in communes we confront both dangers —and try to find a way between them.

I had written that, then left the typewriter to stand by the fire, trying to think of a way of putting it more concretely, when Topher came in. Neither Polly (thirteen) nor Topher (six) were in school, and their older sisters had left school as soon as they reached the legal age to do so. Topher had come into the room to speak to Lisa, who has twenty-eight years of teaching experience in the schools.

"Let's have a lesson now," he said to her.

"All right."

"A long lesson. I'm getting so I like long lessons."

"All right. What kind of lesson do you want?"

"Arithmetic. The kind on the lined papers."

As it turned out, they were working on sets and the commutative property of addition. Earlier this morning Topher and I had a session playing games with Cuisenaire rods. Working with Lisa, Topher draws stars in subsets and translates them into numerals with plus, minus, and equal signs.

Before they could start work, Polly had to clear the schoolroom (a nook off the office) of her cards. She invented a process for making greeting cards with swirling colors by dipping them into airplane oil paints floating on water—using five-by-eight-inch cards, such as we use in research, folded in half; she dips the corners of envelopes also, to match, and wholesales these for two dollars per dozen to gift shops. The cards were drying on newspapers on top of the school desks; so she moved them to hang on strings stretched around the stovepipe which passes through the room. Then she went back to read.

I returned to work, but was interrupted by Herb, a man of twenty-one, doing research for this book—at that moment studying Carl Rogers' chapter on communes in *On Becoming Partners: Marriage and Its Alternatives*. He read aloud:

One aspect which is actually quite natural will seem surprising to many readers: young children accept quite readily the fact that their parents may at times be sleeping with different partners. Children accept their world as it is, especially if that world is acceptable to the others around them. On the other hand, an adolescent who has spent most of his or her life in the ordinary community and has absorbed its norms may be very much troubled or conflicted by the "bad" behavior of his parents.

Herb asked, "Is he being fair?" He had heard, as most of us have, stories about the deleterious effects on children of seeing adults make love. Sometimes they think the adults are fighting—and so on. Is Rogers overlooking evidence of that sort?

Several of us, including Polly, became involved in discussion of that question. In the first place, Rogers may not be referring to children witnessing sexual intercourse. We exchanged anecdotes about instances in which children have, in our own experience, known about their parents sleeping with various partners and shown no particular concern or surprise. Herb told of a little girl who was jealous of him when he was with her divorced mother, mostly because the bed space was otherwise available for the child herself. We went on to discuss the effects on children who see intercourse—of animals, parents, and others. Though we have all heard folklore of its evil effects, none of us knew first-hand of a case in which it had any such effects. In Richard Wright's *Native Son* the fact that children witness parental lovemaking in Chicago slums is, along with rat infestation, given as an example of the degradation in ghetto life. Such attitudes might be partly projection: if adults believe that sex is naughty, they will believe it is therefore bad for children to witness. These attitudes also stem from social oppression: lack of space is associated with intimacy, which makes the latter seem a negative condition of poverty. I asked Polly whether she had ever watched people make love. "No, but I hear it a lot!" She told us about the different rhythms of the three couples sleeping upstairs when she is sleeping below.

If all days were as educational for the children as the last hour has been, I would worry less about whether communal life provides them with an adequate alternative to formal schooling. But each time I see a school bus picking up children on our country roads I wince a little, wondering whether we are neglecting parental responsibility. If Topher and Polly were to go to public school they would trudge the half-mile up the drive each morning to catch such a bus, ride about forty-five minutes each way, putting in longer hours than a factory worker, spending their waking hours largely under regulation and supervision, being shaped to fit society's needs. That seems dysfunctional to me as preparation for life. But I am plagued by doubts. I wonder especially about their social relationships. They live almost entirely in the company of adults. At times both show evidence of a poignant listlessness and loneliness. But so do children who go to school, I argue with myself. Parents whose children are in school never see *their* boredom. To do one thing is to be deprived of another, inevitably, and how can we know which is the more serious deprivation?

Not all communes are so richly populated as ours with educators. There is not always a Lisa when Tophers feel the desire for lessons. On the other hand, most adults have plenty of knowledge to impart, and "teaching skill" in the school system is in large part skill in holding attention (and thus maintaining order), which is unnecessary in voluntary, one-to-one learning. Love is more important than expertise in such education—and probably more effective in purely pragmatic terms. An eight-year-old boy, educated until that age at home, was experiencing his first year of formal schooling when interviewed by a newspaper editor. The parents insist that he and his seven-year-old sister are in no way exceptional children, and that they were given only an hour-a-day of instruction at home. When they entered public school, both tested at seventh-grade reading and fourth-grade math levels. They were placed in the second grade.

Ed. And do you like school?

L. Yes and no. I like the school part, but the kids make fun of me—they laugh at me and they reject me—because I'm different.

Ed. How so?

L. For one thing, we bring our lunches. And Eva and I have whole wheat sandwiches—my mother makes it. And we never have desserts—and we don't eat sugar. Or candy either.

.   .   .

Ed. Since you read at the seventh-grade level, I suppose second-grade reading is easy for you. Perhaps you find second graders reading more slowly than you do. Do you find this tiresome?

L. No, I like the kids, and if they have a harder time with reading than I do, that's ok. I read what I like—I don't think what level it is.

.   .   .

Ed. Do you ever wish you weren't different from others in your school?

L. (quickly) I wish that there wasn't a difference, but I don't want to be like them. I wish they would be like me. I think it's important to be and do what you think is right. So since I think it's right to be the way I am, I don't want to change their ways. . . . I wish more and more people were convinced that what they are doing is necessary to have a good earth.*

This muddles my assumptions. The boy likes "the school part" but in social life he is pained and frustrated—and the

* Interview by Mildred Loomis, "An 8 yr. Old Raps About School," *The Green Revolution*, vol. 10, no. 9 (Sept. 1972), p. 5.

school part itself seems irrelevant to his scholastic development. I am less impressed by his reading and math performance than by his ethical development, his tolerance and yet his clear sense of values—qualities which, apparently, his fellow students have not developed. Do I want my own children educated by peers such as he found himself among in school? On the other hand, what right have I—aside from the question of legal obligation—to make such decisions for them?

To answer such questions one is forced to reconsider the very definition of childhood and, correlatively, of various other categories of dependents and deviants. The problem is addressed by Bennett Berger, a sociologist at the University of California, Davis, who is conducting for NIMH an extensive study of child-rearing in contemporary communes:

This rethinking involves a rejection of the idea of children as incompetent dependents with a special psychology needing special protections and nurturings. Like the big "kids" who are their parents, communal children seem to be just littler kids, less skilled, less experienced, and only perhaps less wise. . . .

In viewing the history of how children are conceptualized by adults, social scientists have thus far emphasized the differences between pre-industrial, agricultural, or sometimes lower-class views on the one side, and industrial or middle-class views on the other. In the former view the status of children is seen as essentially ascribed at birth and rooted in the kinship system. In this view, children are seen as simply small or inadequate versions of their parents, totally subject to traditional or otherwise arbitrary parental authority. The "modern" industrial, middle-class view, by contrast, tends to treat the child as a distinctive social category: children have their own special psychology, their own special needs, patterned processes of growth often elaborated into ideas about developmental stages which may postpone advent to "full" adulthood well into a person's twenties, and sometimes still later. The task of parents and other "socializers" in this view is to "raise" or "produce" the child (the industrial metaphor is often used) according to scientifically elaborated principles of proper child management—a process which in many middle-class families results in the differentiation of family roles in a way that transforms a woman-with-child into a full-time child raiser.

The view that we find prevalent in the hip-communal settings we have studied fits neither of these models with precision. "Young people" are regarded as independent of the family, but not as members of an autonomous category of "children"; instead, their status is likely to be ascribed as that of "person," a development which can be understood as part of an equalitarian ethos, and as complementary to parallel development in the status of females, from "women" (or even "mothers") to "people," and in the status of men, from being characterized in invidious status terms to being characterized as above all a "human being." *

Infants and toddlers up to about age four are primarily tended by their mothers or other mothers with children. Men in communal groups give children more attention than do men in outer society, but there is no norm of expectation—in particular, no inherent obligation for the father to be responsible for his own children, other than as persons in the group. However, some fathers we have seen are as deeply involved as the mothers with responsibility for childcare. One I met, living with a woman who had a child by another man, had taken major responsibility for that child, leaving the mother relatively free. In some cases single fathers take over the child-rearing role completely when the mothers move on, though this is less common than for mothers to be left with children when fathers leave. There is a clear tendency for women to be left with the major responsibility for child-support in contexts in which pairing relations are rather transient—especially, of course,

* *Child Rearing Practices of the Communal Family: Progress Report to NIMH*, 1971, mimeographed, pp. 10–12.

when the children are infants and often breast-fed.* But to have a child without a mate is not necessarily oppressive for the women concerned: many want children, but do not want permanent ties with men—and communes are among the few situations available to them in which they are accepted, have adult help with children and adult company, and work-demands do not necessarily separate them from their children. Since many such women draw Aid to Dependent Children, an adequate subsidy in the economics of most communes—women with children but without mates are welcome additions to many communes.

Because the movement is in its early stages, most commune children are under five. The large number of adults provides for them a rich ambience of security and affection. According to Berger:

But for children older than four or five, the responsibilities of either parents or the other adult communards may be much attenuated. All children are viewed as intrinsically worthy of love and respect *but not necessarily of attention.* As they grow out of primitive physical dependence upon the care of adults, they are treated and tend to behave as just another member of the extended family—including being offered (and taking) an occasional hit on a joint of marijuana as it is passed around the family circle.

Children are usually expected to share in the chores, farming, and industry. Often, as in the case of my children on

---

* In the U.S. Virgin Islands, where I lived for over two years, the norm is that women want children, but are often resistant to having men live with them regularly. The average age for mothers having their first babies is about twelve or thirteen. Since many young mothers work, grandmothers are often primarily responsible for child-care. I have wondered whether the commune movement in the United States might not drift in the direction of such a matriarchal arrangement, since transience and change are more and more characteristic of what Warren Bennis and Philip Slater have called *The Temporary Society,* and the responsibility for care of infants is one of the most stabilizing influences in that context.

our farm, they are relatively isolated from other children
of the same age—and adults vary in their willingness to
take special time with them to play games, tell stories, talk,
or teach. Judged (often justly) from the point of view of
the old culture, this amounts to neglect. Berger quotes a
young mother, "harried with the care of her two-year-old,"
who said, "What I wanted was a *baby;* but a *kid*, that's
something else." Neglect is, of course, rarely deliberate. It
is important for some adults, even mothers, to avoid role
stereotyping, to be free to say they are not "into" children
at some periods of their life, and they may have competitive
childish needs of their own which interfere with giving attention to children. Usually there are enough other adults
around to take up the slack in these circumstances.

Reports of communes are speckled with instances of
child neglect on the one hand and examples of preternatural
maturity on the other. One may create the other. I remember visiting a commune in an old mill beside a shallow, fast
stream. Three or four infants, two or under—grubby, bottomless, unattended—were playing on the bridge over this
stream. I was equally nervous about their welfare and about
intervening, so hovered near them—no doubt polluting the
environment with my old-culture vibes. Nothing happened.
There had never been serious accidents. "We never had to
take a kid to the hospital," a member said, "except once, to
get born. We had to take big people to the hospital three
or four times, who got hurt playing around on the swings
and things." Of another child he said:

The growth of three-year-old Julie in the four or five months
she was here is amazing. When she first came she was extremely attached to her mother; she could barely be without her; she was a very inward person with no sense of adventure. In four months it wasn't uncommon to be sitting
in the mill at midnight when who should walk in by herself
but Julie and ask, "What's happening?" To get to the mill
she had to get out of bed, usually get dressed, and walk down

a rather narrow unlit path about a hundred and fifty feet in the black of night.

As a teacher for most of my life, as well as a parent, I became very confused about the purposes of education. The *teacher's* purpose, particularly as he ages, subtly becomes to perpetuate his job, hence to perpetuate dependency—and parents, too, for emotional rather than economic reasons, are subject to this trap if the context of their lives did not enable them to accept self-worth. It becomes difficult to believe that young people can learn without our supervision, which obscures the fact that the whole point of education is precisely to develop capacity for such learning.

A commune mother in Oregon describes the fine line between neglect and smothering. On the one hand she recognizes that mothers are more likely than other adults on a commune to be aware of their children's whereabouts and safety—"the mommy twitch." On the other hand she sees the emergence of shared concern on the part of the other adults and independence on the part of the child as the direction of educational development.

Mother is often up at the green house or weeding the garden. She doesn't say goodbye each time she goes outdoors. There are lots of strange adults around and they offer to do things only parents are supposed to do.

Kid, crying: "I want my bottle."

Grown up: "OK, I'll make your bottle for you."

Kid: "*No*, I don't want *you* to make my bottle, I want my *dad* to make my bottle!"

Grown up: "Uhhh . . ."

Every child who's ever come here to live has freaked out at first. They go wandering across the fields, yelling at the top of their lungs for "Mommy!" and refusing help from anyone else. When they find mommy she is (ideally) sympathetic but firm. "No, I can't stay indoors all the time. We're living in a new place now, and I want to do some work out of doors. Look, I'm pulling up weeds, so we can have carrots to eat. No, I don't want to sleep in the same building as you every night, but there will always be someone there to take care of you, and I'm not very far away. Would you like to sit on my lap for a while right now?" In real life this . . . is varied with "Goddamit, Larissa, you've got to leave me alone sometimes!" After a month or two or three all the strange adults are not so strange anymore, the garden and meadow are familiar territory, and the tensions ease. Many things come to feel like, simply, the way things are. Once I watched Abe and Woody playing with their blocks. "Now we'll build an A-frame, and next we'll build a dome, and we'll put the shitter right over here. Look, Mom, here's the communal building!" Of course, of course, what else would they build with their blocks? Still, I had never pictured that scene before.*

Just as the word *shitter* may be shocking to old-culture sensibilities, so may be the conscious process of psychological weaning. So much attention is given in our society to child-rearing and education that displacement—away from the "child-centered home"—in the direction of concentration upon adult relationships seems selfish and inhumane. On the other hand, we know, or at least we have often been told, that adults in our society have a tendency to play out the drama of their lives using children as unwitting media. Many of today's young people are in rebellion against the marriages of their parents which, as children, they perceived were desperately strung together using children as the excuse, the surrogate, the compensation for failures in adult relationships. Often what "real" communication took place between the parents—be it disputes or meaningful sharing, about finances, roles, sex, jealousy, aspirations, disappointments—was shielded from the children. Their impression of grown-up conversation was likely to have been

* Elaine Sundancer, *Celery Wine*, Community Services, Inc., 1973, pp. 36–37.

of a flow of abstractions, impersonal practicalities, put-downs, and inexplicably explosive moods, like a scuffle ob-served in silhouette behind drawn blinds in an apartment across the street.

The transparency of communal life opens to children all that was hidden to their parents when they were chil-dren—for better or worse. Last night a tense and sometimes tempestuous meeting was taking place in our living room when I went upstairs to get something. Polly was watching television. "Aren't you glad you aren't an adult?" I asked. She grinned, "Uh-hmm." But, in fact, usually she is drawn to such meetings, rarely participating, but hanging on, lis-tening, learning, reaching her own conclusions, generally ignored as her elders lay open their passions and concerns. At times I cringe, realizing what she is hearing, what candid exposure to adult social reality is forming her mind. It is the pain of contemplation of one's daughter's deflowering, of the disillusionment of growth, of letting children know too early that there is no Santa Claus. Like other middle-aged people, I have been taught that reality is to be re-vealed to children in graduated doses, that in all aspects of life one moves with caution from storks to birds and bees, and the actual flesh encounter is to be as long as possible delayed, finally to take place more-or-less covertly, out of familial ken.

There is no way that can happen on communes. The mere presence of so many adults, with their conflicting views of everything, including child-rearing, dazzles the child with a kaleidoscope of attitudes and behaviors. In place of the impoverished range of adult models in the nu-clear family, amplified by, usually, a female teacher in kindergarten and first grade, then the specialists of later schooling, the communal child finds himself immediately not a witness to but a part of a network of complex rela-tionships, a person among people.

An urban nursery-school teacher observes:

The kids from families have different life-styles and values, they're used to certain clothes, to doing certain things. Often it's basically a financial difference. The kids from communes are used to a looser, more fluid environment, and they're less dependent on their parents. But I've also noticed that it's good to have more than one kid in a commune. It confuses them to have too many authority figures around—or just too many adults.*

In the early days of Berkeley communes, she says, there was little interest in having children—"there were too many white children anyway"—but there is now increasing recognition that people are into the movement for the long run. "More people want kids," she said. "They don't think the revolution will happen next year and they have time for it." Meanwhile the nursery school itself has radical political goals. Unlike schools where individual achievement is stressed, Blue Fairyland engages children in cooperative efforts, urging "the children to work on things together, from drawing posters to preparing lunch. Some of the kids stay for dinner with the parent commune and occasionally a few sleep over, an attempt to decrease dependency on their own parents."

Consistency of treatment and security of sustained relationships have been stressed as desirable by psychologists in our society, but the opposite conditions generally prevail in communes. Of the communal child, Carl Rogers says, "He does not receive consistent treatment, but he lives in a world of real adults, to whose idiosyncrasies he must adjust while finding psychological room for himself, his desires and his activities." In view of the intensity of emotional life in most communes, this may amount to a crash course in the relativity of human relationships. But it seems generally to create self-confidence, responsibility,

---

* Quoted by Steven V. Roberts, "Halfway Between Dropping Out and Dropping In," *New York Times Magazine*, Sept. 12, 1971, p. 60 ff.

and a positive, joyful view of life in most children. Rogers says:

Furthermore, the rural communal child has a place in the group life. As soon as he has the physical strength for it—certainly by age five or six—he can help in the never-ending tasks of a rural existence. He feels himself *useful*, an experience so rare as to be almost nonexistent in the suburban or urban child of our present-day culture.

Much of what I have said of children in communes may be applied to adolescents and adults in need of therapy. Environment that includes a population which is generally accepting and noninterfering is itself a strong therapeutic force. In a New Hampshire commune I was impressed by a beautiful young woman of eighteen who was, it seemed, singing through her days—gardening, cooking, doing crafts—productive and radiant.

After I got to know her better, she told me her story. She had run away from home at twelve. For the next five years she wandered the streets of various cities, became at various times a prostitute, drug addict, petty thief; she was repeatedly arrested and spent many intervals in jails and mental institutions. The expense to society could be compared to that of the education of a professional, but none of society's institutions had been able to help her find peace or to contain her long. Finally she was busted for living in a city commune with a high-school teacher. Her father (who, from her description, seems to have been a psychotically cruel, violent man) had found out where she was living and reported her to the police, getting the teacher suspended from his job. She was sent, again, to a juvenile detention center, where most of the inmates were black girls. They repeatedly beat her up (e.g., for playing a Jimi Hendrix record, which she had no right to play because she was white). Finally she was put into solitary

until, as one of the black matrons put it, "You learn to defend yourself," an unlikely piece of learning to occur in
that situation.

When she was released on probation, she met a young
man from the rural commune where she now lived, ille-
gally left the state, and had been there several months. Mar-
veling at her present psychological strength—which seemed
unbelievable after so short a period—I asked what made the
difference. "This place," she said, gesturing at the surround-
ings of scrub pines and sandy soil. Half-a-dozen young
people had found in some abandoned buildings the space
they needed to allow their natural drives toward health and
fulfillment to emerge.

Many communes have organized themselves as schools,
growth centers, or therapeutic communities, usually with
some degree of professionalism, some distinctions (however nonhierarchical the tenor of daily life) between staff
and teachers on the one hand and students or patients on
the other. The best known of these communities, actually
a chain of communes, is Synanon, which uses an encounter
group method ("the Synanon game," or marathon sessions
called "the stew") as its major therapeutic force. Synanon
has had remarkable success in redeeming addicts of alcohol, heroin, and other drugs, and now attracts many people
without recognized problems who nonetheless find life in
an intensive, communal setting, with continued emphasis
upon working out problems of personal growth and
change, rewarding. The large Jesus Freak communes take
many young people with serious drug problems, as do some
of the other new messianic communes such as Metelica's
Aquarian Concept, Inc., Mel Lyman's Family, and Steve
Gaskin's Farm. The Krishna movement has also established a number of communes in which a life of strict diet,
no drugs, and celibacy for the unmarried attracts many
who have had serious problems in their lives.

NIMH research into problems of heroin addiction has

indicated that when Haight-Ashbury was evacuated by hippies during the late sixties many who stayed in urban settings became heroin and speed users, whereas most of those who went to rural communes did not develop drug problems. (If they used marijuana and psychedelics, they tended to do so in nonabusive ways.) At present NIMH is exploring possible use of rural communes for drug abuse therapy. But to do so may undermine the natural therapeutic effect such communes have. For a community to function as a community, it almost necessarily eliminates distinctions between nonprofessionals and professionals, teachers and students, staff and patients. An extreme example is the group of communes founded by the Philadelphia Association in London, Kingsley Hall being the best known. R. D. Laing and other psychiatrists experimentally participated in these totally egalitarian groups. Of them, David Cooper says, in *The Death of the Family*:

Firstly, there is no psychiatric diagnosis, and therefore the first step in the invalidation of persons is not taken. . . . Some of the people, if they were transposed to the institutional structure of a mental hospital, would be called psychiatrists, others would be called patients. In the communities, however, there are simply people, some of whom are more in touch than others with the changing reality of the group and the changes developing within each person in the group, but the people with this charisma of knowing might well be the "patients" in the conventional setting. . . . The positive center of the experience . . . resides in the guarantee that some other person will always accompany one on one's journey into and through one's self. . . . Beyond this, the antipsychiatry community follows the principles of any other commune.

So far as I know, no study has been made of the relative effectiveness for therapy of nonstructured and structured communes. In the former, communal living is an end in itself, and what therapy occurs is incidental to development of a healthily functioning group. The latter range from halfway houses to schools and growth centers (such as Esalen) which have many communal characteristics, but tend to retain the format of classes and treatments, and to recognize professional status. People in need of education or therapy enter such communes on an explicit, transient basis, often paying tuition or fees in addition to their share of communal expenses, while "permanent" members remain in a distinct class. Study of nonstructured communes would offer serious problems, since their intimate nature would make the presence of observers and use of testing instruments objectionable, as these would alter the definitive elements of the community, including those which have therapeutic effect.

An additional problem in such study pertains to the definition of health. Some critics of Synanon (such as Dr. David Smith, who started the Haight-Ashbury Clinic and has been deeply involved in treatment of heroin addiction) say that Synanon "cures" merely substitute an addiction to Synanon itself for addiction to drugs. Usually one thinks of a therapeutic institution as designed to adapt people to function well outside the institution—in the "normal" world. But typically, those who benefit from the Synanon experience stay there to help the movement grow; and some have the explicit goal of transforming society into an encompassing complex of Synanon communities. Though Synanon is by no means characteristic of the nonstructured communes which are the major concern of this book, it shares with them the belief that the outer society itself is sick, and the commune is not only a haven, but a superior mode of social organization. It is quite true that many who have given up drugs at Synanon might revert to them if they moved to live in the outer environment. Similarly, the woman I described as happily functioning on a New Hampshire commune might return to patterns destructive to herself and to society in another context. At UNITY (described in Chapter V) an engineer is receiving Aid to the Totally Disabled because he has been judged unfit for employment, though he is one of the mainstays of the community in the warehouse. Nearly every commune I have visited contains people who would otherwise be living at public expense in institutions of the straight world—as alcoholics, drug addicts, mental patients—though nothing about their behavior in communes indicates that they have "problems." From the communal point of view, adjustment to the outer society is itself a form of madness. Similarly, one could not easily—by tests, for example—compare the results of communal, noninstitutional education with those of conventional schooling, for education in the two contexts is preparation for incomparably different forms of life.

Whether or not it will be true of communes organized for therapy is impossible to say, but there is a tendency for communes organized as schools to discard formal structures. Characteristic of such schools is one in rural Arkansas, which began as a branch of another communal-type school "for troubled and troubling children." They announced:

Our kids range from 0–13 years; the current boarding students are 11–16 years. There's day care for the students and a fairly unstructured community school for the older ones. A one-room schoolhouse has been turned into an informal learning center where the kids are encouraged to participate in small classes, individual tutoring, and independent work. We have certified teachers and are able to award high school credits and diplomas. . . . We're very strong on talking out problems, both with children and adults; we favor behavior modification practices over authoritarianism.

Within a year such vestiges of structure as that statement implies withered away. Though tuition from students was the primary financial support, there was less and less interest in recruiting and admitting new ones, and other economic enterprises (e.g., raising cattle and rabbits) were undertaken to free the school from its dependence on tuition. Jerry Friedberg's article quoted at the beginning of this chapter, "Beyond Free Schools: Community!", summarizes in its title the evolutionary direction. It becomes impossible to live honestly and democratically together when there are built-in distinctions between classes of residents, some paying, some being supported by the payments, some to be served, some to serve, some with a transient commitment and some making the community their permanent way of life. They tend to shed the structural props associated with educational and therapeutic functions in the old culture and increasingly proceed on faith (rather than any formulated theory) that organic beneficence will provide in lieu of imposed design.

Such reliance on nature is not, however, dogmatic or absolute; it is a tentative and withal modest experimentalism, a trying out, an effort to get in touch with real feelings and needs and to work out responses to these. Instead of trying to farm out children to schools and day-care centers (or even communal children's houses), instead of looking for jobs that will get them out of the house, both women and men in communes seem to prefer to stay home and keep children home. The home is not a trap. Nor is childcare conceived of as a burden. People are inclined to adjust to one another, accepting differences, rather than expecting themselves and others to adjust to external demands and artificial patterns; consequently the need of institutionalization is much diminished. It will be a long time before we will know whether this drift away from structure and design and toward informal, loving association will strengthen or weaken the communes' ability to provide education and treatment, but it seems at present to be the most probable direction of development.

Recently when I was talking to a college audience about communes and my own retirement from professional life, a professor asked me whether I had not found teaching personally satisfying. Indeed I had, I assured him. In my twenty years of college teaching I experienced perhaps twenty classroom hours in which things worked the way they were supposed to—a participative and enthusiastic class, informed and engaged, pulling together toward new insights and knowledge, using well my own professional preparation. Of the thousands of students I had dealt with, perhaps my relations with a hundred were, at least for a time, something like friendships. Antioch is an experimental college and was particularly supportive of me in trying new things, initiating new programs, and, at higher levels of development of educational policy, doing things which seemed significant in changing the very patterns of higher education in this country. In most areas of professional concern—teaching, advising, planning, developing, and publishing—I believe my colleagues would judge me to be exceptionally effective. I know the gratification of functioning well.

Nonetheless, I became increasingly disillusioned, first with the course format, then with the classroom, then with general education design and degree requirements, and finally with institutions themselves. I could not associate the way I was attempting to conduct learning for others with the way I knew I had learned myself, which was almost in spite of the institutions in which I happened to be enrolled (and, later, to be teaching). When I begin a book, I am reading out of interest, rather than obligation; I never know whether I will finish it—let alone what six books I will read next—as, for instance, students often are required to know in courses or in preparing syllabi for independent study. I rarely evaluate what I have done, and avoid like the plague any formal evaluation by others—not because

I resist learning, but because I find such processes dysfunctional in learning. I benefit from criticism and feedback, but only when it is clear that I am utterly free to take it or leave it, when I can amalgamate it with my own responses and a whole range of other considerations my critics may not be aware of. When I think of experiences which matter a great deal to me—whether they be making love, eating a good meal, going to a symphony, or taking a ride on horseback through winter woods—I cannot imagine that a framework of planning, evaluation, and credit would do anything but undermine their essential meaning and value.

When I faced up to the contradictions between my professional life and my personal values, I had difficulty imagining alternatives. In the first place, I rationalized, I had to eat. Like Adolf Eichmann, I was just doing my job. More basically, I had let my self-image become professionally defined. If I weren't a professor, what would I be? Just a man? More self-justifyingly, I thought I had a responsibility to be engaged. Everyone had to have a job. It was doing one's part. It was making the world work. If one were a ditch-digger, a plantation overseer, a professor, I suppose a hangman, there is always a way to do the job better and more humanely, to contribute to social good; but if one had no job at all, he would be a parasite.

Looking back from the perspective of some months of communal living, such considerations seem, of course, absurd. What has been most surprising to me, however, is the degree to which I continue to function as an educator—more profoundly so than at any previous time in my life. I had long heard others say and had said myself that as a teacher I learned most after I left college, that I learn most from my students, and so on: this is conventional, and condescending, rhetoric. What I have learned, however, is the rhetoric's essential truth. If one is truly willing to learn from others, in a situation in which practically no holds are barred and there are few structures to fall back on, when no party sends a report to any registrar, when none are paying to be there and none are being paid, and when, above all, the protective self-images of profession and status have been stripped away, education can, indeed, take place.

It hurts a lot. So far as I can see from here there is no leveling-off place. No degrees are promised. Not even plateaus. Not even vacations or Sundays. To wake every morning to the dawn of infinite possibilities (good and bad) ahead, and no way of retreating to anything behind, is both a joy and a continual torture. All of us are straining to get there, but there is no there to be reached. We hear one another saying, "I'm not ready. I'm too vulnerable." But the awareness sinks in that one will never be either ready nor invulnerable, that for every new acquisition of strength there is a new challenge for which strength must still be developed. I deserve a rest, I sometimes say to myself, and I am right about that; but there is no rest possible, deserved or not.

And I would not have it, could not imagine it, otherwise. One of the reasons I so strongly preferred Antioch to other colleges was that we were always trying something new. It seemed manic at times, for we rarely digested what we had learned from one program before starting from scratch with a new one. There was no way of repeating oneself, of falling into a rut. After awhile that way of life becomes addictive. It keeps one young, forever reaching, never knowing what one is going to be when he grows up.

To be a teacher is to be willing to be taught; to be utterly and forever willing to learn is to have something to impart to others—above all to evoke the same willingness in them. The people who have trouble in the commune are those who even temporarily bind themselves into a self-definition: "I'm the kind of guy who . . ." is a deadly way to start a sentence, deadly for the speaker and the hearer. Something organic has rigidified. No hope there. All of us are doing things we never did before and never thought we could do —building, wiring, plumbing, baking, preserving, gardening. We have started a business, and the house as I write seethes with talk of packing and trucking and machines and invoices and sales. We are engaged in a legal problem regarding our access road, and have been doing research in the county law library, getting neighbors to testify as witnesses, dealing with surveyors and studying old deeds. We are writing this book—and beyond what we learn about the subject matter itself are learning a great deal about the trials and benefits of collaboration. We are dealing with problems of children, of age differences, of habits, of newly recognized needs. Above all, we counsel one another through our days, learning more than we ever dreamed possible—or necessary—about one another's sensitivities and concerns, strengths and weaknesses, annoyances and our capacity to love. We just started. We have a long way to go. We will never arrive.

And that, finally, is the key to our mutual education, to learn to find satisfaction in the process, to dig the doing, to relocate joy in achievement toward joy in achieving, to sense that one is moving steadily and with direction—on a road without end.

When I feel, as I often do, a gnawing uneasiness about the education of my children, I try to reinterpret that as education of myself. Am I learning enough? Enough for what? How would I feel if I knew it all?

10

The New Anarchism

The term *commune* is confusing to many because it seems to suggest communism, though, of course, it is historically (and contemporarily) more appropriately associated with anarchism, the antithesis of such centralized statism as communism often implies. Not many modern communards consciously identify themselves with anarchism, and most who recognize the connection are uncomfortable with it. The term implies politics, a party, the whole mentality of division, competition, and strife—characteristics of the world from which they are alienated. It implies (popularly) fanaticism and violence, disorder and turmoil—qualities at odds with the vision of transcendent coherency, harmony, and integration toward which communalism strives. Probably most communards would describe themselves as apolitical—nonetheless with an implicit faith that their refusal to become involved with recognized processes of politics is itself a political statement with potential impact.

Such faith seems to the worldly-wise sometimes harmlessly, sometimes dangerously, naive. By definition, anarchism provides no means of dealing with the problem of power and so runs the risk of *laissez faire* economics that, in the absence of countervailing restraints at the state or international level, size will surge to gigantism, crushing and obliterating the small and disadvtanged. Against anarchism may be summoned the Hobbesian-Darwinian view of nature, bloody in fang and claw, in which survival is won by aggression and strength. Political power, in this view, abhors a vacuum. Willy-nilly it will emerge, and the alternative to planning is either oppressive injustice or deadly chaos. Human beings, some argue, have a lower nature of lust and greed and selfishness which must be consciously controlled by their delicate higher sensibility, their capability for reason, cooperation, disinterest. The libidinal life-force at the lower level impels man to ravish. But if the bestial flesh is controlled by angelic mind, that force can be transmuted into benevolent, dispassionate *agape*. We can design a society in which an all-powerful central government (corresponding to intelligence) corrects the vicissitudes of power and desire in the body politic. Equality can be guaranteed. Needs can be satisfied.

The central tenet of anarchism, old and new, is that nature is essentially good, and that humanity is also, as part of nature. In the nineteenth and early twentieth centuries, that belief appeared to be a fragile dream, daily contradicted by the relentless facts of human competition and aggression. As fathers perpetually educated their idealistic sons, you can't change human nature. And that nature seemed most safely contained in the zoo of regulated society, albeit the planted foliage resembled the jungle and the bars were invisible or replaced by natural-looking moats. The question raised by the new growth of interest in communalism is whether there are new facts of experience to contradict the wisdom of our fathers. The communal, or anarchist, dream would seem to require almost an evolutionary step in order to be realized—indeed, a demonstrable change in human nature. Are we on the verge of such transcendence?

The major spokesman for the new anarchism, Murray

Bookchin, sees two external factors that he believes sufficiently change the conditions of human life as to prepare the ground for evolutionary transcendence: ecology and technology. In contrast to popular Darwinism, modern ecology emphasizes nature's tendency toward balance and diversity rather than its progress through competition. The welfare of one species depends upon the welfare of all others in its environment, even that of its natural enemies:

A number of studies—Lotka's and Volterra's mathematical models, Bause's experiments with protozoa and mites in controlled environments, and extensive field research—clearly demonstrate that fluctuations in animal and plant populations, ranging from mild to pestlike proportions, depend heavily upon the number of species in an ecosystem and on the degree of variety in the environment. . . . Stability is a function of variety and diversity: if the environment is simplified and the variety of animal and plant species is reduced, fluctuations in population become marked and tend to get out of control.*

The "success" of the human species in taking dominion over the earth thus appears to be suicidal, as it results in such drastic simplification of the environment—particularly in massive artificial population centers—that organic evolution is in fact reversed, leading to rapid degeneration. If the danger of *laissez faire* economics that the rich inevitably get richer and the poor poorer were, indeed, a characteristic of uncontrolled organic growth, the first living species would have annihilated itself in a wasteland of its own spoiling; but, on the contrary, the élan of evolution has been one of proliferation upon proliferation of bewildering variety. In the long view, fitness to survive seems linked to some cosmic intuition of the sort human beings

* Murray Bookchin, *Post-Scarcity Anarchism*, Ramparts Press, 1972, p. 71.

clumsily approximate through systems analysis and cybernetics, an awareness of the interrelatedness of all elements
of the whole. The correctives needed to offset life's tendency toward gigantism are built into organic processes.
Perhaps the human species uniquely lacks a kind of cosmic
intuition or enlightened self-interest which enables other
species to live in the world without destroying it and themselves. The science of ecology is a latter-day development
which might simulate such awareness, like the painstaking
imagining of the visible world a person might undertake
who was born blind.

The emergence of new ecological awareness in the past
few years has been accompanied by emergence of a corresponding technology based on closed systems. Some simple-
mindedly reject all technology on the premise that human
ability to manipulate and control environment is antithetical to ecological balance—the black magic for which man
sold his soul. But, as Bookchin points out, it is precisely
because we have developed a kind of metatechnology based
on cybernetics and computers that we may be able to correct the disproportions of sheerly mechanistic power. The
new technology makes possible a miniaturization, decentralization, and diversification which could reverse the tendency of earlier technology to gigantize, amalgamate, and
standardize. Revolutions and revolutionary thought of the
past have been preoccupied with procuring and sharing
the means of survival and relief from toil. These are what
Bookchin calls quantitative concerns, the realm of Need,
which we now have the capacity to eliminate through
technology. Modes of thought (including, especially,
Marxism) dependent upon a premise of scarcity of necessary resources are now dysfunctional in accommodating
humankind to its future; hence it is a "post-scarcity anarchism" Bookchin predicts, a revolution in which the
major concerns are qualitative:

This quantitative approach is already lagging behind technological developments that carry a new *qualitative* promise—the promise of decentralized, communitarian lifestyles, or what I prefer to call ecological forms of human association.

I would put it more strongly still: human association in the new era must be pervaded by spiritual awareness—of the sacredness of self, others, the environment, the cosmos. Material abundance not only does not exist now for most of the people on earth, but it has become clear that the planet cannot bear such abundance unless there is a radical revision of what is rapidly becoming a universal standard of material welfare. We are stripping the earth to pour goods into the bottomless maw of consumerism, creating hordes seething with envy and pustules of glut. There remains an incompleted task of providing adequate food, clothing, shelter, medical care, education, and amenities for the world population; but this has been confused with the endless process of arousing and catering to artificially created appetites. We suffer more seriously from a spiritual malaise, a problem of values, than from a problem of economics or government or technical ability. In my view, that is the meaning of post-scarcity: we have ventured to the point that we know we could supply, until resources are exhausted and the earth is polluted beyond redemption, material goods for humankind, and can see that the demand will be forever unsatisfied. Post-scarcity does not mean that scarcities have been or can be eliminated; it means that we can now see that we have to stop thinking in quantitative terms about human needs, or, better, circumscribe our ambitions for quantitative increase by recognizing our qualitative needs.

What Bookchin calls "qualitative" needs are those I call spiritual. But the kind of spiritual awareness needed should not be confused with the repressive pietism associated with

conventional religion in our society, nor with the puritanism and work ethic of communist states. Quite the contrary. Bookchin speaks of opening the reservoir of self
which is systematically blocked from expression by both
bourgeois society and those political parties which set out
to overthrow it, characteristically with an ethos of even
greater puritanism and more oppressive work ethic than
that of the society they oppose. Studying European and
Russian revolutions since the eighteenth century, he finds:

Nearly every revolutionary uprising in the history of our
time has been initiated spontaneously by the self-activity of
"masses"—often in flat defiance of the hesitant policies advanced by the revolutionary organizations. Every one of these
revolutions has been marked by extraordinary individuation,
by a joyousness and solidarity that turned everyday life into
a festival. This surreal dimension of the revolutionary process,
with its explosion of deep-seated libidinal forces, grins irasci-
bly through the pages of history like the face of a satyr on
shimmering water.

In another context he quotes a chorus from *Marat/Sade*:
"What's the point of a revolution without general copula-
tion?" The libidinal energy which might make anarchism
possible, like that locked in the atom, is almost impossible
to release and of unimaginable power.

Historically such release has occurred among the lumpen
and *déclassé* elements of society, spreading instantaneously
and briefly to workers and other segments of the population, especially in congested urban areas. Today the primary surge has come from disaffected young people, including increasing numbers of high-school age as well as
college-age people. Now many rural young and industrial
workers who wear long hair and smoke pot are chronically
independent in their attitudes toward their jobs and toward
authority. One of the inadvertent products of the bour-

geois society has been huge numbers of true *déclassés*, both young and middle-aged, who have surfeited on the "benefits" of our civilization and seen to the yawning emptiness at their core.

The uprisings on college campuses and in ethnic neighborhoods of American cities in the mid-sixties evoked savage repressive force from the bourgeoisie, as after the Paris Commune of 1871, the bourgeois "recoiled with the horror and ferocity of a man who suddenly comes face to face with his unconscious drives." (Bookchin).

Given its modern arsenal for control of violence and surveillance of individuals, the modern bourgeois society cannot be attacked head-on. The revolution itself, like the society it hopes to bring about, must be decentralized. Communes, like anarchist affinity groups of other times, tend to be small, familial, scattered, in spasmodic and informal communication with one another, almost impossible to infiltrate, and engaged in no overtly subversive activities. They thrive on the disintegration of a cloyed bourgeoisie—necessarily, as other social classes in our nation and the multitudes of people in less prosperous nations have not experienced the alienation nor developed the awareness which motivates building an alternative society. If the anarchist vision is to be realized, it will probably be nonviolently, as new life springs from decay. But whether or not that happens and whether or not the emergent forms will be stable in their anarchistic diversity depend very much upon whether there occurs, indeed, a change in human nature—a new consciousness better attuned to cosmic purpose and direction and to the human role of creative participation in the evolutionary process, a consciousness enabling humankind to escape what has seemed its fate and to achieve what anarchists have believed to be its destiny.

To review, the new anarchism is:

1. apolitical, at least overtly—dissociated from the conventional processes of social change;

2. ecologically oriented—fostering a diversity of forms in decentralized systems as necessary for the human species to achieve stability in its environment;

3. technologically sophisticated—in a "soft technology," emphasizing means for eliminating scarcity of necessities and at the same time maximizing individual and community control;

4. spiritual—in that quantitative concerns are transcended by qualitative demands for life that is fulfilling for individuals and communities aware of and shaping cosmic purpose, affirming life in all its interrelatedness; and

5. libidinal—which may only be another term for spiritual—deriving energy from release of aspects of self, of dream and desire, repressed in bourgeois society.

These premises are being tested in the daily experience of the new communes, with implications that are sometimes grave and sometimes promising for the realization of anarchist goals in a new world order.

That required change in consciousness will be the subject of the next chapter, but here I would like to address the problems of the new anarchism on the most rudimentary level. I want to tell you about our factory. During the past few weeks I have undergone a crisis of belief regarding the questions I am raising here, and I cannot say with any certainty that as yet my faith is secure. It seems to me a mixed case, that on a small scale anarchistic endeavor is fraught with harrowing ambiguities and tensions and perhaps crippling impracticalities. And to work at all, it must work on a small scale, because by definition it is not a mode of life that can be centrally imposed. One cannot elect an anarchist president or expect HEW to set up a complex of communes for a regional test. Communes such as our own are laboratories in which ideas for the new era are worked out. At the same time, they are seeds of the new crop: if anything is to grow, it must grow from them. Meanwhile, they are made up of flesh-and-blood individuals, people who are simply trying to make a go of it, to find a way to live with their problems and potentialities. Some of the pioneers who settled the West may have spun dreams of bringing civilization to the wasteland, but no doubt most were doing what they had to do—leaving places they had to leave, seeking ways of surviving in the conditions they encountered, getting by. So it is with us. I happen to be writing a book, which carries my head into realms of speculation of little immediate concern to the other people who live here with me. Hence the relevance of the factory—standing fifty yards away from me as I write, but as distant psychically from this book as a plow in a field is from a textbook on agronomy.

Our factory (formerly a two-car garage) produces flowerpots cut from logs. The question it symbolizes is whether a small business, involving a complex process of manufacturing, can operate on anarchistic principles. Those of us (ranging in age from six to forty-nine) working in the factory were inexperienced and unskilled both in business and in operation of the machines. With neither knowledge nor organizational structure, could we produce and sell enough to support ourselves?

I should explain that the term *anarchism* never occurs in our discussions. We are not trying to be anarchists; we are trying to live. But our drift is away from structure and planning, at least in overt forms. We have no illusion that we have cast ourselves loose from society. Had we not been able to buy the farm in the first place (making a down-payment on savings from years of professional life), were there not suppliers, markets, customers, communication and transportation facilities, power sources, laws, credit and currency in the surrounding society, we certainly could not manufacture and sell flowerpots. The structures of that world enable us to exist and continue, but our tendency is to dispose of them or escape them to the extent that we are able, and to replace them subtly with the organic structures that emerge out of our immediate conditions and relationships.

Our business, in short, is a free enterprise in a capitalist economy, and proves nothing about the feasibility of society-wide anarchism. What it does illustrate, or, better, tests, is the capacity of rather ordinary people to cooperate and produce effectively without the arrangements generally assumed to be necessary for such an operation. It illustrates both the problems and potentialities of developing a new consciousness by which individuals function, like organs in the body, as unselfconscious, coordinated parts of a group. During the year in which the business has been underway there have been about a dozen living here at any given time. With many fewer than that (e.g., eight), there would probably not be enough for us easily to take up the slack when one or several, for whatever reason, are not working. With many more than that (e.g., sixteen or more), there would probably be sub-grouping and internal tensions diminishing efficiency to a greater extent than we would gain through added labor. It may be that at least one of the archetypal forms of an anarchist society might be groups of about our size—containing enough variety and energy to sustain an operation which provides subsistence—provided there are other, compatible structures conducting enterprises of greater scale and complexity.

In our early days, before the business started, there were usually more people (up to about twenty) living here. We organized ourselves to get the work of the farm done. There were sign-up sheets for meal preparation, clean-up, shopping, laundry, and other chores. Managers were self-selected for various areas of responsibility (garden, construction and maintenance, kitchen, animals, vehicles, etc.), and our budget reflects these categories. As winter drew on and we diminished in numbers, we gradually shed most of the appurtenances of organization. Now we cook and shop as we feel the need, clean up voluntarily, without assignments. The managerships and budget categories still exist, but have less significance in practice (which sometimes causes consternation and mismanagement). Such organizational forms as sign-up sheets are not inconsistent with anarchism, but the disposition of our group is to prefer spontaneity to structure. Ideally, people will see what needs to be done and do it, each taking a generalized responsibility for the functioning of the houeshold and farm. At least two or three know how to do each job, and though some tend to specialize in certain functions, others can take over easily when there is need. There is no quantitative equality. As in any family, some work harder than others, some are more highly motivated, some are more capable. But with everyone generally committed to one another and the common enterprise, doing what they can and feel like doing, things get done. At least in theory.

In practice, of course, there is considerable bitching and neglect, resentment and guilt. Long ago a man with much experience in communities told me, "If you figure out who is going to carry out the garbage, everything else will seem simple," and it does seem that the greatest tension develops around the most rudimentary chores. A double-bind develops: some do more than their share and resent those who do little. The latter accuse the former of being judgmental, and dig in their heels all the more firmly. A game of stand-off develops, and the house becomes an appalling mess. Group meetings and daily interaction slowly raise group consciousness, but the process is painful. The more one pressures and complains, the less cooperation he evokes. Some seem trapped in paralysis of will or lack of energy for weeks at a time. Those (I am chronically one) who take too much initiative, preempting tasks from others, begin to feel exploited and abandoned—and panicky, for it seems that when the more energetic people slack off there is a real danger that nothing at all will get done. It takes a conscious effort to look around and realize that, after all, a great deal has been achieved and that the routine responsibilities are generally attended to—even by the random accretion of spontaneous effort.

But is this any way to run a factory? I personally love that little postage stamp of a factory—but that affection is not shared by all. The production process involves seven distinct operations, using a tractor-powered cut-off saw, bandsaw, pneumatic nailer, and stapler, as well as painting, packing, and trucking. In addition, supplies have to be ordered well before they are needed. Orders are received and filled, arrangements made for shipping, invoices sent, correspondence answered, books kept, sales made. Machines and tools have to be maintained. The factory has to be cleaned. The truck has to be kept running. The process is intricate and interrelated. For want of a nail (or a box, or saw blade, or invoice form, or storage space when the pots don't move along their little circuit of the garage), production can be paralyzed.

Not everyone likes the work, and there is no community expectation that everyone be involved. As I write, we are just beginning to derive our subsistence from income (remarkably soon—with less than six thousand dollars capital investment). No one has been paid for the hundreds of hours of time put in. We do not anticipate paying wages or relating labor to income. We simply hope to support ourselves, putting what we make into the family budget. Like the garden and animals and woods, the factory is just one aspect of life in the commune—and we want the whole to be harmonious and integrated, with no one activity a central focus. As one woman put it:

The whole point of living here—for me—is not to get things done, necessarily, but to be *happy*. That means making myself a better person in my own eyes. If I'm happy, then everyone else will be a little happier. We've all had first-hand experience of what it's like to have someone we care for being unhappy. It brings us all down. So, it seems to me that everyone's most important job here is to be happy. If we're really meant to be here, then we will not only be happy, but we will enjoy doing all the things that need to be done here. But a person must exercise all his talents to be happy. He also needs time to meditate, if that is what he wants, time to sew, read, walk, look, watch TV—whatever. . . . Why are any of us here *except* to self-indulge? No one came here or stays here for anyone but themselves. That is good. We have enough martyrs in the world, too many unhappy people doing things for someone else.

On a good production day, with half-a-dozen people working three or four hours, we can turn out two hundred and fifty pots. We rarely do that. If we can level off at five hundred pots a week, made and sold, we could live comfortably by our modest standards. No one would have to take outside jobs. We are not interested in expansion or profits beyond that goal. But can even that much be done dependably in the anarchistic mode?

We experimented with schedules and shifts, but (as in regard to house and farm work) these withered away. The industrious didn't need such structure, and those who weren't so industrious would not comply with them. People signed up for work, but they might sleep late, dawdle over breakfast, take off on a trip to town, forget. Those who worked hardest and most consistently were inclined to interpret the sporadic efforts of the others as lack of commitment—to the factory, to the community, to themselves. Whether or not the work actually gets done (and it seems always to get done to a sufficient degree), this question of commitment invariably creates tension. It is a test of love, of worth, of values. Even when it is not, it oppresses the most conscientious, who tend to sacrifice the private (and valuable) activities they might otherwise engage in, such as reading, writing, piling brush in the woods, deep discussion or love time with another, for visible work of measurable community value. Whether we produce pots or not may be critical in determining the economic survival of the commune, but the larger question of whether we want to be here at all is raised when commitment is in doubt. In some cases those who show little interest in working in the factory are also those who neglect the ongoing chores of house and farm. A polarity develops between those who demonstrate commitment by continual, energetic engagement, and those whose efforts are selective and scarce, but who are offended if doubt is cast upon their commitment in spirit, even though that of their bodies is not much in evidence.

My own crisis of belief resulted from that tension. We had found that we could make schedules, and get paper pledges in abundance, but could not adhere to them. Okay, we figured, let's try working when we feel like it, to see whether elimination of the schedules will release energy. It did not. I was reminded of the dilemma many face who try to introduce free programs in schools. If students are dull and unmotivated, that may be because of the routine and imposed standards and discipline. Remove these, and perhaps students will spontaneously begin studying and producing, achieving the results sought by conventional schools, but freely, happily, on the basis of personal choice. This does not happen. Some teachers dabble in such free learning experiments, become disillusioned, and revert to the prescriptive methods they had hoped to supersede. If you want students to work, alas, you have to make them do so, they decide. There are many things besides original sin to blame this on: earlier conditioning, the competition of other demands in the system, the unavailability of truly engaging and seductive learning materials, and so on. But many reach the conclusion that, given present conditions, free learning doesn't work. Nothing happens—but indolence and chaos.

The error in this reasoning is in expecting results comparable to those sought in conventional systems. To return the analogy to manufacture, it is as though a businessman were to hope that if he removed the time clock and the bosses (and wages as well!), somehow the factory would go on and even increase its production of goods. It would not happen. The conventional business model has techniques adapted to its specific purposes, and if one changes, so must the other. In that model, there is no theoretical limit to the amount of production which is desirable, because the real product is not what is manufactured, but money in the bank for the owners, for which the products sold are an intermediate step. Though it is still true for us that profits are an objective, there is an important difference: in our case the workers are the owners. What we want—a satisfying life—is only partly provided by money in the bank. We want to produce enough to sustain ourselves, a concept which includes some savings for future security. But it also includes such factors as amicable relations with one another, a sense of personal self-determination, the gratification of good craftsmanship in making individually beautiful pots, although we know these will bring no better price on the market than mediocre pots, and time for the many other activities and projects on the farm which compete for our energies. It is quite possible for us to be too successful. If, for example, we took a contract to manufacture 10,000 pots per week, instead of 500, we could no doubt gear up to produce them—leasing a building in town, installing a dozen bandsaws, hiring workers from outside the community, and so on. But the point of the operation would be lost, and the additional profits earned would be no compensation. In that context, efficiency must be redefined as overall effectiveness in achieving the whole range of values, incidentally including profit, which the community deems important in daily life. Of course a problem remains of striking a practical balance between the quest for immediate and for deferred rewards, but in the commune, as opposed to conventional industries, the emphasis is relatively stronger upon the immediate.

Does it work? If we had years to look back upon, I might be able to give a more confident reply. We have set up the operation so that each of the seven steps can be done relatively independently, and so individuals can work alone. That is, any time of day or night, weekday or weekend, anyone in the commune can look into the factory and see work to be done that he or she can do. It is more fun, and in some ways more efficient, if several are working at the same time. For example, if the stove is stoked up to heat the place, several might as well take advantage of that heat. If one nails alone, a pile of pots builds up waiting to be painted, and in time there is a space problem. (Of course, that same person can then shift to painting.) So far only a few of us use the saws, so unless we stay ahead of the other jobs, all work stops. But since we all live together anyway, and see one another constantly, such problems of coordination are easy to deal with.

More difficult is the question of whether people will work at all. Laziness and self-indulgence are not the obstacles; or, rather, these are, I believe, merely names for symptoms of deeper disorders. The games of ego can be played with monetary or sexual counters, and also with those of labor. One person's exertion can be interpreted as pressure on others to exert equally. Thus one can develop an ego-stake in *not* working, a resistance to being manipulated. And so on: the variations are endlessly subtle. We have gone through phases (usually lasting no longer than a day) of complete paralysis. Some have stopped working because they felt pressure to work. Others have stopped because they don't want to be perceived as exerting pressure. But their very inaction is seen as only another form of pressure—i.e., if the usually industrious ones are not working, eventually the usually idle ones will be forced to work by necessity. Values and personal worth are threatened. One kind of activity (e.g., working on the production line) may be favored, because it is more visible than another (e.g., working on the accounts). Or all factory work may seem more valuable than such activities as baking bread, cleaning house, beautifying a room. And what about personal reading, embroidery, walking in the woods, or meditating? If a person is simply depressed and spends time alone in his or her room, is that not also a valid use of time, essential as any other for the smooth functioning of the community? These questions are raised again and again, and at the rhetorical level there is agreement that, indeed, our goal is personal freedom that covers the whole range of such uses of time, specifically the freedom *not* to work in the factory. But in action, our commitment to that principle is at least intermittent. Some believe that necessity warrants pressure and manipulation of others. These evoke resistance. The right to freedom of choice is perpetually tested. And the spiral of pulling and pushing, engaging and withdrawing, winds us down into another paralysis.

Laws or rules require police and sanctions. Conventional society devotes a good deal of its energy and resources to the task of making sure that its regulations are adhered to. Anarchism lacks these means of enforcement, and social pressure, which tends to emerge as a replacement, often has the opposite effect from the one desired, promoting deviance rather than adherence to group norms. In the resulting morass of conflict and ineptitude, there is a strong temptation to retreat, to compromise, to introduce just a little structure, just a few sanctions, to prop up flabby nature. But in an anarchistic commune there is, finally, only one sanction which has meaning: exclusion. There are no punishments or rewards except those which are innate in the way of life itself. But it is quite possible for a group to expel a member who is not functioning as the group desires or who is disruptive of its purposes. Thus the dreadful chasm is always present in our awareness. One is either in or out. One fits in—or leaves. While, in fact, expulsion is an exceedingly rare phenomenon in communes, there are often departures resulting from internal tension which amount to the same thing, and these, like divorce, often leave a residue of blame and guilt, casting a cloud over the remaining members, who know it could happen again, it could happen to them.

I emphasize these negative factors because it soon becomes apparent that to the extent that the mind-set of the old culture is retained in an anarchistic communal setting, there will be perpetual inefficiency, paralysis, and emotional agony—and inescapably most of us come into these settings with that mind-set. Unless there is indeed a change of consciousness, anarchism won't work—or will work only with continual propping and compromise and pain. To function without these each member of a commune has to develop an organic, intuitive sense of his relationship to others and to the group, to become an organ in an organism, to recognize at a subliminal level that his own fulfillment depends upon the fulfillment of other individuals and the health of the group as a whole.

Fleetingly, but increasingly, we can see this happening among us. The fact is that we do somehow manage to get out our 500 pots a week, with no specific designation of responsibility, no schedules, no requirements, and that we are becoming happier with ourselves and one another in the process. Certainly the fact that so many in our society are these days exploring anarchistic alternatives—in free schools, encounter groups, and unconventional marital arrangements as well as in communes—suggests a widespread faith in the essential goodness and rightness of human nature removed from the trammels of legislative artifice.

Again and again over the years I have thrown my life into one after another educational and social experiment based on what I now would call an anarchist faith, in spite of knowing the predictable agonies entailed. So many of us make such commitments that I think we must have a spontaneous conviction that there is a link between human intuition and cosmic purpose. It is the faith of Antigone, of Thoreau, of Jefferson, of the Berrigans, indeed of the most ancient political and religious creeds, that the dictates of individual conscience have an authority beyond law. Individual autonomy does not result in social dissolution, but social harmony. Cooperative, constructive effort is most solidly based upon innate impulses, on a transcendent awareness that individuals are linked to one another and to larger nature, and that the good of one is inseparable from the good of the whole. Relieved of social restraints and requirements we are all likely to indulge in shortsightedly selfish behavior or feel the need to protect our tender egos in the unknown climate of freedom. But gradually a new consciousness grows; we hear our own inner voices more clearly, hear them tuned to those of others and to larger purposes beyond us all. That sounds like rather grand rhetoric to accompany the manufacture of flowerpots, but if we discover that consciousness working at such a mundane and practical level, we may sense a renewal of faith on which we can move toward experiments of larger scope. At any rate, to the extent that we go on working this way, in the face of the obvious trials and obstacles which explicit structures, rewards, and sanctions might seem to ameliorate, we implicitly testify that for us nothing else at this juncture of our lives is so clearly worth doing.

11

The New Consciousness

Except that we be born again, it sometimes seems, there
is no hope that we can pass through the looking glass into
the new world order to which communes point the way. Before me are piles of file folders pertaining to such things
as drugs, meditation, diet, ceremony and ritual, music,
crafts, art, extrasensory perception, and new religious cults.
Something is happening—something with an overall unity
—in spite of the diverse range of influences from ecology
and cybernetics to astrology, Jungian and Reichian psychology, yoga, Zen, and Christianity revived—a new culture made up of the remnants of several old ones, piled on
counters at the thrift shop. One may see it especially on
country communes, where life is informed by the seasons,
the needs of plants and animals and people, by a rigorous
economy, and the relative isolation and intimacy of the
members, these disparate streams combining into a coherent
vision and style of life characterized by a casual, familiar,
undemonstrative awareness of human participation in the
universe, an awareness which, after all, involves little mystic
ecstasy, few drug-assisted revelations, or even regular baths
of alpha waves, but carries one into new ranges of experience, illumines a new sense of self, and is sensitive to

the network of relationships linking individual to group and group to environment in balanced systems.

These conclusions are warranted by the evidence we have from communes, and yet seem too abstract, if not pretentious, for the kinds of experience from which they arise. I am fearful of being misled myself or misleading others in matters so critical. Too many messiahs in recent years have announced the apocalypse and an imminent transendence of humankind into an era of new awareness, whereas in essential ways, day by day, the world and people go on much as they have in the past. The risks I and others have taken in committing ourselves to the values of the new culture are too great to permit pursuit of the *ignes fatui* of desperate belief. Meanwhile, as we recognize daily on our own commune, there are bills to be paid—not only those in dollars for groceries and mortgage and gas, but bills for our past conditioning, our insecurities, our distrust, and bills for our present divergence from the norms of the surrounding society. Anarchism and the new consciousness are chic topics for academic discourse, but do they work—with real people in real situations? The grand rewards such as delivering humankind from oppression and saving the planet from despoliation beckon like fantasies; but are there sufficient rewards to sustain us in practice, to get us through dark nights of doubt, to meet our practical needs? Is there sufficient verification along the way to assure us we are not wandering in the desert of madness?

The first discovery of the new consciousness is that we are linked—as were the black and white prisoners in the film *The Defiant Ones*. Before those two men were able to break the cuff chains they wore and free themselves of one another, they not only overcame their mutual hostility and learned to cooperate intuitively (since one could not move without the other), and even used their chain as a tool (e.g., as one lowered another into a warehouse), but they also developed a positive affection and concern. When the chain was finally broken the pair tried to hop a freight. One got onto a boxcar successfully, but the other, wounded, lagged behind, running desperately, and the white hand and black hand stretched toward one another, reaching for help and to be helped, genuine love melded with mutual dependence. Their strength derived from their weakness. Those parts of self which society had repressed and which had become atrophied were reawakened. Human bondage was not weakness nor even unfortunate necessity, but an aspect of human completeness. To be linked is to be whole.

The second discovery is that the more bound we are to one another, the freer we are to be different. Again and again the experience of communes has shown that once basic allegiance is established, individuals are *more* able than formerly to disagree, to disapprove, to judge attitudes and behavior of others. Members of a mutually committed group are not only free to but impelled to criticize one another because of group survival instinct, and serious failures of one member cripple the group.*

---

* Some groups (not typical of the new culture!) carry this principle to extremes. Many have found the virulent mutual criticism of the Synanon game, for example, cannibalistic. One of the messianic communal groups, Mel Lyman's Fort Hill Community (now spread to a number of locations throughout the country) is notorious for the way its members tear one another apart. Both Synanon and Lyman's group attribute essential positive value to this process. Lyman writes: "It is always hard to tell your friend he has bad breath, but if you keep it to yourself you will begin to hate him and wish he would go away. . . . We began to criticize each other. . . . This brought us closer together. Soon a policy of open criticism developed and this created a wonderful understanding amongst us. We improved each other. Now we all know each other so well that we have become as one person" (*American Avatar*, publication of Fort Hill Community, Roxbury, Mass., 1968). Rosabeth Kanter finds forms of confession and mutual criticism significant indices of stability in successful historical American communities (the best known example being Oneida's Mutual Criticism sessions, which were predecessors of modern encounter groups), in *Commitment and Community: Communes and Utopias in Sociological Perspective*, Harvard University Press, 1972.

Such interaction can be purely utilitarian, like that of mountain climbers on the same rope. There have been instant communes on life rafts in the middle of the Pacific, in villages struck by flood, in foxholes under bombardment. When communal living is voluntary, however, the dependency is enhanced by love, and utilitarian interests are enriched by a dimension of genuine, positive desire for each to help each be fulfilled. This is most easily seen in child-rearing. A parent may correct a child because he projects his own reputation upon him, thinking the child's behavior reflects himself. He may do so for practical reasons—e.g., demanding that the child not waste food, damage property, hurt others. He may—as in farm families—want to develop a strong, capable worker in the common enterprise. But there is, in addition to such motives as these, a strong instinctual desire that the child achieve his fullest potential, for the child's own sake, even when that means tolerating or encouraging behavior that is costly, painful, even heart-breaking. Wise mothers often "correct" a son's dependency, even when the mothers find that dependent behavior extremely gratifying to themselves.

In communes the correction may have the same intent, but often is in the opposite direction: the members have to teach one another how to be dependent, knowing how repressed is the need of dependency in American society.* But, conversely, group consciousness does not produce conformity, but actively fosters growth, change, and differentiation. In the courtship period lovers are reluctant to notice differences; they take delight in common interests. Imagine! We are both stamp collectors, both like swimming, both

---

* Philip Slater, in *The Pursuit of Loneliness,* Beacon, 1970, p. 5, discusses "three human desires that are deeply and uniquely frustrated by American culture" and which may be fulfilled in communal life—the desire for community, for engagement, and for *dependence,* "the wish to share responsibility for the control of one's impulses and the direction of one's life."

like to cook! As the relationship matures, the opposite tendencies come into play: diversity of talents and interests makes the corporate unit stronger, more capable, more engrossing, and the emphasis is upon how its members complement (rather than compliment) one another. The communal ideal is that each be able to perform as many functions as possible, so that no one is "essential" as a specialist, and each can take over for another, each radiating the fullest possible spectrum of self-fulfillment.

Some might think that the security of love would lull a group and lure it into the swamp of indolence. One of the myths of capitalism is that people need incentives to grow and change, that without fear of failure or promise of reward, the human condition is to remain inert, static. But in an organic view of life the natural impulse of people is to grow, change, to rectify error as a stalk seeks sunlight, to seek self-actualization through symbiotic relationship with other self-actualizing and very diverse individuals (as healthy flowers require healthy bees, and vice versa). Mechanistic controls and constraints interrupt this process. Conformity, or repression of self, results from surrendering inner motives to external expectations. A farmer does not "grow" (an odd verb in the transitive, as is "heal") his corn by stretching it on a rack, but by fertilizing its roots and clearing the way for it to develop. Given the right conditions an ecosystem will establish itself as a heterogeneous plenitude in which each component thrives.

Three indices of poor communal health, usually apparent instantly to a visitor from the outside (though the members themselves may have let the conditions grow upon them without noticing) are excessive conformity, apathy, and valuelessness. One leads to another. Fear of deviation, in self or others, is paralyzing. Soon nothing gets done. Nobody cares. Anything goes—the rebellious other face of conformity. As in many kinds of psychic disorder, the symptoms may be defended tenaciously. At one of the

free-land communes a visitor returned to his car to find
it being pillaged by a resident. When the visitor objected,
the resident said, "All property belongs to the people, man.
The stuff in this car is no more yours than mine." The
visitor established his claim to the contents of the car with
the threat of physical violence, luckily being bigger than
the would-be thief. When a commune succumbs to such
an ethos, the only redress is escape or violence. The commune quickly dissipates or reverts to a kind of primitivism
tolerable to very few. The atmosphere is oppressive, sullen.
The members feel unable to speak out and helpless to
change conditions that bother them. Often it is the conduct
of one or two members which is bumming out the others,
but (often bolstered by philosophical justification of diversity and freedom) those causing the trouble are increasingly defensive about and even domineering in behavior that others object to, like children begging for
limits. But no one feels free to criticize, because to do so
would raise the horrendous question of rejection. In these
situations, as when our factory is paralyzed, the only hope
is for a change in consciousness. But how can that be
brought about?

Recognition of the need for transcendent awareness is
both intuitive and intentional in communes. Terms such as
"change of consciousness" and "consciousness raising" became current in political activities, spreading over to
women's liberation, black and chicano identity, gay liberation, and other strands of the movement in the late sixties.
Consequently, there has been an effort to take thought and
thereby add a cubit to one's stature—and to some degree
it seems to work. Again, though the analogy was rarely
explicit, the techniques of consciousness changing were
reminiscent of those of anarchist affinity groups of earlier
decades, now strengthened by experience in encounter
groups. Intense, intimate mutual- and self-knowledge pro-

vide a base from which people can move on, with a conscious awareness of purpose and direction, attempting to internalize values which will result in new behavior patterns. A fine balance has to be maintained between indiscriminate acceptance of where one and others are on the one hand, and excessive pressure, or mind-fucking, on the other. Marxists, particularly, denounce the apparent pacification of encounter groups, in which a brotherly understanding emerges (e.g., between militant blacks and police) that obliterates "objective" differences of interest. At the other extreme, the hippie mentality sometimes resists all change in the name of freedom to do one's thing. Wherever one is at is right. A crude conversion process was recognized in protests and mass demonstrations, when peppergas and clubs changed (as well as battered) many heads, resulting in instantaneous radicalization. Confrontation was often sought strategically, not for the effect it had upon the establishment, but for the way it drew liberals over the line into radical consciousness.

The contradictions and frustrations of all such methods of changing values have led many to abandon them. Simultaneous with efforts to bring about intentional change by developing awareness of human brother-and-sisterhood through persuasion and political action there has been a more intuitive movement in the same direction as people experienced consciousness change through the use of drugs and exploration of new religious forms. Never having taken a psychedelic drug (aside from a few experiences with cannabis), I am in some ways poorly qualified to comment on the importance of such drugs in the movement. In other ways, ironically, in view of the prevailing scientific criteria of objectivity, that fact may serve as a credential. But there is no question that especially in its early days the movement was in large part a creature of the drug culture. A man on a commune in Oregon says:

I think all of us have had the Experience. It's from whatever that substance was we all took back in 1965. One way or another this whole thing revolves around LSD-25. You take that stuff, and it takes you all the way back, cell for cell, vibration for vibration, back to the common denominator, that one seed which we all came from. . . . Words just aren't very useful at all in describing it. But everyone knows what everyone else saw. And after that experience you just don't want to live the way you used to. . . . Somebody put this thing into your hand that flashed you into the core of the universe. And a few hours later, there you are again, you're more or less the same person, but you have to figure out some way of living which makes sense in terms of that experience.*

A woman from the same commune, who had left a husband, two children, and a house in the suburbs, said:

I started smoking, and took acid a few times, and I began to look at things differently. Like when I started smoking, I stopped dusting. . . . Then I took acid, and when I put that little pill in my head all of a sudden I understood a lot of things for the first time. I knew what was important, the love and the sharing, and these other things just weren't important at all. But my husband, he still wanted things of his own, and he didn't want to open up the house to others, so we split and I came here.

The term *hallucinogen* for the agents of such experiences is misleading. Though in some cases drug-takers see (or "imagine") things that "aren't there" in the world outside their heads, the core of the experience seems to be an intensification rather than obscuration of reality. Even the hallucinations have the same kind of reality as do dreams, which through symbols and puns and blendings communicate to the conscious mind a highly significant internal real-

* Quoted in Keith Melville, *Communes in the Counter Culture: Origins, Theories, Styles of Life*, Morrow, 1972, p. 162.

ity which may cause suffering if repressed. It is to dreams that psychoanalysts go first to discover what is really happening with their patients.

But much more important than hallucinations are the heightened perceptions of things which are, indeed, there. Psychedelic reality corresponds much more closely to the physical universe described by science than does the highly filtered "common sense" reality available to the gross senses and rational mind. Each object is perceived directly as motion, energy, swirling matter, vivid colors. The perceiver recognizes a continuity between the tissues of his own body and signals of his own nervous system and the external world. A communard describes it:

The world starts moving, like a picture that becomes a movie, in color. Everything is alive. I feel part of a field of energy, at one with the biophysical field. It is like having an electronic microscope strapped to your head, both eyes, seeing into things, becoming akin to the essence of things—and coming down is like having the microscope removed, losing a faculty we once had, or maybe never had, but which shows us how things really are. I remember thinking during my first trip, "This has all been happening all the time that I've been alive, and I missed it." . . .

Tripping is a tremendous ego-loss. I feel a fraction of an inch high, like in a cavern of enormous shapes and textures and colors. At the same time that I see everything is really all one, including myself, I see that every object has unimaginable individuality. Each object is less domitable. I realize that I can't walk into a room without laying a trip on that room, and I don't want to dominate. I see my role not as conquerer, but as receiver; I want to relinquish power. It takes you through the whole trip from denial that I am God to recognition that everything is God, and since I am part of that, I am, indeed, God.

The first time I did it, I woke up the next morning and I was back to myself. Things were in place again, and the trip behind seemed an illusion. The next time I remembered more,

I knew for a longer time that the world really was, in spite of appearances, a torrent of energy and life and that I was part of all that. The next time the vision stayed with me a little longer—and it was maybe a month or more before the humdrum reasserted itself, and reality was no more interesting than before I got into it that way. But it was like falling more and more deeply in love with a woman, getting to know her to the point that I became aware of her at all times, not thrilled by her anymore, perhaps, but aware of how fantastic she was. I became saturated with what seemed the true landscape of reality. It became part of my head-set, and I no longer need acid to remind me. Like, I know the vitality of the universe, and can move in and out of that consciousness with ease.

As with mystic experiences, the vision he describes is non-transferrable, and escapes efforts to describe it in words. A skeptic may resolutely refuse to believe that anything real has been seen. It was only a dream, as we tell children—and sometimes ourselves—waking from disturbing descents into alternative reality. On the other hand we know we cannot escape the bind of our perceptions. Reality is a construct of our consciousness, and that consciousness is fundamentally influenced by subconscious experience. If one permits reality to be structured in this new sensibility, his very self will be changed—and some may undergo this entirely without acid, some after a single trip, and some never, because past conditioning has a great deal to do with whether one is willing to see the world in different terms.

The social effects of the drug culture are as important in changing consciousness as are the effects of drugs upon inner awareness. Through involvement with drugs many —particularly many young people—first became significantly outlaws. The punishments for drug traffic were outrageous in the sixties—in some states exceeding those for any other crime. (Incidentally, there is some correlation between strict enforcement of harsh drug laws and paucity of communes by states; e.g., Texas has many characteristics which would foster rural communes, but the laws used to be more stringent there, and many fewer communes emerged there than in, say, Colorado and New Mexico.) One after another learned that crime does, indeed, pay—in a coin of incalculable value: the experience of transcendence. A web of trust emerged, with a sharp, almost fearful distinction between those in and out (cf., the status of the saved and unsaved on the eve of the apocalypse in Johannine strains of Christianity—as opposed to more rationalistic Pauline strains). If someone in this context is cool, he may be instantaneously accepted as an intimate family member—with all his oddities. One becomes accustomed to deviant behavior from the experience of being in strange mental places and of accompanying others on their trips. He learns that the distinctions between sanity and insanity are relative and based on conveniences of the alien society (hence, in part, the popularity of the writings of the psychoanalyst R. D. Laing and of Thomas Szaz).

This tolerance is symbolized by the growing popularity of astrology. If a person is an Aquarius or a Taurus, or if the moon is in Cancer, certain peculiarities must simply be accepted as beyond rational control. (To some extent this parallels assumptions of scientific determinism, in which personal responsibility is mediated by social background, conditioning, and other factors external to individual will.) A person's trip is to be respected as sacred—provided he doesn't lay it on others. The exotic and peculiar become celebrated as ends in themselves. As Quakers and Shakers in earlier days identified with labels rendered in ridicule, so the term *freak* was accepted with approval by those who took pride in their divergence from social norms. Straights sometimes accuse freaks, with some justice, as having merely invented a new kind of conformity, but I have heard freaks extend their appreciation even to archetypal conservatives in the straight world, as one marveled at an extremely reactionary, rationalistic professor: "I think it's really neat the way he has it together, the way he thinks, dresses, his emotional responses, his politics." This was not sarcasm. Judgment is truly suspended, except insofar as strong individuality and sincerity are admired.

Do those who use astrological categories actually believe that celestial bodies so minutely affect human behavior? Some do, some don't, and in the new culture it hardly matters. Compare this attitude with common acceptance of the *I Ching* as a basis for making a decision. One meditates about a problem or question, then casts yarrow sticks or coins to lead him to a hexagram and its interpretation, usually with astounding relevance to one's concerns. Does he "believe" in the *I Ching*? There is really nothing to believe in. The book itself says take it or leave it. Above all, in this culture one learns there is more in heaven and earth than is dreamt of in philosophy. One's stance is modest before the burning bush.

The soil is turned for the sprouting of belief. What emerges is rather indiscriminate and incongruous—as suggested by this letter from a communard in the Southwest:

Summer & the time of ceremonials/ a week ago Saturday I conducted a peyote meeting to pray for rain—two sick people— three pregnant women—& to bless a trip to the peyote gardens in Texas/ our old Arapahoe friend Pablo helped us/ it was good/ we got a little rain/ the sick people felt good/ & four of us went to the gardens & got back in four days/ miracles/ we drove to Austin in a hippy bus/ borrowed a Mustang with Texas plates to look straight cut all hair & beards sang and prayed all the way/ picked unmolested in the beautiful gardens/ one of the rare places on earth/ SACRED/ driving back to Austin thru San Antonio/ rush hour freeway/ the Mustang becomes obsolete on the second level of a 4 level over-underpass/ the whole thing shaking insanely/ trucks roaring by/ & here we sit with a trunk full of God's flesh/ I run to a phone & call the guy we borrowed the Mustang from/ he sez/ call my brother/ the brother sez he's on the way with a truck & tow chain/ I run back to the underpass to tell the others/ roar & shaking more terrible than ever/ our three are leaning against the guard rail facing a small man with a crew cut & a bible in his hand/ Wade the upholsterer/ crazy as a loon & surely one of God's sweetest angels/ he delivered the sermon on the underpass/ singing & shouting the praises of the Lord/ it was righteous/ at the end he said Are You Saved/ & we told him we were doing our best/ he sd I believe you I know you are/ Let us pray/ & he laid a wonderful prayer on us & a thumping good blessing on the smoking Mustang/ then he left/ Right on/ we sd & just then the brother drove up in the truck hooked up the chain & towed us away/ then fed us/ loaded our cargo into his truck & drove us to Austin where we got in our hippy bus & came home/ Sat. night I conducted another meeting to give thanks for our journey—help some sick people & people in jail & ask for a little more rain/ we had some moisture both Sunday & Monday/ the people felt a little better/ I got sick/ running wide open too long/ what I really want to do is help other people/ but at the same time remember how important it is to stay behind it/ I sure am sick/ it's hard work

I know the correspondent well—and his sincerity is in no way compromised by his sense of humor, just as his capacity for practical straight thinking is not diminished by his interludes—with or without drugs—in the realms of stoned thought. His reverence encompasses an ecumenical jungle horrifying to the orthodox, but it is sustained by his daily experience. It is less a creed than an attitude of credence, an openness to wonder, and wonders, indeed, fill his life.

Within the web of the outlaw culture there is continual reinforcement of such attitudes, continual negative reinforcement of sophisticated cynicism and despair. Ambiguity and ambivalence are accepted. A respect welling into worship for natural process and spontaneity replaces the civilized impulse to control, contain, distinguish, and minimize. The blissful state of positive paranoia (or the belief that the universe is a conspiracy for one's benefit) is fostered, a mystic sense of the interconnectedness of all people and phenomena, of the cornucopia of the Flow, of a cosmic intent to heal and provide bounty. Most of those I know who have had "the Experience" leave drugs behind them entirely or use them only occasionally (and often, then, ritualistically), but they trail clouds of the glory they have known, the tolerance and optimism and affection, the sense of mystery, of ego-loss, of transcendent purpose, which are ingredients of the new consciousness. This state of mind becomes ingrained and constant, achieved without chemical assistance. It seems both a step forward in evolution and a recovery of ancient awareness, wasted and almost lost through suppression and disuse.

It is precisely to released libidinal energy that the new anarchism turns for its motive force. In communes such as I have been discussing, that does not imply saturation in mindless orgies; indeed, heightened sensitivity to one another as persons, particularly in male-female relationships, has something of a deterrent effect upon sexual practice. But that is very different from the repression of sexuality which is built into the old culture, and which, indeed, one is largely released from in communal settings. New inhibitions arise—just as Freud insists are essential for the development of civilization—but these tend to be based on the growing recognition that personal relationships, especially sexual, are only gratifying in a context of mutual respect and welfare. So long as that wisdom is enforced primarily by rules and conventions, it encourages perpetual testing, as an animal endlessly worries the locks and bars of his cage. When it is internalized, becoming intuitive and voluntary, it is a powerful restraint, yet accepted as a necessary and even satisfying part of the process, like the painstaking efforts of a cook to prepare a meal or of a poet to contain content in an appropriate form.

Prophets of the new consciousness such as Alan Watts,

Gary Snyder, Theodore Roszak, and Charles Reich leave me uneasy and skeptical, but hoping and motivated to try. Their academic critics leave me in dry despair. I may be momentarily persuaded, but ask, so then what? As religions of the past have always condemned heretics, these critics do so from a position of orthodoxy, and yet it is an orthodoxy strangely devoid of vision or purpose, a method—like that unreal stereotype of method which some call scientific —without a mission. Doubt seems an exercise somehow morbidly satisfying in itself, though it be the suicidal exercise of policing the Wasteland for impertinent .igns of green growth.

Orthodoxy demands of heretical believers a consistency and coherency inconceivable in the present era of motley flowering of belief. Many years ago a colleague who seemed to me an indiscriminate consumer of psychologies said to me, "I collect therapies like some people collect cookbooks." Today such eclecticism is no surprise. Therapists combine such techniques as nude encounter, psychedelics, meditation, and what have you, selecting from the rich heterogeneity of new-culture gardens. A communard who is also a therapist told me of going herself for therapy to help her cope with moods of loneliness and depression; of her therapist she says:

She was trained at Esalen, among other places, and does a lot with body language and nonverbal techniques, such as eye contact. Being so verbal myself, I find it bewildering to try to relate nonverbally.

So it is with religion and politics of the new age. Self-definition in terms of party or specific persuasion is resisted. One experiments, finds what works, goes into and out of belief loops with ease.

An academic reaction to new-culture eclecticism is that

of Richard King, in *The Party of Eros: Radical Social Thought and the Realm of Freedom,* who says:

In a world of infinite possibility one can paradoxically never make a final choice, and thus commitment remains provisional. One is continually dissatisfied and on the move to another source of pleasure. In contemporary form this is the search for self-fulfillment. And because one can never finally choose, one never has a self, something that is defined by one's choices.

That concept of self, involving final choice, is to my mind a kind of early death: I have seen it happen to people in their teens or even earlier, a weird preternatural settling. The face muscles take a stabilized form. The hair line begins to recede and the midriff to widen. They have made up their minds as one might a bed which is no more to be made love in.

Whether such diversity and protean commitment are compatible with community is a matter to be tested in the communes themselves. Commitment itself undergoes a change in definition. In an older sense it implies a long-term, stable mind-set. Another sense is suggested by the way it is used in automobile racing: a driver commits himself to a turn, at some critical moment making a decision he knows he cannot retreat from to follow out a particular arc for a few suspenseful seconds. Certainly his commitment is whole-hearted, total (or he is likely to fail for lack of nerve), yet it is momentary. Such commitments must be made again and again, at each curve in the track. It is the commitment of the surfer, to the moment, to the experience immediately underfoot. In the temporary society that is increasingly the pertinent skill, the form that profundity and sincerity of belief must take. One must live each moment as if it were forever—at the same time being forever open to radical demands for change.

The orthodoxies have all failed, however oppressively

they continue to wield their sterile power. What we have left to go on is our inner sense of necessities of ourselves in this moment, which includes an awareness of the need of others as they need us. It is possible that no theory derived from cultural history can help us adapt to the future, so rapid are the new demands, but cybernetics and systems analysis and servomechanisms provide what may be a groundwork for a theory of communities in the future. Meanwhile theoretical controversy drones on like a wire in the wind. Our problem is, can we figure out who will take out the garbage?

As I write, the tractor out by the factory begins chugging. A belt to its power takeoff turns the cutoff saw, which sections the logs, to be cored on the bandsaw, to be nailed and painted and sorted and labeled and packed and trucked. Topher, at six, likes to sort and label. He takes pots off the drying rack, measures them with a tape to determine their size, puts on two labels with a pneumatic stapler, and puts the pots on the appropriate shelf for packing. He was afraid of the sound of the machinery some months ago, but has grown accustomed. Recently he and I were the only ones left out there, and I told him I was leaving. "I'll work alone," he said, going on about his stapling. "I have a few more pots to finish up." I thought of child-labor. Topher has no sense of toil—not even that making pots is necessary to survival. It is a privilege. It is fun. It feels good—both the work and the appreciation he gets from others. Polly, thirteen, started the tractor, and now is helping Robb, a twenty-four-year-old former teacher, handle the large logs on the cutoff saw. I wonder in what other context is it possible for people like Topher and Polly and Robb and me to work together, feeling useful, feeling each day the challenge to personal growth and the strengthening of affectionate bonds.

On an experiential level it seems so simple—and yet to

imagine an anarchism built on such principles will require prophets of a radically new world-view. They are emerging, and their vision is being pieced together. Prophets of this disposition do not predict the future so much as they intuit the meaning of the flow of time. The world they describe is one of open-ended possibilities. They are more inclined toward the steady state than the big bang theory of cosmology. They are more of the persuasion of Heraclitus than of Parmenides—i.e., more inclined to imagine the universe in perpetual flux, perpetual evolution, than to see change as the play of illusion upon a ground base of fixed principles. History tells them only of the past, not of the future, not of the essential or determined. Ethologists have attempted to define human nature in terms of its evolution from primitive forms of life, asserting that what we can be is circumscribed by what we have been. But to the new prophets, such scholarship tells us the task of transcendence, not its limits: even our celebrated territoriality is no more definitive than body hair. As the ever-renewed universe leaks its energy to the void, life pulls it into new order, a negentropic force (i.e., a force of negative entropy), forming the formless, anew and anew as forms petrify, in what Norbert Weiner called "enclaves of order." Some scientists have described consciousness as nothing but a rear-view mirror, a sort system for the past disappearing behind us. But in the world-view I am describing it is also an awareness of the *élan vital* welling under us, the wisdom of the surfer making the infinite, instantaneous, subrational choices that maintain balance and direction in accord with our sense of the movement of overwhelming evolutionary power, guessing the future on the basis of our gross yet definite sympathy with the intention of the wave.

This may not be a new consciousness at all, but a prehistoric intuition. The speculation surrounding cave paintings that look remarkably like men in space suits has given rise again to theories that some of early man's sophistication (e.g., the mathematical precision of Stonehenge) may derive from extraterrestial visitation. More simply, we may imagine that the organisms which became human at an earlier stage had primitive awareness, like the communication in a cloud of gnats flying in formation over evening water, which has been lost in our specialized, cerebral development. Current experiments with polygraphs attached to plants suggest that there may be a network of consciousness linking cellular life throughout the universe, a network in which, anomalously, human beings can only participate through the laborious use of electronic instruments, so effective is our cerebral consciousness in jamming the vibrations transmitted to and by our other cells. Whether it be through drugs, or yoga, or meditation, or biofeedback mechanisms or other means of extending awareness, we seem to be on the verge of regaining a capacity to relate to natural processes from which we have been excluded, like black sheep returning to our Edenic home.

Nature, except for humankind, lives in anarchy. Not lawlessly, of course: indeed, it seems that only humankind can violate its implacable laws. But in that environment which we despoil and from which we so desperately shield ourselves, there are no constitutions or hierarchies, no officials, no roles (that world is not a stage), no schedules, no duties —though there are imperative loyalties requiring the mother tirelessly to feed her young, the mate to defend the bower, the species to maintain itself, even by stratagems as destructive to individuals as lemming migrations. In that anarchy, tragedy is linked to bounty irrevocably as winter to autumn, and affirmation to negation with the mindless persistence of March shoots pushing through rotten snow. In political terms anarchy means the abnegation of power, but that belies the reality. Rather it is adoption of the greatest power available, riding the wave of nature's dynamics, identifying with insuperable forces. "Politics,"

Buckminster Fuller once said, "is of the machine age, obsolete." If we can find a way to unleash the new anarchism, with its promise not of chaos but of the supreme orderliness and dependable rhythm of nature, it will make politics unthinkable as warfare is made by the possibility of nuclear holocaust.

Finding a way to unleash it is a slow, sensitive task, like that of bank thieves with sanded fingers sensing the muted fall of tumblers that lock in the mystery. A paradigm for the task is the lesson of love. If I desire you, I must recognize that sexual pressure may be exactly what will drive you away. If I love *you* and not a reflection of myself, I must want you to be what you are, not shape you to my wishes. That may mean I must learn to be glad if you love another, if you choose to leave me. And those hard lessons must be learned in the midst of intense passion, not through diminishment of feeling, but through its increase, by learning to care enough not to destroy.

The world beyond the looking glass will seem much like the one we leave—or at least the one on blueprints produced by humane intelligence. Only the motives will be reversed, and the fruit looking just like perfectly manufactured wax will, strangely, be real, edible, perishable. The factory will run—without pressure, without wages, its profits absorbed by the community as unceremoniously and uncompetitively as air is breathed and water drunk. People will make pots as they prepare and eat a meal, sleep, make love, sweat, defecate—as something that must be done, that one can learn to like to do.

Or so we hope. For those of us who have lived long on the wrong side of the glass, adjustment to the reversed world will no doubt always be somewhat self-conscious and awkward, like immigrants who even after many years in their new home still dream and count in the old language. For Topher it may be different—if we have wisdom and love enough to let him become, and to learn a little from him.